Public
Private Worlds

Public &
Private Worlds

WOMEN IN CONTEMPORARY NEW ZEALAND

Edited by Shelagh Cox

Allen & Unwin
Port Nicholson Press

First published in 1987 by Allen & Unwin New Zealand Limited in association with the Port Nicholson Press, Private Bag, Wellington, New Zealand

Allen & Unwin Australia Pty Ltd, NCR House, 8 Napier Street, North Sydney, NSW 2060, Australia

Unwin Hyman Ltd, 40 Museum Street, London WC1

Allen & Unwin Inc, 8 Winchester Place, Winchester, Massachusetts 01890, USA

ISBN 0 86861 467 X

Cover painting: 'Interior', 1986, acrylic on canvas, 6' × 8', by Jane
    Zusters, reproduced by permission of the artist
Cover design: Missen & Geard
Typeset in Bembo by Graphicraft Limited, Hong Kong
Printed by SRM Production Services Sdn Bhd

Contents

List of Illustrations

Preface

Shelagh Cox

This book started with the experience of living two lives in one. My daily existence involved private life, whether I was a daughter, wife, mother, friend or woman alone. It also involved life in the public world. Both private and public life always mattered but living one fully seemed to entail living the other partially or in secret. In order to live well at home I did things and thought in a certain way. In order to do well in the outside world I became a different person. As long as I kept my two selves separate, I got by. But whatever means I developed for reconciling the two, there was a hidden complexity. The half of my life I was failing to acknowledge was present in the other. Sometimes its presence distracted or disturbed me and sometimes it nourished me. Aware as I was of this double existence, I could make very little sense of it and felt I could do nothing about it. I wondered if other people fared better and, if so, how they managed it.

Both men and women live at home as well as in the outside world but it is women who have traditionally taken the weight of private life. They still do. So the division of the world into public and private spheres tends to be of greater concern to women than to men. The contributors to this book are women. Each contributor has a specialist field of knowledge and experience which she has brought to her reflections on public and private worlds.

The chapter called 'The Theoretical Background' is intended to explore basic ideas and issues. People have tried to make sense of divisions between the public and private worlds throughout western history and feminists are doing so today. The questions they ask are raised in this chapter. Why is social life organised in this divided way? How have particular forms of this organisation been justified? Is a society's way of dividing up human lives necessarily the right way? If we don't like what we've got, what can we do about it?

'The Theoretical Background' does not need to be read first.

Claudia Pond Eyley, Shield for Mary Cassatt, 1983, acrylic and photocopy image, 114 × 155 cm. Private Collection, Auckland.

PREFACE

Each chapter is self-contained and weaves together theory and information. The chapters allow the reader to draw back from the immediacy of facts, figures and personal experience and see the social grid as a whole. Rosemary Novitz writes of the task of identifying patterns in the lives of individuals, 'patterns which suggest that our personal histories are not solely the product of individual choice, and that our "free" choices are often made between a very limited set of options.' In seeing patterns, we see the power of the constraints upon our lives and that can be disheartening. But identifying constraints is the first step towards doing something about them and in most of the chapters of this book there are proposals for change.

Certain themes are heard throughout the book. One is the satisfaction women may find in aspects of private life which are commonly thought to be mundane and uninteresting. Anne Kirker writes of the artist Joanna Paul and her concern for 'the great meaning of ordinary things'. Kirker sees much of the current work of feminist artists as an exposure to public view of the hidden aspects of private life. Another recurrent theme is the invisibility of the private sphere and thus of women's work, life and thought. The conflict between home life and their art has affected all women artists and silenced many. Representations of a denigrated private world tends to have low status in the public world of the exhibition.

The neglect of women who work for 'love' at home rather than money in the outside world is explored in Marilyn Waring's chapter 'The Invisible Women'. International and New Zealand systems of accounting leave out women's unpaid work. Official ways of assessing the economic value of work lead to the 'invisibility of the majority of the human species by way of statistical treatment. The family of man avoids confronting the absence of well-being in the family of women.'

The invisibility that Alison Laurie writes of is overt and punitive: the suppression of lesbianism in our heterosexist society. Suppression goes beyond prejudiced attitudes and discrimination against lesbians. The very existence of lesbianism can be denied in the attempt to keep it invisible. 'Making lesbianism visible is a very difficult and dangerous business under patriarchy.'

As a child, Cathy Benland was excluded from the 'sacred space' during religious services. Only boys or men could serve mass at the altar and be seen by the congregation. Women could go into the sanctuary only when they became invisible through their domestic role. 'In private, when no one was in the pews, no liturgy was taking place and there was menial work to be done, females could enter the sacred space.' The public and private spheres are often thought to be independent of one another. But when they are investigated closely their essential interdependence becomes apparent. Bev James writes about mill workers' wives in Kawerau, drawing on the women's understandings of their private lives and their experience of their husbands' work. She demonstrates the power of a strike in a one-industry town to bring into question commonly accepted ideas about the autonomy of women's domestic lives.

Jan Robinson starts her chapter on prostitution by revealing a similar dependency. 'The mode, style and structure of sexual discourse derives directly from public sphere activity ... the fact that sexual acts usually occur in private should not deceive us into conceptualising them as being privately determined.' She exposes economic and social realities in the public sphere that underlie the private acts and myths of prostitution; they are realities that prostitutes themselves often recognise when other people don't.

Rosemary Novitz looks at another way in which the public and private interpenetrate. Exploring the relationship between paid and unpaid work, she highlights women's increasing involvement in the public world of paid work and the apparent lack of a corresponding involvement of men in housework and childcare.

Prevailing ideas about the two spheres are often muddled. Kay Saville-Smith examines the 'apparent incoherence of state policy and action' as it affects women. She exposes the contradictions implicit in the administration of the domestic purposes benefit (DPB) in New Zealand. It is in the state's economic interest to keep a solo mother at home rather than provide expensive childcare, yet this conflicts with the wish to punish women who claim independence from men. So the state encourages women to live on the DPB because it saves public money while, as guardian of the moral order, it makes life unpleasant for them.

Women's association with the private sphere affects not only their daily lives but their creative powers. Aorewa McLeod discusses women's fiction writing and asks 'Can it be that the possibilities offered by our lives must limit the sort of fictions we construct?' She argues that many New Zealand women writers explore female identity in terms of romantic love and an ultimate fulfilment through intimate relationships. 'The resemblances and interrelations between our fictions and our lives, the fact that the paradigms of one reflect and influence the other, suggest perhaps that in order to write differently we will have to begin to live differently.'

Recalling her Tuhoe childhood, Rose Pere writes of a world that is not divided into public and private spheres. In her experience, this allowed women to grow up as whole people. 'Within my own tribal groups women are of paramount importance.... There were no distinct or formal boundaries for men's and women's work habits or patterns.' Rose Pere says she has been exposed to 'very positive female models' from the descent-lines of both her natural parents.

All the Pakeha contributors to this book advocate change in the construction of the public and private worlds as they exist now. Most want the change to be radical. 'We can only live other lives by changing the structures which prescribe our choices and rethinking some of the understandings which prompt us to act in certain ways' (Rosemary Novitz). No one thinks the change will be easy. It may not be very manageable: 'once a few pebbles are thrown it's not long before you have a whole avalanche bearing down upon you' (Cathy Benland).

In working on this book I have taken a long journey from perplexed beginnings. I have lost the innocence about the world in which we live that protected me when I started. But the journey, taken with the women who have contributed to the book and the woman who published it, has brought me to a new and more realistic understanding of our divided world and to a readiness to take up the tools of reconstruction.

Shelagh Cox
January 1987

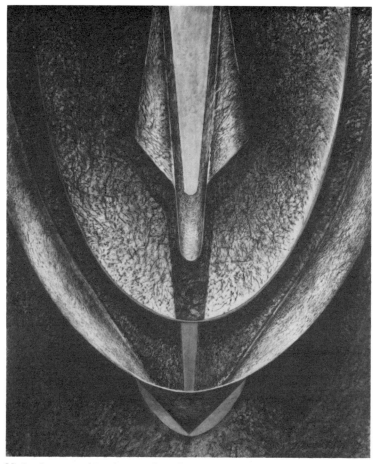

Vivian Lynn, working drawing for Asherim, *1984, charcoal, 108.8 × 91.2 cm, National Art Gallery, Wellington*

Chapter 1

THE THEORETICAL BACKGROUND

Shelagh Cox and Bev James

We all inhabit two realms, the public and the private, and they shape our lives. The division between the public and the private has important social and economic consequences. It allows us to structure our lives in a workable way, to bring order to the potentially disordered, so that tasks as necessary as the protection of children and the control of criminals are possible. In the world in which we live, public is separated from private life along lines that further our economic interests and the need for efficiency. The production of goods, on which a capitalist economy rests, takes place in the public sphere; the provision of food, shelter and human maintenance – without which capitalist production cannot continue – takes place in the private sphere.

Men's and women's lives, too, are separated. It is widely accepted that men belong primarily to the public and women to the private sphere. The requirements of a capitalist economy keep men in the work of production in the outside world whereas women's childbearing capacity keeps them at home. This separation is thought to be unavoidable, even if some women find a legitimate place in the outside world.

The division is taken as natural. As such, it is not considered a proper subject for social investigation: we cannot go beyond our existing knowledge to question the relationship between the spheres, how they are constituted, or the preconceptions which underlie them. But our existing knowledge is lopsided. We know a lot about what goes on in the public marketplace and in the life of the state; we know something, and conjecture a lot, about what goes on in the private sphere of the family. But we don't know much about the relationship between them. The way we approach the two realms tends to be different. We reserve our full analytical armoury for the public sphere; we are more willing to content ourselves with descriptions of the private sphere. We assume that the public sphere is open to scrutiny; it is important and challenging enough to call for the attention of the finest minds. We see the private sphere as veiled, comparatively inaccessible, and of secondary importance. It is the proper field of study for those who are not quite up to studying affairs of state and the economy. And we assume that the relationship between them is unproblematic.

These are the assumptions that feminists are beginning to question. They are seeing the known world as artificially restricted. They are making it clear that the map of society, long accepted as an accurate guide to social life, has been made by phallocentric cartographers. The result is that we have good guides to the public world but little accurate mapping of private life.

The authors of this book are seeking to extend the known world of social analysis to encompass private life. They also believe that the division of the world into public and private spheres is a social construction and not a natural imperative, that we can question and analyse it and that consequently we can find better ways of organising our lives.[1]

Public and private are words that people think they understand: 'a public figure', 'a private person', are not phrases that cause puzzlement. But the clearly delineated surface conceals complexity. In using the words *public* and *private* we are not talking about one pair of opposites alone. They epitomise other pairs of concepts which divide the world into dualistic categories: society/family, work/domesticity, production/reproduction, culture/nature, outer/inner, impersonal/personal, freedom/necessity ... the list is not complete. The opposition between the concepts of the public and the private is both powerful and vague. Its power breeds a cluster of associated oppositions; its vagueness leads people to assume that oppositions which are merely similar are in fact the same. So within each broad realm, distinct ideas are seen as one.

It is on this basis that men are equated with one side of the dichotomy and women with the other. Attributes associated with the public sphere – the impersonal, paid work, the outside world and so on – are assumed to belong to men, their

2

opposites to women. The cluster of attributes, unanalysed, forms a densely constructed whole.

The public and the private, men's and women's realms, are taken to be twin monoliths, not to be questioned and not to be changed. They are used to justify the sexual division of labour: men work in the outside world and get paid for what they do, whereas women are housewives who don't get paid. This assumption is still powerful, but it is no longer unquestioned. Women's participation in paid work is increasingly recognised. But there is still an odd form of double-think when it comes to accepting the presence of women in the outside world.

Women's place in the workforce may be recognised and allowed for in some of the arrangements for daily life and in some government policy. So, at one level, a changing pattern in the sexual division of labour is acknowledged. However, old attitudes shape expectations of who does what, and who gets paid. Most women in the paid workforce find themselves carrying a double burden – their daily housework as well as their work outside the home. The assumption that women will be responsible for work in the home is supported by assump-tions about male and female characteristics. Women are thought to have certain womanly traits, which make them especially suited to domestic tasks. They are nurturing, sen-sitive and good at jobs requiring an eye for detail. In contrast, men's competitiveness, ambition and toughness equip them for the outside world. So a sexually divisive moral code, lying deep in the minds of men and women, tends to exist beneath surface readiness for change and, very often, undermines it. The result is often a bewildering set of contradictions.

Women are at the forefront of the investigation undertaken in this book because, traditionally restricted to the private sphere, their identities are bound up in the new analysis. Powerful men, who have found their identities in the public sphere while having a recognised place in the private, do not have the same need to investigate the two together. The oppressed have a sharper eye for the mechanics of oppression than the oppressors.

The concept of a divided world is embedded in our understanding. In the western European tradition it can be traced back to the Greek thought that has shaped much of our own. Greek ways of separating public from private life shed light on assumptions that underlie what we do and think

3

today. Aristotle wrote in the fourth century BC: 'the male is by nature superior and the female inferior, the male ruler and the female subject....'[2] Misogyny underlay the basic social arrangements of Greek society so that the lives of free men and women were effectively separated.[3]

Why were free men superior to women? According to the Greeks, there were two spheres of human action – the sphere of freedom and the sphere of necessity. The life of free men was best but it was dependent on getting certain essential things done. There must be a sound material base for the free life, and it was to be found in the household. All the mundane human activities took place there, whether they were the production of goods or the reproduction of the species. Both were necessary evils and the proper occupation for lesser human beings, either slaves or women. So the appropriate attitude of a free Greek citizen to his household and its members was a blend of dependence and contempt. For him the sphere of necessity permitted the freedom of public life, and its value lay in its unavoidability. For free men a life with women was the inescapable prerequisite to a better life without them.

Male superiority was justified by an appeal to the different natures of men and women. Women were not fitted for the higher offerings of the sphere of freedom because they lacked powers of reasoning; correspondingly, they were naturally fitted for the sphere of necessity. Only women could bear children and so, by an extension of logic which sounds familiar today, only women could rear them. Both activities, as well as the provision of all other everyday goods and services, were to be found in the household. So women belonged with slaves in a devalued world. Aristotle's view of women had its place in this context.

The systematic devaluation of women can also be seen in the Greek view of procreation. Menstrual blood provided the prime matter of the embryo, but it was semen that imposed form. 'In birth,' Tertullian said, 'the whole fruit is present in the semen.'[4] In a society in which matter drew contempt and form belonged to the realm of the rational and the spiritual, such an argument reinforced the misogyny of Aristotelian philosophy.

These two oppositions – freedom and necessity, form and matter – allowed for a separation between the lives of free men and women, and a rationalised basis for granting men superiority. Susan Moller Okin puts it like this:

> ... women's purpose is seen to be the reproduction and rearing of men, and their nature is prescriptively defined in terms of the optimal characteristics for the performance of their functions ... [Aristotle] relegated the vast majority of people, both male and female, to the status of means, whose purpose was to enable the few to pursue their truly human ends.[5]

Okin is referring to Aristotle's version of a widespread and influential belief: that biology is destiny. The biological determinism expressed in Greek thought shapes the lives of women today. At its core is the assumption that since women bear children, it is their destiny as human beings to rear them. Moreover, all the aspects of life that are associated with childrearing in a particular society – from providing food and physical safety to caring for other adults and making day-to-day life pleasant – are the province of women.

Biological determinism is closely associated with functionalism. The functionalist approach equates women's identity with their purpose. What are women for? To produce children and to do the tasks associated with that function. Where do women belong? In the private realm where they can devote themselves to their life-purpose. In the private realm they can be protected from the uncertainties and responsibilities of public life at the same time as they are excluded from its privileges. By fulfilling their function, women are true to their nature and attain moral goodness. It follows that they should be where they are.

The Aristotelian justification for women's lesser position in society underlies much of our thought. But there is another forceful theme in our philosophic heritage. It is the belief that men and women are equal in their natural endowments. Of course, such a conviction cannot be reconciled with a belief in women's inferiority; women cannot, by their very nature, be both less than men and men's equals. We are heirs to a powerful double strand of unreconciled thought about the right relationship between men and women. The inconsistency is seldom confronted.

Two philosophers who tackled the question of the relationship between men and women were Plato, writing in the

Greece of the fifth century BC, and John Stuart Mill in nine-teenth-century Britain. They are widely separated in space and time but will be considered together because both looked at the misogynist social ordering that marked their societies and thought about alternatives which gave some women more equality.

Plato defined two kinds of women – those who fulfilled the function of reproduction in the home and those who shared with men the capacity to function as citizens in the public sphere.[6] He thought that women who would join men as guardians ruling in the ideal city must be separated from women in private life. The guardian class, Plato argued, must include women because some have qualities which make them worthy of positions of power. Such women must, like men, be selected and trained for rulership. To be admitted to the guardian class is a privilege afforded to exceptional women. Once included, they are expected to cast their abilities in the mould set by the men who have established the criteria for membership. Women guardians must be totally unlike private wives. Women admitted to the responsibility and power of guardianship must be trained, presumably, in qualities which are the complete opposite of the submissive attitudes appropriate to domestic life. Similar issues of gatekeeping are with us today. When women are admitted to the arena of male power, their initiation may well involve a difficult and painful resocialisation into many of the qualities women are taught to see as unwomanly and unsuitable in private life.

Plato backed away from the implications of the double standard he set. So do we. In our world there is a clear–cut line of demarcation between successful professional and business women on the one hand and women in the private world on the other. We, too, are sometimes unwilling to face the discomfort of attempting to understand fully not only the differences but the inequalities that exist between women identified primarily with either public or private life.

Like Plato, John Stuart Mill called for the emancipation of some women on the grounds of the usefulness of their contribution to society. Mill, however, went further than Plato. Imbued with the egalitarian ethos that was part of his Christian and humanist background,[7] Mill argued passionately for the presence of women in the public world as a matter of human rights. There are no slaves in Britain, he said, except the wife of every household. The subjection of women 'is not felt to jar with modern civilisation, any more than domestic slavery among the Greeks jarred with their notion of themselves as a free people'.[8] According to Mill, all women should be free to attain the qualifications that admitted them to power in the outside world: education, the vote, equality before the law, admittance to the professions.

Recognising that the barriers to the public world must be broken down is relatively straightforward. But Mill went on to identify a much more difficult problem. He said that when women were confined to the private sphere they developed certain undesirable characteristics and ways of behaving. Women who lived a life that was mainly domestic were often thought to be 'mobile, changeable, too vehemently under the influence of the moment, incapable of dogged perseverance, unequal and uncertain in the power of using their faculties.'[9] These characteristics were a consequence of limitations imposed on them in a cloistered private world. Emancipation would allow them to discover their true natures in the free environment of the outside world.

Mill opened a door on a fascinating but complex question. It is a door that has not really closed again, or not for long. He saw that while public and private worlds might be built by men, this did not mean that the barriers between them could be removed by enlightened men with the interests of women at heart. The worlds might indeed be truly separate, in the sense that they produced different kinds of human beings. If it is admitted that men and women are socialised into different characteristics by their occupancy of different worlds, the question becomes infinitely more complex.

Mill was 'a brave and far-thinking feminist'.[10] But he did not question the assumption that the day-to-day care of the family was women's unpaid work. For Mill, women should have right of access to the world beyond the home, but they were also uniquely responsible for childcare and domestic work within it. He could not envisage the absence of the private sphere and women's traditional place. Mill did not say this directly; he simply left a lot unsaid. Many analysts today also fail to ask how the family, with its valued qualities, can be safeguarded at the same time as women are freed to enter the public world. Fear of the loss of the traditional family comes in the way of a clear, unemotive analysis of the problems it presents. We can analyse the marketplace and the state without the unconscious warning that we must not analyse them out of the possibility of existence. We resist suggestions for restructuring the family, fearing we may lose it altogether.

Frederick Engels argued not only for the abolition of a particular economic system, capitalism, but also for the form of the family associated with it.[11] Like Mill, Engels was writing in nineteenth-century Britain. Both men were concerned to show how environment rather than biology affected the position of women, but they had very different starting points. Mill focused on the implications of the domestic life for women, and was concerned with their political rights. He was primarily interested in the position of women of his own class, the bourgeoisie.

In contrast, Engels' work revealed stark distinctions between the lives of bourgeois and working class women. Engels explained the origins and nature of women's oppression in terms of economic imperatives. Like his associate Marx, Engels thought that human beings create themselves and their society through work, or production. Productive activities, he argued, in turn affect the organisation of marriage, family life and the relations between the sexes. Engels' analysis focused on the public and private spheres in terms of a separation between production and reproduction. By production he meant the manufacture of goods necessary for survival. In reproduction he included human reproduction and the activities involving the care and nurture of human beings.[12]

For Engels, the oppression of women is most acute in capitalist societies. There, the institution of private property is highly developed and consequently the divisions between public and private spheres are entrenched. In looking at the relationship between capitalism and women's oppression, we need to consider briefly the transition from feudalism to capitalism which occurred in Western Europe over the sixteenth to nineteenth centuries.

This transition represented a major upheaval in the organisation of economic life. No longer were the processes of production and reproduction to be found under the same roof, as they often were when artisans worked from the place where they lived, and peasants carried out a range of economic activities within their household. Instead, production became centralised in factories and workplaces, relegating the household to the periphery of economic life. This was made possible by an increase in capital accumulation. Also, the eviction of peasants from the land provided the labour force necessary for the growth of capitalist industry. The implications of these changes for the position of women and the relations between the sexes were profound. Society was now divided into public and private spheres, with men perceived as belonging to the first and women to the second. Michele Barrett suggests that capitalism exacerbated sexual divisions, and greatly increased the dependence of women on men, in all social classes.[13]

The concepts of public and private are historically constructed. While they were prominent characteristics of classical Greek social life, these divisions did not become meaningful in most of Europe until households were transformed by the development of capitalism. In European feudal society there was far less distinction between public and private than there was in classical Greece or nineteenth-century capitalist England.

Engels saw that, just as private and public divisions alter from one period to another, they are experienced differently from class to class. Bourgeois women in nineteenth-century England led very privatised lives. Engels saw the bourgeois English woman as reliant on her husband for her livelihood and social standing, and confined to domestic activities. The bourgeois marriage, he claimed, had very little to do with love. In return for her husband's economic support and status, the bourgeois wife provided her reproductive capacity. Her oppression was, therefore, the result of her husband's economic supremacy. Bourgeois marriage was above all an economic relationship, concerned with the inheritance of private property. The family, and women's role in it, served to reproduce that class and its economic, social and political privileges.

Contemporary socialist feminists, interested in the psychological and emotional forces of private life, have compared the nineteenth-century ideal of womanhood with that of today. Barrett argues that the nineteenth-century bourgeois conception of family life is apparent in today's image of the family as a private refuge, ideally consisting of the male breadwinner with financially dependent housewife and children.[14] This approach underlies the curious conflation of attributes that constitute the 'ideal' housewife and mother. She manages the house, does its menial work and provides moral and psychological guidance. She combines roles that are seen to be quite separate in the public world – administrator, charwoman, counsellor, teacher and priestess.

In the nineteenth century the bourgeois image of women as financially dependent and totally domestic also affected the working class. However, the need for working class women to participate in the labour force threw up many contradictions between this ideology and their actual household arrangements. Peasant women and women of the emergent working class were hit badly by the shift in productive activities from home to factory. The complementary productive unit of husband and wife, based on the household, was shattered.[15] Women's dependence on marriage increased as they became less able to provide financially for themselves and their children. Women of the new proletariat were often faced with destitution. They had few opportunities in the home to produce goods for sale; the demands of childcare often prevented them from going out to work; if they were able to enter employment, they earned less than men. During the seventeenth century, desertion of wives and children was increasingly common.[16] Families became liabilities for men who were forced to rely on wage labour alone to support themselves and their dependants.

Even today, women of all classes are constrained in their choices by economic dependence on men. Though there is equal pay legislation and a welfare state, women stand to lose economic security and social status by moving out of the protection of the traditional patriarchal family.

Engels considered women of the nineteenth-century proletariat to be economically oppressed by the bourgeoisie. He strongly condemned the exploitation of women as a cheap source of labour. In deploring women's plight, Engels frequently referred to the adverse effects of the mother's employment on the whole family. He considered that the quality of proletarian family life would be greatly improved if women were to remain at home.[17] The same is often said today.

Engels' analysis of gender relations in the nineteenth century rested solely on economic explanations. Men belonging to the bourgeoisie owned property and their power rested on that. Married women were not legally able to own property, nor to earn their own income. They had no means of support, except through a husband or male relatives. Proletarian men, however, did not own property[18] and thus, according to Engels, the means for men's economic dominance over women was absent. As working class women were also employed in industry, and so were provided with their own means of economic emancipation, Engels concluded that the sexes were more or less equal in the proletariat.

Engels' work has become a significant reference point for contemporary socialist feminist analysis which locates the oppression of women in the organisation of production and reproduction. Socialist feminists agree with Engels that the existence of separate public and private spheres is associated with a particular type of economic system, and furthermore that there are important economic differences and inequalities among women, as well as between women and men. They are, however, also critical of Engels' analysis.

In concentrating on economic explanations, Engels failed to realise that patriarchal forces would also be at work. He did not see that men have power over women because of the status and privilege accorded their sex by society. Only incidentally did Engels confront the problem of patriarchy by mentioning working men's brutality towards their wives. His attention was given largely to the public sphere, and women's access to it. This meant that he did not consider the nature of women's reproductive capacity, its significance in the private sphere, and its relationship to women's place in the paid workforce. Nor did he look at the way labour is divided between men and women in the private sphere; like John Stuart Mill, he took the sexual division of labour for granted. Women as childbearers and childrearers were not subjects of his analysis – and yet these roles are central to women's experience.

Engels' analysis is based on Marxist theory. As a theory of society, Marxism provides many insights into the nature of power, conflict, inequality and change that can be applied to relations between men and women. The failing of Marxist theory is that many inequalities between women and men go unexamined, because they do not fit within the framework of the capitalist relations of production.

Contemporary feminists, concerned with issues of sexual inequality, are critical of assumed divisions between public and private. They are critical of both the ideology which limits women to the private sphere, and of the actual divisions which women experience as problematic. The activities of women, as keepers of domestic order and harmony yet at the same time participants in public life, expose the contradictions inherent in the ideology of separate spheres. Above all, feminists regard it as basic to their task to examine critically that realm of emotion and intimate relations, private life, which is usually deemed to be beyond analysis and politics.

In confronting these issues, feminists too have to face the difficulties arising from the way biological reproduction is incorporated into society. First, they have to separate biological reproductive functions from social roles that become identified with them. Secondly, they have to find ways of acknowledging the necessity to society of reproductive activity without acquiescing in any social arrangement that confines women to the private sphere.

Radical feminists[19] have explicitly attempted to tackle the issue of women's reproductive biology by arguing that women's unique ability to become pregnant, give birth and lactate are central to their oppression. Women's reproductive biology seems so fundamental to their oppression that some radical feminists want to transform it altogether. Shulamith Firestone assumes childbearing to be inherently oppressive to women and argues that they need to be freed from the 'tyranny of biology' through reproductive technology.[20] Firestone advocates conception outside the womb and the use of artificial placentas, so that women are completely dissociated from conception, pregnancy and birth.

Writing in the late 1960s, Firestone epitomises early radical feminist ideas that gave new vigour and direction to feminist theory. For Firestone, women's oppression is primary, widespread and fundamental; it is therefore more basic than class or race oppression. She argues that men and women form two opposing 'sex classes'[21] and that their struggle is the key moving force of social change. Firestone's solutions challenge the social structure as a whole. If artificial means of reproduction were implemented, the link between women bearing children and rearing them could no longer be made. Such a solution questions accepted ideas about the value of the family, and the primary role of women as mothers.

However, attributing women's oppression solely to their reproductive biology ignores power relations between the sexes in other areas, including those of politics and economics. There is, for instance, no guarantee that women would gain control of artificial reproduction or that they would be involved in deciding who could use such technology and for what purposes. Recent feminist work indicates that new reproductive technologies are controlled by both capitalist and male interests.[22]

Other radical feminist work has treated biology differently. Cultural feminists, for example, assume antagonism and polarisation between the sexes, as Firestone does, but they do not see women's reproductive biology as the source of oppression. Rather, it is society's ideas and understandings about women's reproductive functions that oppress women. Cultural feminists think that women's true nature needs to be discovered and fostered. They wish to revalue motherhood and to demonstrate what they believe to be the intrinsic moral superiority of women. Cultural feminism seeks social change by isolating and defining specifically 'female' attributes, and according them status and value. This is seen as part of constructing a distinctive women's culture.

Cultural feminism seeks to change the way people think about activities and attributes traditionally associated with women. This approach can involve political activity in the public arena. In a similar way, nineteenth-century liberals used public channels such as the media and parliament in their attempts to change attitudes about women. But cultural feminism's solutions also tend to be expressed as personal, individual ones which eschew contact with political and economic structures and concentrate on a psychological inner world and the development of a separate women's sphere. The women's culture movement celebrates qualities and values ascribed to women – nurturance, sensitivity, emotion, ability to relate to others, intuition, pacifism and so on. The establishment of a separate world is seen as a way of protecting female values from the contamination of the male-defined public sphere. Such a viewpoint is reminiscent of the nineteenth-century patriarchal ideology of women as protectors of the domestic realm and guardians of virtues threatened by the public world. By advocating a retreat into the private sphere and accepting its confines, cultural feminism leaves the divisions between public and private worlds intact. Hester Eisenstein defines cultural feminism as 'a feminist version of the eternal female'.[23]

There has been no consensus among feminists on how to examine the social implications of women's reproductive role, nor how to deal with associated inequalities. Attempts at understanding the relationship between reproductive biology and social arrangements are hampered by characteristics of feminist thought itself. Certainly, feminism is critical of many aspects of women's traditional social position; it presents values which oppose prevailing values, and promotes alternative visions of society. But feminist critiques have not so far provided us with a detailed analysis of women's reproductive role, nor of how it can be given social status and value.

Feminist theory has its roots in a culture characterised by sex inequalities. In constructing its theories and world-view, feminism has been influenced not only by women's experiences as members of a subordinated group, but also by ideas developed in a male-dominated and male-defined world. As feminists, we have been shaped by the very world we struggle to transcend. Many of its ideas are ours, often without our being fully aware of our own conditioning. Therefore, it is not only crucial to examine women's reproductive experiences from the point of view of women. It is also essential to examine critically all assumptions about biology, whether feminist or non-feminist. While there is much work to be done on the question of reproductive biology, some important ideas can now be put forward.

The basic issue is: to what extent do biological differences inevitably result in significant social differences? Three ideas are important. First, there are similarities among certain groups of men and women. Although the sexes have different biological experiences, they share similar social experiences. While men and women appear to inhabit separate worlds, as members of the same classes and ethnic groups, they also share common experiences and interests. For example, shared work, neighbourhood, family life and schooling bring them together. Nevertheless, it is important to remember that these shared experiences are still gender-defined.

Secondly, members of the same sex may be driven apart by their social positions. For example, the assertion by black women that feminism is mainly a middle class movement, concerned only with white women's experiences and interests, illustrates that there is no single, all-encompassing women's perspective or vision of a just society.[24] There are significant

14

social differences between women, as well as between women and men.

Thirdly, although women may share the same reproductive organs, they can have different experiences as a consequence of their biology. It is perhaps especially in the private realm that differences among women bring into question the idea of a united women's consciousness. For example, the experience of motherhood is neither available to nor chosen by every woman; nor does it have the same meaning for all women.

Women's world-views, then, are shaped not only by biological experience but also by social conditions which are shared by men, and by the hierarchies that structure social relations. Yet it is still widely assumed in our society that biological differences between the sexes are easily and inevitably transformed into the social arrangements of the public and private spheres. By accepting biological difference as a major structuring principle in our lives, we obscure the complex ways in which a whole range of social requirements – from production and reproduction, to the needs for intimacy and association with others – are organised. Explanations reducing complex social arrangements to neat biological imperatives condemn us to the divided world as we know it.

So far we have looked at ways in which public and private worlds are structured, both in theory and in everyday life. We have discussed difficulties that have prevented full analysis of public and private divisions, pointing out that these divisions are often assumed to be justified by the different reproductive biological functions of women and men. Our argument, however, is that the public and private worlds are social constructions that can be examined and need to be changed. Both the ideology of separate spheres and the real experience of separated lives are damaging to women.

We shall now consider ways of thinking that might lead to a better understanding of the public and private worlds. However, we are wary of formulating a theory to be laid neatly and definitively over the terrain of the public and private. There is always the danger, in developing new concepts, of appearing to establish a premature orthodoxy. Our ideas must be tested by the changing experience of women of all classes and ethnic groups. It is not easy, either, to change habitual ways of thought, even if new ideas appear convincing and just. Trans-

lating intellectual conviction into practical and personal contexts often challenges deep-seated cultural habits and dearly
protected parts of our identities.[25]

We have identified four different ways of dealing with the
public and the private. The first two alternatives are:
1. Allowing women to enter the public sphere.
2. Rethinking and remaking the private sphere.
Both rest on the basic idea that private and public worlds are
unalterable and accept them as basic divisions in social life.

The second two alternatives are:
3. Abolition of the private sphere.
4. Challenging the divisions between the public and the
   private.
These last two alternatives confront the structure of the division into public and private realms, the third strategy by
ignoring private life and the fourth by questioning the very
assumptions that underlie our perceptions of the two realms as
separate.

The first course, crossing the border from the private to the
public, is one that feminists have followed in working for legal
and civil reforms since the nineteenth century. Such reforms
meant great advances for bourgeois women and accomplished
many of John Stuart Mill's aims. Women were allowed into
higher education and the professions and benefited from
changes to the matrimonial property laws.

Working class women, however, could not take advantage
of many of these changes. Their conditions at home and at
work were not appreciably altered. As Engels starkly revealed,
they still had to contend with low rates of pay, dreadful
working conditions and the burden of childcare.

Securing legislative equality and the entry of women into all
areas of public life is only a partial solution, and one that does
not lead to full sexual equality. The private sphere, and thus a
large part of women's lives, remains untouched. Bringing
women into the public sphere has the limitation of the
traditional liberal view, which argues that the public sphere is
independent of the private. Carole Pateman comments: 'liberal
principles cannot simply be universalised to extend to women
in the public sphere without raising an acute problem about the
patriarchal structure of private life.'[26]

The second possibility, remaking the private sphere, entails
both internal reconstruction and more social recognition.

Re-creation of the private sphere may be seen as a way of enabling women to gain more power in the family, and, by implication, society. At first glance, promoting women's role in the private sphere is an anti-feminist position. The notion of women having power within the private sphere is part of the cult of domesticity. It is characteristic of the movement of conservative women wishing to protect traditional values which defines women's identity primarily in terms of the family and private life. It endorses the idea that women's influence in family relations and domestic matters constitutes a complementary power base to that of the public sphere: 'the hand that rocks the cradle rules the world.'

But the anti-feminist, conservative legitimation of women's power in the family must be distinguished from its opposite – feminist concerns to identify and examine possible sources of power for women in the private sphere. Some recent feminist work has looked in a different way at domestic life. It has focused on the productive and socially necessary nature of housework,[27] and promoted the idea of women being paid for their domestic work. This is regarded as a solution to women's economic dependence and inferior status.

In fact, paying women for their domestic services would not necessarily ensure them power or autonomy. This suggestion assumes that domestic work is like work in the outside world. It is an attempt to analyse domestic work with concepts applicable only to paid work and to the productive relations of the marketplace, rather than asking *why* women do housework and rear children. It therefore implicitly supports assumptions about the 'natural' characteristics and capabilities of women, and does not challenge women's identification with the private sphere.

The 'wages for housework' concept is based, also, on the false premise that money will give women power in the private sphere. But the nature of this power must be examined critically. It is often circumscribed; it is informal, as opposed to the formal power of the public sphere; and its success relies on the tactics typical of subordinated groups – persuasion, cajoling and manipulation.

The private domain is not an autonomous realm. As well as through economic imperatives, home and family life are subject to intrusion from the public sphere in the form of the law and governmental policies. The state actively promotes a certain form of the family and of gender relations: a nuclear family, with the husband as head of the household and main income earner, a necessarily heterosexual institution, preferably based on European, Pakeha culture.

Women are unlikely to gain power and influence through their family activities when the ideal of the family promoted by the state reinforces the separation of the public and private spheres, and supports the subordinated role of women as primarily wives and mothers. The ideal family is promoted by the state in many ways: in the images of the family contained in policy statements, for instance, in the distribution of material resources to families, or in favouring the male wage earner over the female. As telling are the areas where the state neglects the family – for example, the unsatisfactory legislation on wife abuse and rape and the narrow mono-cultural focus of social policy.

Re-creation of the private sphere may be regarded quite differently, not as a means of finding status or power within society but as a means of women creating a self-determined existence, separate from the male-defined world. This is the aim of cultural feminism.

Certainly, the private sphere requires redefinition and re-valuation according to women's experiences. But re-creation should not identify women with unique characteristics which are portrayed as essential, innate and unchanging. This is rigid thinking that confines women to one sphere of life, and ignores both real divisions among women and connections between women and men.

Enlarging women's investment in domestic life will not assure them increased power and status, nor equality with men. Both the cult of domesticity and the cultural feminist movement rest on illusions about the private sphere. Both grant it more autonomy than it really has. It is seen as a place where distinctive values can be fostered and developed, and these values are seen as either having no connection with the outside world, or as being in opposition to it.

The private and the public cannot be separated in this manner. The private is in thrall to the public sphere. Among women who identify themselves with domestic life, there is some recognition of this fact. In the private sphere, as it is traditionally defined, women trade a secondary position in society as a whole for security and supremacy in the household. The transaction is less obvious, but no less real, for cultural feminists. While taking a step away from patriarchal control, they remain bound by patriarchal structures through their isolation in the private sphere. Women who subscribe to the cult of domesticity accept a disadvantaged role; cultural feminists often fail to see that they are saddled with one. They do not realise that the private world, which they see as theirs, is dependent upon the male-dominated public world. In effect, the separate spheres are used not only by men to keep women down but by women to keep themselves down.

At one level this is a wise form of protection. Women value their domestic and emotional strengths. They do all they can to maintain them and find meaning in them. In the world as they experience it, only the private sphere seems to offer them the opportunity to live as they wish.

What they do not realise is that retreat into domestic and emotional enclaves often involves costly bargains. The first is to do with power. By retreating into the private sphere and fostering its values, women connive at their own exclusion from formal and legitimated centres of power. The second bargain is to do with thought. Intuitive thinking is seen as distinctively feminine. It is perceived as being in opposition to the rational thinking that is taken to be distinctively masculine. Ruthless logic is perceived as the only kind of thought possible in a world dedicated to competitive efficiency. It is seen, by women who find their identity within the private sphere, to be both a male prerogative and dehumanising. Women, therefore, should have no part of it. Indeed, it is felt, they must exercise a moral guardianship of the expressive, the transcendent, the ambiguous. Women must protect all the officially repressed but humanly essential qualities that are driven out of the world of masculine thinking. Retreat into the private sphere can entail a retreat from rational thought.

Separation on the basis of gender, with all its damaging consequences, is not inevitable. But strategies for change will mean letting go of the short-term advantages of the private and public worlds as they are, and seeking out the possibilities for fundamental alteration and human gain. Reconceptualisation is the first step, but it is not possible if some of the basic tools of thought are forgone by the very people – oppressed women – who have most need of them.

The third option, abolition of the private sphere, recalls

Engels' solutions to women's oppression. His idea was to abolish the domestic sphere through socialising housework and childcare, and through bringing women into public industry. These strategies are echoed in contemporary feminist demands for good quality, publicly funded childcare, equal opportunities for women in the labour force and a more equitable sexual division of labour in the home.

Engels' solutions suggest a radically altered society. Reallocation of childcare responsibilities and alterations to the domestic division of labour would bring widespread change to both public and private life. Long-held assumptions about women's responsibility for childrearing would be questioned, and resources in the public sphere would be redistributed in order to implement collective responsibility for childrearing and domestic work.

The sexual division of labour has damaging consequences for people confined to or defined by the private sphere. But valued aspects of our lives are also located in the private domain. It cannot simply be abolished. We need to separate scrubbing floors from the warmth and love that can flourish in the private world. The difficult question is: how are people to satisfy their needs for affection, security and intimate relations, if not in some form of private life? Currently, any critical analysis of the family is often met with hostility and resistance. Many women's antagonism towards feminism results largely from an assumption that feminism denies any value to personal life.

As Barrett points out, women seek in a contradictory manner to reproduce the very family structures that oppress them.[28] Family life has many rewards, and the allure of the family is felt no less by feminists. This makes it even more difficult to break through dominant ideas about 'what families should be' and to conceive of new ways of living that promise personal fulfilment, intimacy and security. Fear of losing what we most value stands in the way of full analysis.

But different forms of family and personal life are being explored. Barrett and McIntosh argue that it is not only important to strive for changes in the public sphere – in the law and institutions; people can change their own lifestyles too.[29] They suggest that both sexes benefit from less oppressive relationships based on a greater sharing of childrearing and domestic chores. It is important for people to have choices so they can develop different ways of life at different times and be free to decide not to conform to social expectations such as marriage, heterosexuality or childbearing.

The three strategies so far discussed provide some opportunities for reconstructing gender relations. But they are inherently limited because they do not concentrate their attack on the ideology of separate spheres. Indeed, they work within and confirm existing ways of conceptualising and organising the public and the private. They still accept the doctrine of separation.

It is difficult to burst out of and journey beyond the bounds of the public and the private. The concrete realities of these divisions dominate our lives both as structural constraints and as ideas that have conditioned our thinking. Yet we must find new ways of understanding the two worlds; only if we see more clearly can we act more effectively.

A connection must also be made between activity in the outside world and awareness of the inner world. Feminists have not been wholly successful in bringing together personal and political understandings in the struggle to see afresh. There have been difficulties in placing 'feelings, experiences and consciousness on the agenda for political action'.[30]

The idea that the personal is political is as central to an understanding of the public and private worlds as it is to other forms of action-directed knowledge. Women, as traditional and principal inhabitants of the private sphere, have the advantage of familiarity with it and the disadvantage of being oppressed by it. It is not surprising, then, that women, rather than men, want to try and understand the private sphere. The idea of a 'woman-centred perspective' has been advanced as a crucial element in feminist theory and strategies for change.[31] It is particularly relevant to the ideas discussed in this book. In learning to see the public and private spheres fully and clearly women must at the same time come to know and define themselves and the place they occupy in a male-dominated and male-defined society.

What should we seek to know? First, we need to have a better understanding of the private sphere itself. We must seek to take it apart and separate out its characteristics. Only then can we analyse these as fully and as seriously as we analyse the characteristics of the public sphere. Once we have a clearer picture of what goes on in the private sphere, and how its various components are interconnected, then we can achieve an analytical balance in considering the public and private spheres.

Secondly, we must consider the public and private worlds together. We have argued that our perceptions are shaped not only by the content of the public and private worlds, but also by the very existence of the categories themselves. Their inter-relationship is basic. Solutions to women's oppression are to be found neither solely in the public sphere, nor solely in the private. We can only start to challenge gender inequalities if we concentrate on the point at which public and private separate to become meaningful categories. We must direct our attention to the indeterminate and unchartered borderland between public and private life where inconsistencies in the ideology of separate spheres are likely to be revealed. For change to occur we must identify the contradictions in men's and women's lives. Feminists need to contest the limitations of the sexual division of labour throughout society. It must be challenged in the kitchen, in the workplace and in the House of Representatives. To strive towards a women-centred perspective we have to take many factors into account. It is simplistic to regard New Zealand principally as a patriarchal society. Instead, we need to realise that it is structured along several lines of hierarchy and conflict. Class and race separate women from one another. Therefore we may have to consider the possibility not of a single integrated woman's perspective based on issues of gender alone but of several, compatible women's visions.[32]

This book is an attempt to promote discussion about the public and private worlds in New Zealand society. It is an attempt to start constructing new ways of seeing these worlds both through intellectual understanding and through enquiring into women's experience. It is an attempt to make a contribution to the task that faces feminists in New Zealand, the task of rebuilding the worlds of women and men.

Chapter 2

BRIDGING THE GAP
Paid and Unpaid Work
Rosemary Novitz

It takes me twenty minutes to get home at the end of the day. I like that time. I enjoy being suspended between my job and the need to confront what we will have for dinner, whether there are clean school shirts for tomorrow, and the dwindling supply of milk tokens. This is my time for bridging the gap between the public and the private. The separation between these spheres is marked by my movement from one place to another. Yet these two aspects of my life, these worlds of 'work' and 'home', are also inextricably linked.

For one thing, like most people, and especially most women, I 'work' at my paid job and in my home. Both spheres generate tasks I like and those I would rather avoid. Both also provide opportunities for conversation, humour, conflict and emotional support. I am called at 'work' if my child is sick or has an accident. Phone calls also penetrate the supposedly private retreat of my home, and draw me into the concerns of my paid work and community activities.

Where I live, what I eat, my leisure activities and those of my household are determined by the type of work I do and how much I get paid. The sort of job I do, and the time and energy I can give to it, is in turn limited by the needs of the people with whom I live. My public and private worlds can be distinguished, but they also interpenetrate, feed on one another, are mutually influential, and exist at times in tension.

This chapter explores the relationship between the 'public' sphere of paid work and the 'private' sphere of the unpaid work people do at home. The focus is on differences in the nature and extent of women's and men's involvement in each of these spheres. The lives of both men and women span the public and the private, but they tend to do different things and

23

Photograph by Marti Friedlander

spend different amounts of time in work inside and outside the home.

In this discussion women's lives receive more attention than the lives of men. For women, more often than men, must work to bridge the gap between the public and private worlds we all inhabit. It is they who adjust their hours of paid work to fit in with the time their children are in school, or clean office buildings at night while their partners care for their pre-school children. It is mainly women who organise after-school and school-holiday care, and give up their jobs, for a time at least, when a new baby arrives. They link their households to the local community through Plunket, playcentre and kindergarten committees and their voluntary work in schools. As a result, many mothers feel increasingly like worn elastic, endlessly stretched between their jobs and demands on them at home.

Women experience the pressures of 'bridging the gap' personally and individually. Yet those pressures have their source in the way paid and unpaid work is organised, and in deeply ingrained ideas about women and men. This is the context within which we experience both the separation and the connection between the public and the private. Understanding that context requires that we look both at the history of the relationship between paid and unpaid work in New Zealand and at the contemporary situation.

Ideas about the division between public and private worlds were elaborated in the nineteenth century against the background of the development of capitalism, industrialisation and the increasing tendency for paid work to be located outside the home. The experience of 'going out to work', and the understanding that men should be involved in paid work while women engaged in unpaid work at home, were brought to New Zealand by British settlers.[1]

From the start, the view that women should be economically dependent on men was inconsistent with the fact that many of the first women settlers were single women who arrived to earn their own income. They were employed as domestic servants, agricultural labourers, textile and clothing workers. These women were often encouraged to come to New Zealand in the hope of finding a good husband. But, as Julia Millen suggests, 'they were needed primarily as workers', and 'were employed to do much of the hard and dirty work in the colony' for the lowest of wages.[2]

Clearly women then, as now, were needed both as paid and unpaid workers. There is some evidence that the economic value of married women's unpaid domestic work received more recognition in the later nineteenth century than it does today. Those who sought to convince young men of the advantages of matrimony argued that:

> ... the wife is a great saving to her husband; if he is poor, she cooks for him, makes and mends his clothes, keeps his home in order, looks after the poultry and does a host of little things that he must willingly resign if deprived of her assistance.[3]

Among Pakeha settlers the home was increasingly seen as a haven into which men could retreat at the end of the day, sustained by the labour and love of wives.[4] Jock Phillips has suggested that the pursuit of this ideal of the secure family base, dependent on a male breadwinner, helped to convert tough male pioneers into disciplined wage earners.[5] Employers had an interest in men's acceptance of their responsibility to work in the public sphere in order to sustain life within the private sphere of the family.

This distinction between public and private worlds had little relevance for Maori people whose households were still the sites of work on which they depended for food and shelter. It also did not reflect the experience of many rural Pakeha families attempting to transform bush into farmland using the labour of every able-bodied member of the household.[6]

Even in urban households largely dependent on wages earned outside the home, women worked to contribute money to the household income. Although only a minority of married women were officially in paid work, many women supplemented their husbands' wages by dressmaking, taking in washing, caring for other people's children, or providing meals and accommodation for boarders.[7]

The association of paid work with the public sphere and unpaid work with the private sphere would have meant little to many New Zealand women who, in their homes, integrated work for love and work for money. They would move from their own washing to laundry for which they were paid, put the lodger's food on the table as they served their own family, and, when their husbands were unemployed or deserted them, they would throw themselves once more into domestic service or factory work.[8]

Women's experience of public and private divisions is clearly affected by their class position, and by the earning capacity of the men with whom they live.[9] It is usually in middle class households, essentially those that can be supported on a single wage, where paid work is most closely associated with the public sphere, and unpaid with the private.

In the nineteenth century many women whose households depended on their earnings worked at home sewing flour bags and clothing for large firms. They were supplied with materials, and paid on a piece-rate basis. Women were more likely to do this work in their own homes because they were house-bound by childcare, yet often needed to earn a living. There were considerable advantages to employers in this arrangement. It was a means of evading the Factories Act which bound employers to provide certain minimum conditions of work.[10] Outwork also made it very difficult to unionise the labour of the lowest paid workers.

The 'sweating system' is a good example of how women's position in paid work is an outcome of the interaction between the interests of employers and demands on them in their homes. Sweating was a way of extracting the maximum amount of labour from workers with the minimum cost to employers.

The Coal Mines Act (1891), the Shop and Shop Assistants Acts (1892, 1894) and successive Factory Acts (1891, 1892 and 1894) attempted to curb this exploitation of women workers, sometimes by introducing restrictions on the employment of outworkers, sometimes by limiting women's hours and conditions of work or excluding them from certain jobs.[11] While many New Zealand men never actually earned a 'family wage', the idea that men were entitled to earn enough to support a dependent wife and children for years depressed the wages of women. Single women were seen as merely biding time until they were married and supported by their husbands. Married women were defined as just supplementing the family income, rather than making a vital and necessary contribution to it. Yet the low rates of pay they received were seen as a threat to the employment of the 'legitimate breadwinner in the family – the father'.[12]

The women who received the lowest rates of pay in the 1890s were those working as domestic servants, who usually also worked the longest hours. It seems more than coincidence that the rates of pay were lowest for women when they were doing the work most women did in their own homes for no pay at all. A woman would earn 11s or 12s a week as a sock-knitter, but only 7s 6d a week as an underhousemaid.[13] Women doing similar work to that of men were paid considerably less for their labour. The average skilled tailoress would earn 20s a week. A tailor, however, could earn £3 10s.[14]

Given the fact that young women could barely earn enough to pay for food, clothing and shelter, marriage became for many of them an economic necessity. Their marriage and withdrawal from waged work, of course, perpetuated women's low earnings, and reinforced ideas about women's marginal position in the workforce. Thus beliefs about a woman's place, material necessity and daily experience interacted to reproduce inequalities between women and men in paid employment.

Women in the late nineteenth century were concentrated in domestic service and the clothing and textile industries, but they became increasingly absorbed into clerical work and sales work after the end of the First World War in 1918.[15] While these were relatively new occupations, the expectation that women in paid work were either waiting to get married or supplementing a 'family wage' was again used to justify their low rates of pay.

Veronica Beechey has argued that the concept of the 'family wage', and the special responsibilities women have been expected to assume at home, have often led to a situation where women are paid less than they need in order to sustain themselves, let alone other members of their family. She refers to this as women being paid at rates 'below the value of their labour power'.[16] This means that even women in paid work are often economically dependent on their male partners. It creates still more severe problems for women who live alone and have children to support, since their earnings may barely cover their needs for food, shelter and clothing.

Women's low wages have been both a product of ideology about the family which assumes women's economic dependence on men, and a source of that dependence, for women's earnings have seldom been sufficient to support themselves and their children independently of a male partner or the state.

Ideas about the private sphere of the family thus mould experiences in paid work, and those experiences in turn convert ideas about family relationships into the reality of dependence. Meanwhile some employers benefit from the opportunity to buy women's labour for less than it costs to meet their daily needs.

The definition of women, and especially married women, as marginal to the world of paid work was highlighted in the Depression. During the 1930s married women teachers were refused employment by the Education Department and single women received virtually no unemployment relief.[17] Significantly, when unemployment relief was established for single women through the Women's Employment Committees, it involved a six-week course in cooking and sewing, and the expectation that the women involved would find domestic work in the homes of more prosperous families.[18] Economic crisis seemed to require that women should go back to the home, whether as unpaid or poorly paid domestic workers.

Men were seen as the 'breadwinners' and women were told that they should give up their jobs if they could be done by men.[19] Few women in employment could in fact be replaced by male workers, because women and men were concentrated in different occupations. Men did not have the skills to replace typists, sewing machinists, laundry workers, telephonists and nurses. Gender-specific skills had become an integral part of the New Zealand labour market. The continued association of certain jobs with men and others with women makes it difficult for men to replace women in paid work today.

The Depression exerted contradictory pressures on women. The ideology of women's domesticity was used to discourage women from entering paid work. At the same time the practical necessities of meeting their families' needs pushed women into trying to find paid work regardless of their personal inclinations.

According to Eve Ebbett, for many New Zealand women the Depression did not end with the election of the Labour Government in 1935 and the development of their social security programme. 'The hard times lasted until the war began and jobs for obvious reasons became freely available.'[20] As men vacated jobs, women, who ten years before had been told to remain at home, were encouraged to enter them. The ratio of women to men among those in full-time employment rose from 27:100 in 1936 to 34:100 in 1945.[21]

Women who had seldom been encouraged to do jobs other than machining, food processing, clerical and sales work, nursing or teaching were needed as agricultural labourers and process workers in factories.[22] Under the threat of war, the ideology of women's place in the private sphere started to crumble, together with the association of men with certain jobs and women with others. At the same time many men away at war were sustained by the thought of their homes as retreats from dirt, death and destruction, held together by the efforts of women who devoted themselves full-time to other members of the family.

During the post-war period attempts were made to reassert the view that most women, and especially most mothers, should be involved full-time in caring for their families at home. In the late 1940s, as in the Depression, women were urged to vacate their jobs for men, or were simply replaced by returned servicemen. Women themselves often embraced the security of domesticity after the insecurity of the war years.[23] But as Helen Cook has indicated, there were tensions between this focus on home and family and women's actual involvement in paid employment.[24]

Meeting post-war expectations that families should have fridges and washing machines often required that married women sought paid work.

> ... the new prosperity was vested in the incorporation of more
> workers into the economic machinery, in particular the
> spending of more and more money on domestic consumption.
> This required the incorporation and retention of more wives
> and mothers into the paid work force; their pay packets could
> then enrich their own domestic budgets so that they could
> afford to buy the goods being produced.[25]

While attempts were being made to revive nineteenth-century ideals of the domesticated woman, the proportion of women in full-time employment who were married rose steadily be-tween 1945 and 1956. The total number of women in employ-ment increased throughout the 1950s, and the percentage of all married women in full-time employment almost doubled during this time.[26]

There is also some evidence that not all women meekly

accepted the injunction to devote themselves full-time to their homes and families. Helen Cook has found evidence in the *New Zealand Woman's Weekly* that many women were critical of conditions of work for women at home. As one woman argued:

> It seems to us that the new unpaid servant class, who seem to have no redress, no let up from enervating toil and stupid restrictions are the New Zealand women as housewives and mothers. Life has not become easier for them as it has for the male worker.[27]

Other women noted how a young woman was often 'an absolute captive of her babies' and argued for crèches to relieve women of the 'unremitting demands made on them by small children'.[28] The unpaid work women did at home was increasingly compared with paid work and found to be more demanding than most jobs.

It would be wrong, however, to explain the increasing numbers of women in paid work in the 1950s exclusively in terms of their interest in purchasing the consumer durables which were required in post-war households. There was also an expansion of jobs in fields which had been traditionally defined as 'women's work'. The tertiary sector of the economy in New Zealand, as in other countries, expanded in the post-war period, generating jobs in clerical and sales work as well as personal services.[29] New jobs in health and social welfare, for instance, were seen as ideally suited for women. Women were drawn into employment because, just as in the late nineteenth century, there was a demand for their labour.

The involvement of women in paid work gathered momentum in the 1960s. The proportion of all married women in full-time paid employment rose from 8 per cent in 1945 to 13 per cent in 1956 and to 20 per cent in 1966. Currently 36 per cent of married women are in employment for twenty or more hours a week.[30] While many New Zealanders may associate women with the private sphere of the home and men with the public sphere of paid employment, women are clearly deeply embedded within both spheres, and never more so than in the 1980s when one in every two women of working age is in some form of paid work.[31]

Yet the nature of the work done by women and men still differs, and men remain more extensively involved in paid

31

work. The majority of women in employment are concentrated in the occupations in which their mothers and grandmothers were involved. Women are to be found in clerical and sales work, nursing, teaching, and clothing manufacture, as well as in service work where they predominate among those who clean, cook, launder and wait on tables.[32] Almost half of all those in professional and technical occupations are female, but three-quarters of these women are either medical, dental or veterinary workers, or teachers. Only a third of male professionals do these jobs. Men are found in a much wider range of trades, factory work, professional and technical jobs, as well as being 92 per cent of all those in administrative and managerial work.[33]

Job segregation on the basis of gender is being challenged by many younger women. Almost 50 per cent of those enrolling for medicine are women; an increasing proportion of the student population taking courses in law, commerce, veterinary science, agriculture and forestry is female.[34] More women are also becoming apprentices in a range of trades where they are to be found training as fitters and turners, telecommunications technicians, painters and paper-hangers, carpenters and printers.[35] If these trends gather momentum, encouraged by positive action programmes such as the present financial incentives for employers to take on female apprentices, differences in the nature of the paid work done by women and men will become less obvious. At the moment, however, the contrasts remain stark, for 74 per cent of all women serving apprenticeships are still to be found in ladies' hairdressing, and only 10 per cent of practising lawyers are female.[36] The tendency for many women to be found in occupations which mirror their unpaid work at home also persists, and contributes to the definition of this work as unskilled or semi-skilled.

A focus on the distribution of all women in employment can, however, distort the experience of particular groups of women. While a third of all women in full-time employment are in clerical or related work, only 22 per cent of Maori women workers do this type of work, and an even smaller percentage of Pacific Island women. Maori and Pacific Island women are much more likely to be production workers in factories, transport equipment operators or labourers. Almost half of all Pacific Island women in full-time employment are in this category, compared to 38 per cent of Maori women, and 15 per cent of the total female full-time labour force.[37]

Maori and Pacific Island women are those most likely to be paid to do the domestic work which women do unpaid in their own homes. Thirteen per cent of all women with full-time jobs do service work. Nearly a quarter of all Maori and Pacific Island women are in these jobs. They are also much less likely to be involved in professional and technical occupations.[38] An exclusive focus on the differences between women and men in paid employment can distort differences between women. These inequalities arise out of differences in the sort of jobs they do, the amount they get paid for their work, and the levels of power they have in their workplaces. The jobs in which Maori and Pacific Island women are concentrated make them among the lowest paid workers in New Zealand and those most vulnerable to lay-offs and to seasonal fluctuations in the availability of paid work.

Men tend to spend much more time in paid work than women. Just under half of all women in employment spent thirty or more hours a week in paid work at the time of the 1981 census. In contrast 87 per cent of male workers were on the job for over thirty hours each week.[39] Only 2 per cent of men in employment worked less than twenty hours a week in 1981, compared to 17 per cent of all women in the workforce.[40] According to census definitions of what constitutes part-time employment, this type of work is overwhelmingly the sphere of married women. While part-timers are defined for census purposes as those who are usually in the workforce for less than twenty hours a week, the Department of Labour classifies as part-time workers those who are in employment for less than thirty hours a week. This leads to some confusing and inconsistent conclusions about those in part-time work, depending on whether the source of the information is the census or the surveys of employment conducted by the Department of Labour.

Recent information on part-time work available from the new quarterly Household Labour Force Survey indicates some significant changes in the composition of the part-time labour force between 1981 and 1986. The labour force survey is based on a sample of households rather than information from the entire population, and defines as part-timers those in the labour force for less than thirty hours a week. A comparison of the results of the labour force survey done in the first quarter of 1986 and 1981 census figures reveals that there was an increase of nearly 60 per cent in the incidence of part-time work between 1981 and 1986. The growth in full-time employment was only 3 per cent. According to the most recent survey, one in five employed people work part-time compared with one in eight in 1981.[41]

Most striking is the discovery that, while part-time employment is engaged in by people of all ages and both sexes, male part-time employment has increased by 193 per cent compared to a 34 per cent increase for women. These men tend, however, to be under twenty or over sixty, while the involvement of women in part-time work peaks for married women who are in their thirties and have young children.[42]

The hours women spend in paid work also varies between Maori, Pakeha and Pacific Island women. Maori women with children are least likely to be in any form of paid work, but when they do enter employment they are more likely to work full-time. Pacific Island mothers are more likely to be in some form of paid work, and also more likely to work full-time than part-time. Pakeha women with children under eighteen years old are most likely to be in paid work for less than twenty hours a week.[43] This is probably a consequence of inequalities in the distribution of earnings between Pakeha, Maori and Pacific Island men. Women living with men on lower earnings have greatest pressure on them to contribute to the family income. This pressure interacts, of course, with the difficulties women experience in finding jobs and solving the problems associated with the care of their children while they are away from home.

Part-time work often appears to be the ideal means whereby women can bridge the gap between paid work and demands on them at home. Frequently, however, it means temporary employment and low pay, with minimal opportunities for training and promotion, coupled with the continuing expectation on the part of their families that they will assume the major responsibility for childcare and domestic work.[44] Susan Shipley has also revealed that part-timers are those most likely to experience unemployment.[45] They are also less likely to belong to a trade union or professional association, and therefore least likely to receive the support of any collective action by other workers when they are unfairly dismissed or poorly paid.[46]

Women in part-time jobs are often over-qualified for the work they do.[47] Typists and shop assistants, bookkeepers, telephonists, nurses and machinists frequently take work as cleaners, ward-maids and kitchen hands after the birth of their first child. This is an international trend in women's employment which is given particular expression in New Zealand.[48]

Interviews with Christchurch women in factory and service work have revealed that the need to get work which fitted in with their childcare responsibilities was the main reason for women accepting work which was lower paid and less skilled than the work they did before having children.[49] Part-time work in their previous occupations was often much more difficult to obtain.

Employers are often seen as accommodating themselves to women's desire to spend time at home with their children during the day yet involve themselves in paid work. However, it is important to recognise that employers also have an interest in providing this type of work. As Sylvia Dixon has argued, it is necessary to look at the demand for part-time workers as well as the reasons why women want part-time employment.[50]

The demand for workers who will clean office buildings at night when those who work in them are relaxing at home, the need for round-the-clock nursing care in hospitals, or extra people to wait on tables when restaurants are heavily patronised, all lead employers to offer part-time work. The expectation that mothers should care for their own children during the day, the lack of inexpensive quality childcare services, and the persistence of the view that women should be responsible for cooking, cleaning and washing within New Zealand homes explain why some women often accept the part-time work which is offered.

The demands on women as unpaid workers within their own homes therefore interact with some employers' interests in hiring people to work shorter hours. This produces the contemporary distribution of women and men in part-time employment, and the tendency for part-time workers to be concentrated in certain occupations. Part-time workers tend to be found in community, social and personal services, the wholesale and retail trade, restaurants and hotels because there is a demand for part-time work at what are often considered 'unsocial hours' in these sections of the labour market, or for a fluctuating number of workers on the job at various times.[51]

Those in part-time jobs are often low paid because they do work which has traditionally been done by women. Arguments for equal pay for work of comparable value are challenging the tendency to neglect the skills involved in the work women do and forcing comparisons of traditionally 'male' and 'female' jobs in terms of education, experience, responsibility and the ability to work independently.[52]

Part-time employment is, of course, not inherently poorly paid, temporary work with little prospect of training or promotion. As Sylvia Dixon suggests:

> It is more fruitful to acknowledge that the quality of part-time jobs is primarily a function of the market position and social status of the occupation in which they are embedded, rather than presume in advance that part-time workers are likely to be disadvantaged.[53]

She stresses the variation in the conditions of employment for part-time workers in different occupations and argues that there are 'high quality' and 'low quality' part-time jobs.

This raises the issue of what would constitute 'high quality' part-time work. It would involve permanent employment on relatively high rates of pay as well as access to sick leave, family leave, holidays and bonuses comparable with those of full-time workers doing the same job.

There are positive moves towards better quality part-time employment, yet problems remain. At present, most part-time work is insecure and poorly paid. Part-time work does not make women financially independent within households which include another full-time earner. There is also recent evidence that the growth in part-time work is at the expense of full-time jobs.[54]

Inequalities between households are likely to be heightened when some families include two earners in full-time 'high quality' jobs, while others include one or two people in 'low quality' part-time employment. Those in part-time employment may increasingly be working shorter hours and earning less because it is in employers' interests to offer this type of work, rather than in workers' interests to take it. Many part-time workers would work longer hours if jobs were available, or if it was easier to combine full-time employment with the care of young children or other dependent relatives.[55]

Part-time employment is, therefore, not a simple solution to women's or men's desire to combine paid and unpaid work. It may enable some people to do interesting and satisfying paid work for less than thirty hours a week. It also has the potential to intensify divisions in the labour force between women and men, low paid and highly paid workers, and people at different stages in the life-cycle.

Women earn less than men because they are involved in different jobs and spend fewer hours a week in paid work. As we have seen, the lower rates of pay for occupations in which women are mainly located grow out of ideas about women's place in the home which were elaborated in various ways in the late nineteenth and early twentieth centuries. The earnings of contemporary women workers in clerical and sales work, clothing manufacture, nursing and domestic services are a legacy of the expectation that those who did this work would not have to support a family. As a result, despite the passing of the Equal Pay Act in 1972, women in the 1980s still earn approximately 76 per cent of the average weekly ordinary time earnings of men.[56] The gap between women's and men's wages widens still further when overtime earnings are considered. Men's overtime earnings are on average three times those of women.[57]

While men's longer hours in paid work generate higher earnings, they also have the potential to cut them off from intimate contact with those for whom they are earning this 'family wage'. The negative consequences of this for many men has been poignantly captured by Alison Gray. The pressure to be 'good providers' drives some men to such long hours on the job that they scarcely have time to enjoy contact with the children for whom they worked to provide a home, bicycles, presents, holidays, or just school uniforms and visits to the doctor.[58] Some of the men she interviewed expressed this lack of involvement clearly:

> I come home and I go to bed and I think, 'I've hardly said a word to the kids'.

> For five years, while I was getting the business going and so on, I never saw the kids. I figured that at that particular age, from

say three to eight, a man's input is not as important as it is from now on.

I was out working. Let's face it, the wife brings up most children.[59]

While many men are trapped into the expectation that they will be 'breadwinners' and 'good providers', expectations of economic dependency and low earnings trap women as well. Their economic dependence on men, whether they are full-time or part-time workers, may keep them in unhappy or violent marriages rather than face a lower standard of living on the domestic purposes benefit or on their own earnings. Research has revealed much joint decision-making on economic matters within New Zealand households.[60] Yet women's equal participation in these decisions, and their access to their partners' earnings, depends on men being prepared to give women authority over money the women have not themselves earned. This confers power on men within households, whether or not they choose to exploit it.

The tendency for women's jobs to involve less skill and shorter periods of training than the work in which men are concentrated is sometimes offered as a reason for their lower rates of pay. If this is the case, the solution to the problems posed by women's lower earnings lies in the improvement of women's vocational skills. So it is clearly necessary to widen the range of apprenticeships, on-the-job training, professional and vocational courses done by women.

It is also necessary to look critically at claims that women on the job are less skilled than men. Occupational skills are 'socially constructed'; what is regarded as skilled work is an outcome of negotiation between employers and workers. A job may involve skills which are not recognised as such by employers or society, but nevertheless draw on years of informal training and experience. Thus childcare workers, without formal training, but with years of practical experience, may be employed as unskilled workers. Professional cleaners may be defined as unskilled, although they use training they began to acquire perhaps before they even started school. Sewing machinists may require little training on the job because they have been trained at home and at school in the use of their machines. Objectively this work could be defined as skilled; in fact it may be considered semi-skilled or even unskilled because the skills involved are widely distributed and often taken for granted among women in New Zealand.

In the last ten years there has been increasing recognition that the classification of many women's jobs as unskilled, and men's jobs as skilled or semi-skilled, has only a minimal relationship to the training or knowledge required. As Anne Phillips and Barbara Taylor have expressed it:

> Skill definitions are saturated with sex bias. The work of women is often deemed inferior simply because it is women who do it. Women workers carry into the workplace their status as subordinate individuals, and this status comes to define the value of the work they do. Far from being an objective economic fact, skill is often an ideological category imposed on certain types of jobs by virtue of the sex and power of the workers who perform it.[61]

Recent research in New Zealand on the impact of the introduction of computer technology in the newspaper industry highlights the way skill is socially constructed by certain groups of workers. It also illustrates how some workers can restrict the access of others to certain skills, and hence to higher rates of pay.

During the process of transition to 'cold type' printing using computer typesetting rather than the old linotype machines, female telephonist-typists at a city newspaper were retrained to use visual display terminals to type advertisements directly into the computer system. Male printers were able to use the trade union structure to ensure that these former clerical workers acquired only a limited range of typesetting skills when they were retrained as 'telead operators', using terminals very similar to the ones used by the printers themselves. They were therefore able to limit the access of other workers to new skills, skills which were crucial to the definition of their own work as a highly skilled craft, and therefore worthy of higher pay.[62]

On the basis of her fieldwork, Roberta Hill has suggested that the male printers tended to minimise the skills of women telead operators, who both dealt with customers placing advertisements and typed the advertisements into the computer system.[63] The women were essentially doing two jobs, under considerable pressure to cope with as many calls as possible, and making decisions about which print formats were appropriate for certain advertisements. They felt that their work demanded increased skill and responsibility, and often recognised that attempts by the men to undermine their confidence had their source in printers' interests in retaining their jobs, and the recognition of these jobs as skilled trades-work. As one woman put it:

> He keeps trying to put us down – expecting that we'd make a mess of things. Complaining about our punctuation.... Well, they see us taking over their work. Their work is diminishing and they see we can do it.[64]

Women workers may therefore be doing work which is defined as less skilled than that of men because male workers have sought to limit their access to certain skills. Female vocational choice is clearly not the sole restriction on women's access to work which is recognised as skilled. Men's failure to appreciate the demands on those who do 'women's' jobs also has implications for whether the skills the jobs require are recognised by employers. The retrained telephonists became members of the Printers Union, dependent on male trade union officials to negotiate on their behalf with employers. The interests of male printers lay in maintaining the definition of their own work as superior in skill and responsibility to the work of the former clerical workers.[65] Significantly, the women's earnings did increase as their work became more like that of male printers and less like that of female typists.

It is also significant that the printers often justified their continued right to work within newspaper production on the basis of their role as 'breadwinners' within the family. One of the printers expressed his sense of outrage when he read the comments made by newspaper management on the labour-saving potential of the new technology. His comments reflect the links between men's public lives in paid employment and their private commitments within their families:

> I yelled out to my wife.... She came running. It's really worrying. I'm the breadwinner in our family. Some families have TWO wage earners but in our family there's just me.... What upsets me is the idea that they've used us to iron out all their problems and then they'll just bring their fancy women in.[66]

Men's defence of their privileged position in paid employment may sometimes be at the expense of women workers, but at the same time, in their eyes at least, justified in the interests of the particular women to whom they are bound within the private sphere of the home. Thus, the economic dependency of women in the home who are unpaid has implications for women who are involved in paid work outside the home.

Shirley Dex has suggested that male-dominated craft trade unions have often perpetuated skill divisions between women and men in order to enhance men's earnings and job security.[67] Research has also revealed that some men see women as being disposable in a time of recession.[68] This idea rests, of course, on the expectation that they will, when unemployed, retreat back into their homes to be supported by their husbands. However, unemployed women will not necessarily be supported by a male earner. Usually they and their households need the money the women have been earning.[69]

Unemployment for women represents not just the loss of money for 'extras' in the household but real problems with respect to mortgage payments, grocery bills, money for visits to the doctor or new shoes for children. Financial reasons were those most frequently given by unemployed women seeking work in Palmerston North; boredom and the wish to find personal fulfilment were secondary.[70] While women may often be seen as economic dependants, they clearly see the need to make a financial contribution to the household income as a crucial part of their commitment to others within the private sphere of the home.

Women have become increasingly involved in paid work in New Zealand during a time of economic recession and high unemployment. At times women are perceived to be taking jobs which might otherwise be filled by male 'breadwinners'.[71] However, the persistence of job segregation on the basis of gender serves to make this as untrue today as it was in the Depression of the 1930s. Women's involvement in paid work has increased because there has been an expansion in the sectors of the labour market in which women have traditionally worked. Male workers have neither had the skills to do this work, nor sought to acquire them. At the same time the areas of mining, manufacturing and construction which employ more than a third of all male workers have been particularly hard hit during the present recession. The Department of

Statistics has recently concluded that male unemployment 'has been quite unrelated to women's movement into the labour force.'[72]

There are severe difficulties in accurately measuring current levels of unemployment among women or men. However, available figures tend to suggest that unemployment rates are higher for women than for men. The Population Monitoring Group has concluded that, since peaking in 1983, male unemployment has been declining. At the same time female unemployment, especially for those aged between twenty-five and fifty-nine, has increased considerably between 1981 and 1986. Expansion of jobs in the spheres in which women have been traditionally involved cannot keep pace with their increasing participation in paid work.[73] Recession, rising prices and the decline in the real value of wages draw women into paid work and into unemployment.

Some women are much more likely to find themselves unemployed than others – young people under twenty, for instance, and Maori and Pacific Islanders. In 1981, 16 per cent of women under twenty and 12 per cent of men were unemployed, while the rates for Maori and Pacific Island women in this age group were 44 per cent and 38 per cent.[74] Unemployment is also higher among divorced, widowed and separated women than it is among married women. Single women are those least likely to be unemployed.[75] Those with higher levels of education were also less likely to be unemployed, except that, according to the 1981 census, men are more likely to be employed than women with the same level of education.[76]

Women's vulnerability to unemployment arises out of a number of different factors, and cannot be explained solely in terms of direct discrimination. One of the most significant factors is, however, the constraints deriving from the special responsibilities they are expected to assume for children. The most recent Household Labour Force Survey revealed that many women in the 13 000 households surveyed were unable to find suitable childcare.[77]

Problems with respect to childcare have led a number of women to bridge the gap between paid and unpaid work by doing outwork in their own homes. Just as women in the late nineteenth century produced clothing at home on a piece-rate basis, so today women make curtains, bedspreads, cushions, dresses, skirts and jackets in their own homes. These tasks are fitted in between cooking, washing and childcare as these women integrate in their homes work for pay and work for love. As one woman expressed it:

> You're your own boss ideally, that's the thing, but the work here becomes the boss.[78]

Legislation controlling outwork was introduced in New Zealand in the late nineteenth century, and by 1936 factory owners could only employ one outworker for every ten factory workers. The outworkers were supposed to register with the Department of Labour and receive union award rates for their work. In 1981 the Factories Amendment Act ended these controls on outwork. The government of the time justified this move on the grounds that approximately only 25 per cent of all outworkers were registered. Since the Act could not be enforced, controls were lifted. As a result no figures are available on outworkers since 1981 and it is virtually impossible for unions to contact those who do this type of work. Just as women's unemployment is often disguised, and women's unpaid work is hidden, so women's outwork remains largely invisible.[79]

Like part-time employment, outwork is attractive to women because of their childcare responsibilities, but is only available because employers find it an inexpensive way of employing women. Those doing outwork often supply their own sewing machines, they may pick up and collect patterns and cloth, they provide the space, heating and light in which the work is done. At the same time they may be paid less for their work than factory workers doing the same job.[80]

Outwork is attractive for employers because it maximises output for the lowest rates of pay, just as it did in the late nineteenth century. In 1984 some women outworkers reported working for about 50 cents an hour before tax. In contrast, one of the 'best firms in town' was reported to pay nearly $6 for one and a quarter hour's work.[81] This fluctuation in rates of pay is a consequence of lack of union control over this type of work. Women have to accept the levels of exploitation involved in 'private' paid work because they often find no other way to make money. The ideology of women's place within the private sphere of the home interacts with employers' real material interests to produce a set of workers who are the most vulnerable and the lowest paid members of the workforce. Their experience shatters the middle class ideal of the separation of 'home' and 'work', and illustrates once again the constraints on women over the last hundred years as they manoeuvre to integrate paid and unpaid work.

A young woman caring for two pre-school children, and consumed with domestic activities for eighteen hours a day states that she 'is not working at the moment'. The census excludes questions on the time people spend on housework and child care, but explores in great detail the hours New Zealanders spend in paid employment. Much unpaid work is invisible, taken for granted, and rarely recognised as 'work' even by those who do it. As a result we know very little about the time people spend washing, cooking, ironing, reading stories, growing vegetables, listening to the problems of teenagers, or feeding the baby at 2 o'clock in the morning.

Yet it is this work which ensures that millions of people each day are able to sally forth into their jobs, fed, clothed and rested. This is also the work which prepares another generation to take their places in what is officially referred to as 'the workforce'. Employers and the state tend to assume that habit, love, or sheer necessity will ensure that this essential, but unpaid, work is done. As Marx recognised in the nineteenth century:

> The maintenance and reproduction of the working class is, and must ever be, a necessary condition for the reproduction of capital. But the capitalist may safely leave its fulfilment to the labourer's instinct of self-preservation and of propagation.[82]

Feminists have attempted to make domestic work visible through documenting women's experiences of pregnancy, childbirth, the care of young children and daily household chores. Looking at these activities as 'work' has opened up the possibility of applying to them forms of analysis usually associated with paid work. The status of housework as an occupation, job satisfaction, and the experience of fragmentation of tasks among housewives have received attention.[83] Still more challenging have been analyses of human reproduction which mirror Marxist analyses of the production of things rather than people.[84]

The production of commodities, or goods for exchange, involves those who do not labour to produce these goods acquiring rights in them because they have paid for the labour of those who do this work. When human reproduction is considered, it is women who emerge as the producers of children. Men are those who acquire rights in these children, but are often non-producers, or non-labourers, absolved biologically from the efforts involved in pregnancy, lactation and the labour of childbirth. They are also likely to expend less effort, time and emotional energy in the work which goes into the conversion of babies into adults.[85] Their freedom from this sort of work often enables them to be the major income earners in their households, generating the money on which women depend in order to engage in this usually unpaid reproductive labour. This dependency is a major source of men's power within households.[86]

What evidence do we have that the labour involved in childrearing is so unevenly divided between women and men, and how are tasks like cooking, cleaning and washing allocated in New Zealand households? Is there evidence of change in the distribution of unpaid work between women and men, just as there are changes in women's involvement in work outside the home?

Despite the paucity of research on unpaid domestic labour in New Zealand, we do have some evidence that it is largely 'women's work'. Women were 99 per cent of those whose employment status was 'household duties unpaid' at the time of the 1981 census. While less than 1 per cent of all adult males are in this category, just over 41 per cent of all women over fifteen years old classified themselves in this way.[87]

Questionnaires from a random sample of women drawn from electoral rolls in 1984 revealed that 30 per cent of those who responded did all the housework in their homes, while nearly 50 per cent said that they did most of the household chores. This suggests that 80 per cent of the 252 women surveyed did all, or most, of the cooking, cleaning, washing and other housework in their families. Only 5 per cent of these women thought that they received more help from their husbands or partners than they got a decade ago, and only 14 per cent suggested that housework was divided equally between themselves and other members of their family. When men did participate in housework they were likely to be seen as 'helping', and the overall responsibility still rested with their partners. As one woman put it: 'My family help a bit, but I have to organise it.'[88]

The men who responded to this questionnaire were more likely to think that men now participate more in household chores and family life. They also thought that this was most likely to occur when women are in paid work outside the home.

Other studies also provide some evidence for increasing involvement by men in domestic work as the women they live with become more involved in work outside the home. Some of the men Alison Gray interviewed for *The Jones Men* indicated that they spent more time with their children when their wives entered paid work. This was often a real source of pleasure rather than a chore. As one man said:

> I've got a tremendous relationship with the kids now because my wife works Friday, Saturday and Sunday nights, sometimes Monday too. So I get home from work – just to say goodbye to her, then she's off. Then I've got to cook tea, bath the kids and put them to bed. My daughter thinks the sun rises and shines on me....[89]

Significantly, however, these studies still tend to reveal that it is women who fit their paid work into the times when husbands, other family or friends will be available to care for their children. Men are much less likely to adjust their paid work to their children's need for care. Their involvement in childcare is often at the expense of leisure activities, time with other men, reading or TV watching. Seldom do they try to find a job which fits in with the time their partners will be at home at the end of a day.

The Family Networks project which involved an in-depth study of sixty-eight randomly selected families in the greater Wellington area revealed that women with children under five tend to adjust their hours of paid work to the times husbands, family or friends were available to take over the care of young children. As a result, the main caregivers in these households, usually women, worked irregular hours, 'most commonly ... arranged to fit around the family.'[90] Their partners were usually in full-time employment.

Only one of the women in this study said that her husband had adjusted his hours on the job to fit the needs of his family.

Overall, this research confirmed the findings of other studies by indicating that, when children are young, women fit their paid work around the family, while men tend to fit time for their families around their involvement in full-time employment.

The pattern for men to 'help' with domestic work rather than assume equal responsibility for it, and for women to fit their employment around their family's needs, emerged in a number of studies done in the mid 1970s. These studies also indicated that men were much more likely to be involved in the care of their children than they were to cook a family meal or do the housework. Interviews with 200 women in Christchurch with children under sixteen years old did, however, suggest that the more women became involved in paid work outside the home, the more likely they were to want the tasks of childcare, cooking and cleaning to be shared equally between themselves and their partners.[91]

The gap between how people would like to divide tasks in their households, and how these tasks are actually divided, is neatly illustrated by some recent research which compared expectations before marriage with who did what a year after marriage. The responses showed some significant shifts towards more traditional patterns during that year; even couples who expect to divide tasks equally may find this difficult to accomplish in practice. Most likely to share domestic work were men and women who accepted feminist ideas about female equality and the need to avoid stereotypes, those with mixed flatting experiences, and those in households in which women had experienced high levels of education.[92]

Research into unpaid domestic work in New Zealand consistently suggests that, while men may be spending more time with their children,[93] and husbands of women in paid work spending slightly more time on housework, the major responsibility for unpaid household work and childcare still rests with women, even when they are in full-time employment. Garth Fletcher's study of fifty Hamilton households revealed that, when hours of paid and unpaid work are combined, women in employment for over twenty hours a week had a longer working week than either their husbands or women not involved in employment. He concluded that it is women in paid work rather than their husbands who adapt their patterns of household work to the demands on them in their jobs. They adjust to the situation by spending less time during the week on housework and childcare, and make up for this at weekends by spending, on average, five hours each day on housework. Their husbands spent half this time in household chores over the weekend.[94]

Men in New Zealand do, however, have a strong tradition of involvement in a range of unpaid practical tasks other than childcare and housework.[95] They may spend more time in various do-it-yourself activities like home decorating, carpentry and car repair than they do washing or vacuuming. Yet the time men spend on these tasks is miniscule relative to the vast amounts of time women spend on housework and childcare. These do-it-yourself activities also have the advantage of leaving a tangible product, one which can often be given some monetary value. A month of meal preparation and nappy washing leaves little evidence of the effort which has been expended.

Women still seem to be those most involved in work for 'love' rather than money within the private sphere of the home. This, as we have seen, has important implications for the nature and extent of their involvement in paid work. Their lower earnings and shorter hours of employment in turn reinforce expectations that they will do more domestic work, give up their job when there are prospects of promotion for their partner in another town, or take time off when children are ill.

As those investigating the 'new home economics' argue, we can expect that 'necessary time inputs into the household are likely to be done by the partner whose forgone earnings are lowest'.[96] Since women's earnings are usually lower than men's, they tend to be the people in the household most likely to sacrifice their earnings in order to meet their families' demands for care. Women's position in the public sphere of paid work therefore both moulds and is moulded by their life in the home.

It is also women rather than men who assume responsibility for the care of elderly people within the family.[97] Many women start caring for an elderly parent just when their children's needs start to decrease. This unpaid work may keep women in part-time employment or lead them to give up their jobs and sacrifice their earnings just when they are reestablishing themselves in the paid labour force. Responsibilities not only for parents but also for children has an effect on the extent of their involvement in work for pay.

Much of this discussion has focused on households composed of two adults and their children. In fact, only 38 per cent of all households in New Zealand now consist of a man, a woman and one or more dependent children. Almost a quarter of households are composed of men and women who live together without children, and there has been a rapid increase in the number of people who live alone (17 per cent of all households in 1981). Six per cent of households consist of solo parents and their dependent children.[98]

An increasing number of women are living alone with their children, assuming responsibility for their economic support as well as performing the traditional caring tasks. More men are living alone or flatting with non-family members and doing a range of tasks often done by their mothers in the households in which they grew up. People are postponing the birth of their first child, and therefore spending longer periods of time living together, with both partners equally involved in paid work.[99] While there is little statistical information on the proportions of households consisting of gay men and women, they are also undoubtedly increasing, and inevitably challenging the traditional division of labour between women and men.

At the same time, there are growing numbers of women in paid employment, and these increases are most obvious among married women with young children. All these trends lead us to expect some significant changes in the distribution of work in the home between women and men, and in the association of housework and childcare with women. Research evidence for a shift towards a more equal division of work in the private sphere remains scant. There have been few studies in this field, and possibly they have focused too much on households which are likely to be least innovative in their allocation of unpaid work. But people may also be adapting rather more slowly than we might expect to the changes outlined above.

One possible solution to the difficulties women experience as they try to bridge the gap between paid and unpaid work is that women should simply become more like successful men. This would mean consigning the care of their children largely to others and devoting themselves to achievement in the public sphere. If enough women did this, there might be similar proportions of women and men in the most privileged sections of the labour market. Some women might be better off than other women, but inequalities between women and men might become less glaring.

However, many feminists have been critical, not just of inequalities between women and men, but of the way work is organised, of wage gaps between those in different jobs, and of power hierarchies in the workplace. Opportunities for a few women to live the lives of highly paid powerful men, freed from domestic responsibilities, is seldom seen as the solution to the problems faced by the majority of women. Rather than focusing on the incorporation of women into the structure of paid work as it is presently organised, feminists have argued that we need to question the sanctity of the eight-hour-a-day, forty-hour week and find more collective and collaborative ways of organising the workplace. There is also increasing recognition that powerful economic interests are served by the continued concentration of women in low paid jobs with little job security. The interaction between women's involvement in paid and unpaid work has made available workers whose low wages contribute to employers' profits. Real change in the situation of the majority of women workers will inevitably challenge the economic interests of those who employ them.

The changes many feminists seek are therefore not just strategies whereby individual women might increase their earnings and exert more power in a male-dominated society. They are changes which will transform the structure of this society, the way it is organised and the economic and political relationships between people within it. Our society tends to elevate individual choice; people are expected to control their own destinies, to determine the shape and colour of their lives. We are brought up to believe that choice, individual effort and unique opportunity are all that lie between us and a different, possibly better life. If, however, our lives are not solely determined by ourselves, but are the outcome of an interaction between our individual inclinations and the way our society is organised, then we can only live different lives by changing the structures that limit our options, and rethinking some of the understandings which prompt us to act in certain ways.

While we may dream of big changes, small changes which lead to modification of the system rather than its transformation are still important. There have therefore been struggles for permanent part-time work in the public service, for equal pay for work of comparable value, for incentives for employers to take on female apprentices, and for job-sharing and flexible hours of work. There has also been increasing pressure for the provision of a variety of inexpensive childcare services.

Despite some initiatives in these directions, it is still very difficult to combine paid and unpaid work in ways that go beyond the stereotype of the nine-to-five job within a hierarchical work environment in which people receive very unequal rates of pay for working equally hard at different jobs. While more men are becoming convinced that they should increase the time they spend in childcare and domestic work, the burdens of trying to juggle time between the spheres of paid and unpaid work are still primarily borne by women.

Ann Oakley has seen this as a consequence of the persistence of the male model of 'a career'. Women, she suggests, have not been able to develop an alternative model of involvement in both paid and unpaid work which does not carry with it substantial penalties, traps and pitfalls:

> For them [women], the problem, since the present social structure was established in the eighteenth and nineteenth centuries, has always been to reconcile the conflicting demands of home and work in such a way that they appear to be conforming either to the feminine housewife model or to the male career model. An acceptable alternative pattern has yet to be established – either for women or for men.[100]

Women's experience of the double burden of paid and unpaid work, and the realisation by many men that they do not, and will not, earn a 'family wage', lie behind an increasing questioning of the inevitability of female domesticity. They also generate challenges to traditional ways of organising employment and family life.

Many of us have developed individual strategies for combining paid and unpaid work that daily test our ingenuity and our energy. Through these strategies we try to accommodate demands on us as parents, and the children of our parents, as well as employees, husbands, wives, lovers and friends. Changes to the way paid work is organised and the division of work between women and men (in the home and outside it) are necessary if we are ever to bridge more creatively the gaps between our private and public worlds.

Chapter 3

TO US THE DREAMERS ARE IMPORTANT

Rangimarie Mihomiho Rose Pere

E hine! hei ona wa
kā kite koe i te puawaitanga
o te moemoea, te wawata
Kā rongo hoki Koe
I te pumanawa – pumau...
E hine! e Kore e Waikura e.

Young girl! the time will
come to pass when you will
realise our dreams, our hopes,
you will also experience the
deeper meaning of intuitive
intelligence, creativity –
innate qualities.... Young
girl! these do not perish with
time.

Picture if you will the following analogy. A team of women is working on a tukutuku panel.[1] The chief designer has told the women working in the front of the panel what designs they need to use to symbolise her dream. These women pass threaded needles back and forth through the slats to partners at the back of the panel. The dreamer knows how the whole design will eventually look – she represents the pure intellectual. The women working in the front of the panel initiate the design and see it unfolding as the needles pass back and forth at strategic points – these women represent the academics who set up the 'blueprint' within society. The women at the back of the panel are an important part of the process, but the vision that unfolds before them is cluttered and blurred – these women represent the 'masses'.

I have had dreams for as far back as I can remember, and I continue to have dreams. For me life's moments are to be savoured whether they be good or bad. For me dreams enable me to capture the magic that comes with each day. The dreamers are important.

Lake Waikaremoana. National Publicity Studios.

Born in Ruatahuna a half-century ago, I was strongly influenced by my natural mother's kinship groups. I was transferred from my natural mother to my maternal grandparents soon after birth. I regarded my maternal grandmother as a mother. The word mother has a wide range of meaning. In Maori kinship terminologies, no distinction is made among the related women of one's parents' generation. One's aunt in English becomes one's mother. In Maori an individual uses matua (father) for all male relatives, and whaea (mother) for all female relatives in his or her parents' generation.

Up to the age of seven I lived with my maternal grandparents on an ancestral block of land called Ohiwa, approximately 20 kilometres south east of Waikaremoana. Ohiwa is a 270-hectare block of land that was originally cultivated and settled by Ngati-Hika, a sub-tribe of Kahungunu. Several pa sites, burial grounds and various artefacts remind me and my kin of its sometimes turbulent history.

A brief account of my ancestry is also important to me as a Maori. It establishes my rapport with readers. Te Iriheke, who was my maternal grandfather, was himself the son of a Kahungunu father by the name of Te Rangi and a Tuhoe-Potiki Ngati Ruapani mother, Ngawini. My maternal grandmother, Mihomiho, was herself the daughter of an Englishman, Fenton Arundel Lambert, and a Tuhoe-Potiki mother, Te Au Mihomiho. Some of these forebears lived and farmed on Ohiwa along with elders and other relatives. Many other people used Ohiwa as a meeting place, and a place for stopping over when travelling through on horseback.

I slept, ate, played, worked and learnt alongside four generations, and was never excluded from anything my grandparents were involved with, including attending celebrations, tangihanga (ceremonial mourning) and many other gatherings. I learnt through observation and participation. It was my grandparents' generation, and older, who influenced most of my learning in those formative years. After my grandfather died in 1944, I joined another part of the family at Waikaremoana so that I could attend the Kokako Native School; but my grandmother, Mihomiho, continued to influence my life until her death ten years later.

I should also acknowledge Ngati Rongomaiwahine, Ngati Kahungunu and Ngati Porou, my father's tribal groups and in particular members of the following hapu (sub-tribes): Ngati

Hika and Ngai Tahu-Matua. Harry, my paternal grandfather, who died in 1931, was the son of Bertram Lambert and Teia of Ngati Hika. Wiki, my paternal grandmother, who died in 1983, was the daughter of Tu Kapuarangi and Ani Karaitiana. Through Ani I am united to Hauiti Tuatahi and Hine-te-Ra of the Tairawhiti tribes.

As a female, I have been exposed to very positive female models from both my natural parents descent-lines. The most senior men and women in my immediate kinship groups set the example of complementing, respecting and supporting each other. They made it quite clear from the legacy they left that men and women, adults and children, work alongside each other and together. Retaining this close interaction of all members of the extended family during the waking and working hours of the day is extremely difficult and often quite impossible in the urban situation. There are few services or social occasions in the wider community that encourage and allow for extended families of all age groups to participate together on a regular basis. The role of parenting is left to one person in many instances (usually the mother). Social and economic pressures, including other implications, can also be added to further complicate such an important responsibility. Within traditional Maori society, parenting and following through the development of a child were the responsibility of the whanau as a whole.

The adult models to which children are exposed in their formative years dictate and influence the way people later think and feel about themselves. My Maori female forebears, before the introduction of Christianity, and the 'original sin of Eve', were extremely liberated as compared to my English tupuna. With the exception of slaves (male and female), the women were never regarded as chattels or possessions; they retained their own names on marriage. Retaining their own identity and whakapapa (genealogy) was of the utmost importance and children could identify with the kinship group of either or both parents. The clothing and ornaments of traditional Maori men and women were very similar in both texture and appearance, particularly over-garments, such as cloaks. Clothing was loose-fitting and flowing so that pregnant women were never restricted by the 'fads of fashion' that for English women could include tight corsets. Conception was not associated with 'sin'; childbearing was not seen as a 'form of punishment and suffering' but rather as uplifting and within the natural order of life.

Assault, which could have included rape or an insult to women, involved a penalty of death or some very severe punishment for the offender. For example, a woman of Tuhoe-Potiki had her back badly injured by her third husband. Her kinship group, one of whom was the 'head' of one of her hapu, declared the husband 'dead'. This punishment was worse than physical death because he was completely ignored and boycotted by the whole community, including his own immediate family. Children persecuted and abused him because he was a 'non-person' and when he finally died he was buried without ceremony.

As a grandchild who was truly blessed and loved, I am drawing extensively on my own experience and on the knowledge that has been shared with me by my immediate elders. Most of the information in this study is from whanaunga (relations), and from consulting the work of other research workers and writers.

It is not simple to share information and knowledge about the way people consider the type of preparation their children should receive in order to fit them for the role of adult life. My intention is not to give answers or solutions to questions that this generation or future generations might have, but rather to experiment in the use of new methods of analysis and the furthering of new understandings.

An over-simplification of the diversity of Maori institutions not only produces the errors inherent in averages but disregards the vivacity of the Maori people themselves. Their lives and institutions were far from static and consistent before the arrival of the Pakeha, and have certainly not been so since. But it is convenient for the Pakeha to collectivise 'the Maori' and restrict an understanding of the conflicts between us to 'agreed' areas. But such an approach hardly reflects the realities of human interaction. My own small contribution to resolving these difficulties is to share at least a part of my knowledge with you. I have no intention of sharing it all. Tribal histories are not public matters; but the memories of childhood experiences coupled to the position of women in my own descent-lines may be particularly topical today.

My views on this matter resemble those expressed by John Rangihau, a Tuhoe-Potiki kinsman, and give a timely warning for anyone who sets down hard and fast rules about Maori institutions and concepts.

> There is no such thing as Maoritanga.... Each tribe has its own way of doing things. Each tribe has its own history. And it's not a history that can be shared among others.... I can't go around saying because I'm a Maori that Maoritanga means this and all Maoris have to follow me. That's a lot of hooey. You can only talk about your Tuhoetanga, your Arawatanga, your Waikatotanga. Not your Maoritanga. I have a faint suspicion that this is a term coined by Pakeha to bring the tribes together. Because if you cannot divide and rule, then for tribal people all you can do is bring them together and rule ... because then they lose everything by losing their own tribal identity and histories and traditions.

When Elsdon Best wrote the tribal saga of *Tuhoe*, he decreed that the ancestral gods should determine whether the book should keep the tribal canoe afloat or whether it should flounder on some hidden rock. A tribal canoe needs far more than a book to keep it afloat; it needs people to believe that it can transport them to new horizons. The Urewera and all that it conveys to those who visit, and the way that it intrigues and inspires those who 'belong', helps to assure me that the tribal canoe is still afloat even in these very challenging, turbulent times. Indeed, all the tribal canoes are afloat – the current resurgence of tribalism makes it quite clear that we know from whence we came and that we want to chart our own direction into the future.

Many of us identify ourselves with the awe-inspiring beauty of the Urewera bush, a domain that is made up of different families of trees from the young to the ancient, with their roots deeply entrenched in Papatuanuku. While there are also many other New Zealanders, who appear to be symbolised by the Kaingaroa Forest with its one family of pine trees standing row after row in their sameness, one is ever hopeful that the schools will contribute to their growth by way of diversity.

I also identify with Hine Pukohurangi, the heavenly mist maiden who mantles everything she gently embraces! The following song was composed by my daughter Katherine Ngarangi Tautuhi on 6 February 1984:

| Hine Pukohu | Beautiful Mist Maiden |
| te ngahere | O'er the trees |

nga maunga	O'er the mountains
te moana	O'er the sea
He taonga miharo	Beautiful vision
na te Kaihanga	From the Maker
Nana nga mea Katoa	Maker of all things
he taonga miharo	beautiful vision
Na te Matua?	from the supreme.

I know that traditional Maori institutions are often criticised and attacked for being sexist, and yet for me the language, with its values and beliefs, clearly indicates otherwise. Our tribal traditions are serving us well, and it is time to break down some of the myths espoused by Maori and non-Maori people who are either ill-informed and ignorant, or who are playing their own power games.

Within my own tribal groups women are of paramount importance and this is symbolised through positive concepts being associated with females: wahine (identifying with the first female parent, Hine-Wao – unlike 'women' from the womb of man), Papatuanuku (mother earth), hapu (pregnancy, large kinship group), awa tapu (sacred river of life – menstruation), whare tangata (house of humanity), waka tangata (the canoe that is the lifeline of the family and the transmitting of a heritage). In Tuhoe-Potiki the women are the first communicators on the marae and no official occasion begins without them. No self-respecting Tuhoe male will go on to a marae without a woman. I am more than familiar with this important role and have carried it throughout the country because other tribal groups also recognise its significance. Within Ngati Kahungungu I have been given full speaking rights on the marae and spoke just recently on the marae at Waipatu, Hastings, as a lead into a wananga for young Maori women from all over New Zealand. These young Maori women were deeply moved by the whole experience. The majority of them did not know very much about their own heritage. Maori women from traditional backgrounds have always had the role of mediators and learn to develop communication skills to a very high level. In international conferences I have attended there has been acknowledgement of the work of Maori women as social scientists.

In contrast to coastal tribes, Tuhoe-Potiki had a harsh hinterland environment. Resources were sparse and limited.

The rhythms of their life reflect that situation. Both sexes and all age groups were trained to know their environment and were expected to utilise its resources. A person, no matter of what age or sex, was expected to perform, or at least to attempt, any task that confronted them. The survival of the individual and group depended on this type of philosophy. As a child in Waikaremoana, I saw both men and women performing the same tasks – from delivering and caring for babies to fencing, ploughing and digging roads. In consequence there were no distinct or formal boundaries for men's and women's work habits or patterns. The girls and boys played the same games – including rugby at school, did the same chores, and fought together in feuds amongst whanau. One learned to assume responsibility and think independently at an early age. It was as a total person, rather than as a male or female, that one came to recognise oneself.

I also wish to share a part of my philosophy with readers. This statement is about the total development of the individual within the context of the family. The symbol that is being used to define this totality is Te Wheke (the octopus). Only a limited interpretation of my basic beliefs can be given in English. It thus involves the hermeneutic difficulty of expressing the concepts of one culture in the language of another. There are twelve stages of learning that I know of from my immediate forebears, and I am still at stage one. There are so many things that one can take for granted from one's own heritage. I have only realised the full significance of what my immediate elders tried to share with me as a child through comparing it with what I have seen from a western university in New Zealand. I was very fortunate to receive the teachings of a people who could traverse the universe through the aristocracy of the mind.

TE WHEKE (THE OCTOPUS)
An explanation of the symbol is as follows:

The body and the head represent the individual/family unit.

Each tentacle represents a dimension that requires and needs certain things to help give sustenance to the whole.

The suckers on each tentacle represent the many facets that exist within each dimension.

The eyes reflect the type of sustenance each tentacle has been able to find and gain for the whole.

The intertwining of the tentacles represents a merging of each dimension. The dimensions that have been mentioned need to be understood in relation to each other and within the context of the whole because there are no clear-cut boundaries.

I will now make reference to each tentacle by beginning with:

WAIRUATANGA (SPIRITUALITY)
Sustenance is required for the spiritual development of the individual, the family. The Creator, the Great Parent, the Supreme Influence is of the utmost importance. The Creator, the most powerful influence we have, is recognised as the beginning and the ending of all things. The Creator has planted a language and given a unique identity to me and my Maori forebears. We have given this identity an earthly form. Our forebears transmitted numerous incantations, beliefs to help give sustenance to this spiritual existence.

An absolute belief in a Supreme Influence has always been a part of my Maori heritage. The closest I can get to the Creator is to retain and uplift the unique identity he has given me. The world view of the Maori is that people are the most important of all living things in the physical world, because we believe we are in the image of the Creator. We do not support the Darwin theory and do not classify ourselves as belonging to the animal kingdom. The sacred seed of life and the sacred river of life are from the Creator. My natural parents link me up to the beginning of humanity. I was baptised in and born of water – my mother's.

MANA AKE (UNIQUENESS IN THIS CONTEXT)
Just as one is aware of a child's heredity from forebears, there is also an awareness of those things that make a child absolutely unique. This absolute uniqueness is a part of the individual's own mana as a whole. *As long as humanity has existed there has never been any one who is exactly the same as any one else.* This concept also applies to the family unit. If a family receives sustenance that gives them a positive identity with their mana intact, then that family will have the strength to pursue those goals and those assets that can uplift them. A balance has to be kept between individual and group

61

endeavour. My elders only gave me guidelines to help me
through life because they had the utmost respect for my mana
ake – my absolute uniqueness.

MAURI (LIFE PRINCIPLE, ETHOS)
If great importance and support is given to the mauri of each
individual in the family, in time the individual, the family, will
appreciate the mauri in other people, the mauri in meeting
houses, the mauri of traditional courtyards, the mauri of trees,
the mauri of rivers, the mauri of the sea and the mauri of
mountains. The traditional courtyards and the mountains of
New Zealand have heard and felt the mauri of the language as
spoken by our Maori forebears before the intrusion of any
other. The mauri of the language and the mauri of everything
else that has been mentioned is very important to the family
unit and the way it can withstand negative influences. Respect
for the natural environment and conservation are important
aspects of the whole.

HA A KORO MA A KUI MA (THE 'BREATH OF LIFE'
FROM FOREBEARS)
The 'breath of life' mentioned here relates to the heritage that
has come down from Maori forebears. Sustenance from
knowing one's own heritage in depth is important. A basic
belief is that one's future is linked up with one's past so that if
the heritage is firmly implanted then the members of the
family will know who and what they are, the unique identity
that they have, will remain intact. Families who have had their
heritage transmitted to them have a strong central core that can
enable them to become universal people.

TAHA TINANA (THE PHYSICAL SIDE)
The family must receive sustenance for its material and bodily
needs. The general guidelines required would relate to
medication, suitable foods, suitable and appropriate clothing,
appropriate means of shelter, different types of recreation
including physical education, everything that pertains to
physical survival. The body is regarded as sacred and requires a
set of disciplines. The head is regarded as the most important
part of the body and has its own set of restrictions, tapu,
placed on it. If one does not take care of her or his head, then

worrying about everything else pertaining to the body is pointless. The genital region is also regarded as very tapu, particularly in women – the sacred 'houses of humanity'.

Tremendous respect is given to the body and the way one should use it. A mother cherishes and nurtures her child in the womb, and when one is old enough to take over the responsibility of his or her body, then this cherishing and nurturing must continue. As a child and grandchild I remember the physical warmth, the tremendous flow of love that I received from my many parents and grandparents. They taught me to adjust and to accept change – to think things out for myself. They taught me to realise that my physicalness as a human being would be a constant challenge to me.

WHANAUNGATANGA (THE EXTENDED FAMILY, GROUP DYNAMICS, SOCIAL INTERACTION)

Whanaungatanga is based on the principle of both sexes and all generations supporting and working alongside each other. Families are expected to interact on a positive basis with other families in the community to help strengthen the whole. Families receive sustenance for this dimension when they feel they have an important contribution to make to the community they live in. Genealogy, whakapapa, is an important part of whanaungatanga. It is the basic right of the child to know who his or her natural parents are even if he or she is adopted out. The spirit of the child amongst other dimensions begins from conception and relates to the child's forebears. A basic belief of the Maori is to expose a child to his or her kinship groups as soon as possible and throughout the whole of his or her lifetime.

The extended family is the group that supports the individual through a crisis or anything else of consequence. Kinship identity is most important. Affection, physical warmth and closeness of members of a kinship group is encouraged and fostered. Traditionally men and women who did not produce children of their own could foster a relative's child or children. Some of our most famous ancestors and Maori people of more recent times did not produce any issue of their own, but were still regarded as most outstanding leaders and tribal parents. The concept of Matua-Whangai – foster parents – is becoming prevalent throughout Maoridom again. Today some of us extend whanaungatanga across the world community; for example, I have been adopted by a Cherokee family and am addressed and known as White Eagle.

WHATUMANAWA (THE EMOTIONAL ASPECT)

Sustenance and an understanding of emotional development in the individual, and the family as a whole is considered important. Children are encouraged to express their emotions so that the people who are involved with the parenting know how to support, encourage and guide the children. Crying for joy or sadness by both sexes is regarded as natural and healthy by the Maori. This form of expression is not regarded as a weakness. Emotional involvement and interaction are regarded as important meeting points for human beings. Creativity, which is innate in each person, can often be developed through this aspect of total learning. Human emotion is still one of our most powerful forms of body language and the Maori, among other Polynesians, acknowledges it in a very positive way.

HINENGARO (THE MIND – 'THE HIDDEN LADY' – THE SOURCE OF THE THOUGHTS AND EMOTIONS)

Approaches of learning that arouse, stimulate and uplift the mind are very important. My immediate forebears believed in the aristocracy of the mind and despised anyone who tried to tamper with the mind. The mind if nurtured well knows no boundaries, and can help one to traverse the universe. Intuitive intelligence is encouraged and developed in some individuals to a very high degree. There is a strong belief in exercising and using all of the senses on a regular basis. First-hand experiences are most important to the whole notion of learning. Thinking, knowing, perceiving, remembering, recognising, abstracting, generalising are all processes which refer to the intellectual activities of the hinengaro. Emotional activities such as feeling, sensing, responding and reacting are also processes of the hinengaro. There is no doubt in my hinengaro that intuitive intelligence has helped me to remain fairly intact in myself as a total person.

WAIORA (TOTAL WELL BEING)

If each symbolic tentacle receives sufficient sustenance for the whole then the eyes of the individual and the symbolic family unit will reflect total well being. Waiora is my definition of total well being as shared with me by my elders. If people from the wider community wish to help Maori people face up to the challenges confronting them in today's world, then I feel that some cognizance must be given to the philosophy I have tried to share within the limitations of English as my second language.

As a human being I have the basic right to seek enlightenment, to extend my own mauri, my life force, in every possible way. I have many limitations but the influences of my early childhood in Ruatahuna (my birthplace) and Waikaremoana make me strive to go forward, to learn, and to face up to the challenges that confront one in today's world. I remember one of my elders saying that if I stood tall, my ancestors would also stand tall. I can respect and appreciate other cultures, including other traditions, because of the way I feel about my own. I am learning to understand my own culture by comparing it with others and I am proud to be able to share and to contribute something that is from my own heritage. While humanity has many universals, the Maori people have their own unique contribution to make to the fellowship of peoples.

Sylvia Siddell, Intruder, *1983, pencil drawing, 64 × 46 cm. Private Collection*

Chapter 4

PRIVATE LIVES AND PUBLIC FICTIONS

Aorewa McLeod

I have been teaching *the bone people* by Keri Hulme as part of a course on twentieth-century women writers. I have talked about it as a novel by a woman writer and a novel about sex-roles, gender stereotyping, the nuclear family and the violence inherent in parent–child relationships. I have talked about it as a novel that deconstructs the binary thinking of our culture – male/female, black/white, parent/child, mind/body.

It's a radical and innovative novel in New Zealand writing, but particularly so in the context of women's fiction. When Hélène Cixous, the French Feminist theorist, writes of the concept of *écriture feminine* she suggests that as yet it's an ideal, only a utopian possibility, and that most women are still writing within the terms of male discourse. But the radical and utopian nature of Hulme's text closely parallels the image the French feminists give of the *écriture feminine* of the future, when they describe the metaphysical feminism which moves past and negates all concepts of gender difference as being part of the phallocentric symbolic system. Cixous begins her article 'Sorties', looking for the new woman:

Where is she?

Activity/passivity,
Sun/Moon,
Culture/Nature,
Day/Night,

Father/Mother,
Head/heart,
Intelligible/sensitive,
Logos/Pathos.

Form, convex, step, advance, seed, progress.
Matter, concave, ground – which supports the step, receptacle.

Man
——————
Women

Always the same metaphor: we follow it, it transports us, in all
of its forms, wherever a discourse is organized. The same
thread, or double tress leads us, whether we are reading or
speaking, through literature, philosophy, criticism, centuries of
representation, of reflection.
Thought has always worked by opposition,
Speech/Writing
High/Low

By dual, *hierarchized* oppositions. Superior/Inferior. Myths,
legends, books. Philosophical systems. Wherever an ordering
intervenes, a law organizes the thinkable by (dual,
irreconcilable; or mitigable, dialectical) oppositions. And all the
couples of oppositions are *couples*. Does this mean something? is
the fact that logocentrism subjects thought – all of the concepts,
ʼthe codes, the values – to a two-term system, related to 'the'
couple man/woman?
Nature/History,
Nature/Art,
Nature/Mind,
Passion/Action.

Theory of culture, theory of society, the ensemble of
symbolic systems – art, religion, family, language – everything
elaborates the same systems. And the movement by which each
opposition is set up to produce meaning is the movement by
which the couple is destroyed. A universal battlefield. Each
time a war breaks out. Death is always at work.

Father/son   Relationships of authority, of privilege, of
                  force.
Logos/writing   Relationships: opposition, conflict, relief,
                  reversion.
Master/slave   Violence. Repression.

And we perceive that the 'victory' always amounts to the same
thing: it is hierarchized. The hierarchization subjects the entire
conceptual organization to man. A male privilege, which can be
seen in the opposition by which it sustains itself, between

activity and *passivity*. Traditionally, the question of sexual difference is coupled with the same opposition: activity/ passivity.[1]

The bone people opposes and negates the two-term system, related to 'the' couple man/woman. It takes the basic romance format (the narrative form which focuses on the creation of the couple), and opens with the woman alone and unhappy, introduces the right man and then refuses the conventional conclusion. Joe, late in the novel, describes Kerewin as 'someone of past or future, an androgyne' – someone who doesn't conform to our culture's binary definition of gender. This is after Joe realises he's been following the false 'idea that lovers are, and marriage is, the only sanity'.

Kerewin Holmes challenges male/female polarities. She reverses and displaces, to use Cixous's terms, hierarchical binary opposites. She has those qualities usually defined as male: she's strong, skilled at fighting, aggressive – 'me killer instinct'. She fishes, builds, wields both a hammer and language like a good kiwi joker, and can drink anyone under the table. At the end of the novel she gives Joe and Simon the protection of her name as the husband/father traditionally does. She refuses the qualities by which women are defined: sexual love, sexual relating, procreation and mothering. She is sexless in terms of our society's definition of female sexuality. Although Kerewin mockingly describes herself as looking like 'the ultimate in butch strangers', and although she's called a 'stinking leslie', she's not homosexual. There's no word in our present culture for what she is. When she describes the strange person who helps her recovery in her struggle with death Kerewin thinks of her invention of the neuter personal pronouns 've, vis, ver'. But unlike Marge Piercy's 'per' in *Woman on the Edge of Time* (per for person), it remains a concept, unused and unusable. The 've' reminds me of Simon Peter's 'up you' V gesture of defiance. In *the bone people* that basic postulate of woman's fiction – the couple – is given the V.

In the beginning of the novel, which is also its end, we read:

They were nothing more than people by themselves. Even paired, any pairing, they would have been nothing more than people by themselves. But all together, they have become the

heart and muscles and mind of something perilous and new,
something strange and growing and great.
Together, all together, they are the instruments of change.[2]

This has something of the same millennial tone as Cixous and
the French feminists. Cixous writes:

> writing is precisely *the very possibility of change*, the space that
> can serve as a springboard for subversive thought the
> precursory movement of a transformation of social and cultural
> structures.[3]

In an article on *the bone people* Shona Smith discusses the
various religious images used in the novel, describing it as 'an
eclectic mixture of Maoritanga, Christianity, Sufi mysticism,
Japanese aikido'.[4] She points out the resemblances to the
Christian Holy Family – there's Joseph, the Virgin Kerewin,
the boy child, Simon Peter, born to suffer. There are also
parallels with Maori mythology. Kerwin calls Simon 'sun-
child', one of Maui's names – Maui, washed up from the sea
wrapped in hair, like Simon, Maui Potiki, Maui the runt, the
cast-out child.

The novel provides an alternative to the nuclear family. As
Kerewin is unwomanly, so Joe is unmanly. He has a bisexual
past and has what our society defines as 'feminine' traits – he
loves cooking, weeps easily and openly. But he's also violent.
The father-son relationship exemplifies what Cixous describes
as a 'relationship of authority, of privilege, of force'. It's a
mutually destructive symbiosis which Kerewin breaks into –
not as the lover, not as the wife, not as the mother.

As well as rejecting conventional male/female pair bonding
the novel breaks down and reverses the binary black/white
hierarchical opposition. The parent is Maori and the cuckoo
child is Pakeha. The Maori parent treats the Pakeha child in a
way that echoes the Pakeha's treatment of the Maori – in-
dulgently allowing him tobacco and alcohol while punishing
him brutally, punishing him to the point of extinction for not
conforming to their standards. The child is dumb. Like the
Maori he has lost his language. The novel ends in a vision of
communality, of black and white families relating. It's the end
of Kerewin's journey from her condition at the beginning –
alone in her tower:

> it was the hermitage, her glimmering retreat. No people
> invited, for what could they know of the secrets that crept and

chilled and chuckled in the marrow of her bones? No need of
people, because she was self-fulfilling, delighting in the
preeminence of her art, in the future of her knowing hands.[5]

Instead, at the end of the novel, fulfilment and future turn out
to be in responsibility, in loving – caring for the blind cat, the
brain-damaged child and her and Joe's extended families. But
not loving sexually, as our society expects a woman to love.

Does Kerewin represent Cixous's new woman? Cixous
writes:

> she cuts through defensive loves, motherages and devourations:
> beyond selfish narcissism, into the moving open transitional
> space, she runs her risks. Beyond the struggle-to-the-death
> that's been removed to the bed, beyond the love battle that
> claims to represent exchange, she scorns? at an Eros dynamic.[6]

The novel's form, with its mixture of style and genres, of
realism, mythology, mysticism and romance fits Cixous's
concept of a heterogeneous open ended form – 'that will wreck
partitions, classes and rhetorics, regulations and codes.' Cixous
sees this as the female form of the future.

There has been another notable woman's novel about a
different sort of family and a different sort of loving: Patricia
Grace's *Potiki*. Maui Potiki is rescued from the sea, crippled,
deformed, the natural son of the 'natural' May. He becomes
the symbol of the people's attempts to reclaim the vestiges of
their land. Like *the bone people*, *Potiki* fuses myth, realistic
narrative and social commentary. It's made up of a collection
of stories, and in itself is partly about the importance of story
telling, and of narratives that arise out of the community and
the individuals in it. One story is Roimata's, the story of her
leaving home as a teenager and returning years later to marry
the man who waited for her. It's a reversal of the traditional
male quest, or male *Bildungsroman*; here the hero is the woman
and the waiting and passive maiden is the male.

Like *the bone people*, *Potiki* is an excitingly new and different
novel for New Zealand. Particularly striking is the refusal in
both novels of the narrative paradigm that has constrained
most New Zealand women novelists. Both novels end on
visions of community, not the couple. And I can't help but
note that both are written by Maori, not Pakeha.

It fascinates me that the two innovative, experimental and
different New Zealand women novelists, Frame and Hulme,

are so oddly similar. The 'eccentricity' of their lives has intrigued media and readers. Both live alone, neither has married, had children, or indeed, as far as we know, lived in any sort of couple bonding. It's not the conventional, or expected life for a New Zealand woman, which has made me question just what is the relationship between our private lives and the fictions we create for the public?

Can it be that the possibilities our lives offer us must limit the sort of fictions we can construct? The more often asked question is perhaps how far do the fictions we read affect or limit the possibilities we see for the ways we can live?

The bone people highlighted for me a basic sameness in most other New Zealand's women's fictions, perhaps because the basic pattern for many women's novels is the *Bildungsroman*; they are novels about the development of the protagonists' minds and characters as they pass from childhood through varied experiences into maturity and a recognition of their identity and place in the world. And as commentators on women's fiction have noted, women's public identity and place have been restricted.

For most women private and public roles are often the same. Women, defined as relational beings, find that their fulfilment comes through relationships – as lovers, wives, mothers. Colette Dowling, in *The Cinderella Complex: Women's Hidden Fear of Independence*, writes of women's 'excessive "affiliative needs", by which is meant the need to experience relationship above all else.'[7] Dowling begins from the premiss that in our society autonomy and high self-esteem are positive goals and ones that women find it difficult to achieve, indeed are conditioned not to achieve. Carol Gilligan, in *In A Different Voice*, is more hesitant about accepting autonomy and separation as positives. She says women's 'identity is defined in a context of relationship and judged by a standard of responsibility and care.' 'As opposed to [the male voice] which speaks of the role of separation as it defines and empowers the self [the female voice], speaks of the ongoing process of attachment that creates and sustains the human community.'[8] Gilligan sees women's relational attitude as different from, but not inferior to male autonomy.

Whether, with Gilligan, one believes it is a good thing, or, with Dowling, that it is a limitation, women's fictions are, and have been historically, about couple relationships. Who does the woman love? What happens to that love? Who does she marry? It's a pattern that is not very different structurally in Jane Austen or Mills and Boon romances.

Recent New Zealand women's novels, like British and American ones, have tended to be about women aged forty to fifty looking back on their lives. The shape of those grimly realistic fictions is similar. There is a relationship to one man, or a series of men, marriage, or marriages, children; and often the loss of the man or men, but the permanence of the children. After the publication of her successful *Breed of Women*, Fiona Kidman was overwhelmed by women telling her that she had written about their lives.

Whereas the romance – both the 'serious' nineteenth-century variety, and our twentieth-century popular descendants – ends in marriage and the affirmation of woman's cultural identity, much serious twentieth-century women's fiction ends in dis-illusionment, the broken marriage and the backward look to 'what went wrong?' However the narrative structure and pos-sibilities remain the same – a realistic *Bildungsroman*, progres-sing from girlhood to marriage, and now beyond.

Marilyn Duckworth's early novels, *A Gap in the Spectrum* and *The Matchbox House*, were surreally claustrophobic accounts of women's psychic imprisonment, both in love relationships and the nuclear family. After a long silence she wrote *Disorderly Conduct* (1984). It is a realistic account by a forty-year-old mother, with several children by a succession of husbands, of the break-up of two affairs, one casual and one long term. It's about failed and family relationships and a woman whose life is shaped by those relationships. Then, in 1985 Duckworth published *Married Alive*, a futuristic science fiction novel set in New Zealand after an epidemic, which renders everyone potentially insane, unexpectedly violent and dangerous. As its title suggests, the novel is a metaphor for the dangers of close personal relationships, all of which are to be avoided. If you live with anyone they might run amuck and injure you. Yet the novel ends with the wife leaving her maniacally murderous husband and going off with her new lover into the happy-ever-after:

'We've got things to say to each other,' Adam says.
'Have we?' She watches his mouth, mesmerised.
'Yes. I've thought about you a lot. We're going to get to know each other. And fall in love. And be happy.'
'For God's sake – ' She turns her face away, disbelieving.

He turns it back. 'No. Don't do that. Give it a chance. You know you want to.'

'That's what my boyfriends used to say about sex when I was at school,' she says, laughing.

'I'm talking about love.'

Her insides begin to melt.[9]

I'd like to interpret this as cynicism but it doesn't read like it. And even if it is, Duckworth is suggesting we are all conditioned to repeat the same pattern. To me it reveals the woman novelist's problem in escaping the fiction and life paradigm.

In Lauris Edmond's *High Country Weather* (1984) the fifty-ish protagonist looks back to the time in her past when she decided to give up the possibility of extra-marital romance for her children and 'real' life. But how does it end? With this description of the two lovers spending one night together:

> But I can say that they went together into some remote region which most of us enter rarely, if at all, even when making love and knowing it is love. Or believing it is. Now I am on the brink of the most elusive definition in the entire language; but since Louise at that time had got no further, I think I must leave that too. It's enough to say that 'love' as glimpsed, fought for (and against), finally realised, between Nigel and Louise was love in one of its better definitions. One of its best, in fact.
>
> That's why they could go together in those few hours, on a starless summer night, to a place to which no one can give a name, because if any of us are allowed to enter it we can do so only by losing ourselves entirely and re-discovering the names of things when we come back to the world of places and people, time, information and rational awareness.[10]

It's a eulogy of love as the positive ideal that few of us are able to achieve, but all dream of.

Elizabeth Caffin, in a recent review of McLeod and Wevers' *Women's Work: Contemporary Short Stories by New Zealand Women*, wrote:

> To call these stories simply domestic would be to deny their insistent context – one is struck by the mental loneliness of many of these women, a solitude of a very different kind from the physical inarticulate isolation of 'the man alone'. This female loneliness or inner secrecy is particularly intense because it usually occurs in close relationships.[11]

And while some of us are reading these often depressing stories what are the young women of today reading? Mills and Boon's ubiquitous and highly popular *Sweet Valley High* series – romantic novels about how to capture the most desirable boy. A typical blurb reads, 'Will Jessica steal Tod from Elizabeth? – they're both popular, smart and gorgeous. But that's where the similarity ends.' The perfect relationship and 'love' is something to be striven for, something on which our women's fiction is based. Yet the actuality portrayed by the older 'serious' women novelists is a life in which women are trapped by the paradigm and unhappy because of it. But there seem to be no alternatives.

It's a critical cliché that fiction arose with the bourgeoisie, with capitalism, with the nuclear family. And at the very origins of eighteenth-century fiction was the romance, written for women and increasingly by women. And the romance suggests that the couple relationship, marriage and the family are woman's social and cultural fulfilment.

Rachel M. Brownstein, in her study of nineteenth century novels about women, *Becoming a Heroine*, writes of the ways women's lives are intimately interconnected with their fictions:

> The novel about a chaste heroine and her gender-determined destiny raises and ponders such still-pressing questions as whether intimacy and identity can be achieved at once, and whether they are mutually exclusive, entirely desirable, and, indeed, other than imaginary. It explores the connections between the inner self and its outward manifestations – between the personal and the social, the private and the public – by focusing on a woman complexly connected to others, who must depend, to distinguish herself, on the gender that delimits her life. The protagonist of the classic English novel is at the center of a web of questions about how much her fate is just a woman's, or characteristically a heroine's, or authentically her own. Her self-consciousness is compelling because it mirrors the posture of the reader who looks in a novel for a coherent image of herself.[12]

Brownstein reads the novels as learning experiences for women who are necessarily limited by their gender in a society that allows that gender only certain well-defined public manifestations.

She is writing about authors our literary canon would

classify as 'serious' – Austen, Eliot, Brontë, Woolf, and indeed
Meredith and James. But Janice Radway, in her incisive and
important critical study, *Reading the Romance: Women, Patriarchy and Popular Fiction*, comes to conclusions about popular
fiction that seem equally relevant to serious fiction. She
argues that popular fiction has a narrative structure that 'demonstrates that despite idiosyncratic histories all women
inevitably end up associating their female identity with the
social roles of lover, wife and mother'.[13] For Radway the
romance format denies women the possibility of refusing a
relational destiny. Indeed, it confirms and justifies what Dowling desribed as women's 'excessive "affiliative needs"', and
denies them the possibility of autonomy and independence.
Radway, however, does not condemn the romance. Her
study sees it as satisfying and fulfilling a basic female need.

There are, of course, differences between the formulaic
stereotypical characters and plot of the popular romance, and
serious fiction. In the subtlety of a Jane Austen novel the
romance can move beyond a simple confirming message of
how to find social acceptability, into the intricacies and complexities of making a choice of the man who will determine
your self.

Kathleen Brake, in *Love and the Woman Question in Victorian
Literature: the Art of Self-Postponement*, writes:

> the women's movement finds so much to repudiate in times
> past and is so committed to future change for the better that this
> can erode sympathy with earlier periods and literature. Two
> works which particularly interest me because they share my
> concern with women and love in Victorian literature, Jean
> Kennard's *Victims of Convention* and Patricia Stubbs' *Women and
> Fiction*, are strongly inclined to condemn the love-story plot as
> an arbitrarily imposed literary convention that worked women
> no good. Not considering its development as in large part a
> response to the real conditions of women's lives, they rather
> simply and severely wish to have done with it. But instead of
> depreciating, one can explore the love story and come to
> recognise the depth of its significance for women and the
> complexity of the critique that can arise within it.[14]

For Blake, the love-story narrative is 'a response to the real
conditions of women's lives'. But, while I accept Blake's comments, I'm arguing that we do need alternatives to the love-
story plot. I agree with Radway who says:

The romance is an account of a woman's journey to female personhood *as that psychic configuration is constructed and realised within patriarchal culture*. It functions as a symbolic display and explanation of a process commonly experienced by many women. At the same time, because the ideal romance symbolically represents real female needs within the story and then depicts their successful satisfaction, it ratifies or confirms the inevitability and desirability of the entire institutional structure within which those needs are created and addressed.[15]

I remember Adrienne Rich in her essay on the death of the poet Anne Sexton by suicide, writing:

> We have had enough of suicidal women poets, enough suicidal women, enough of self destructiveness as the sole form of violence permitted to women.

But she ends her essay affirming Sexton as a survivor:

> I think of Anne Sexton as a sister whose work tells us what we have to fight, in ourselves and in the images patriarchy has held up to us – as Tillie Olsen has said, 'every woman who writes is a survivor'.[16]

Perhaps this is a way to read the love-story novel – as works by survivors, helping those of us who exist in our culture's version of women's roles to survive. Margaret Sutherland's *The Love Contract* is such a novel. It's a small, sad and honestly realistic novel about falling in love:

> They believed they loved as few others could. They suffered that extreme egoism bred by total involvement – the splendid selfishness of the bond cocooned them.[17]

But it goes on past the happy-ever-after – it's also about marriage, childbearing, and their consequences.

> Perhaps, thought Kate, I don't love Rex.
>   Sly, her mind came back to the idea, like a child to matches. Do I love you? she would think, serving him mashed potatoes. The question, once so simply, obviously answerable, was now complex and unfathomable, like infinity, like those mathematical equations she had never been able to solve because she had not grasped the fundamental process they illustrated. Do I love you? she would hear her thoughts insist, while he pointed to the spoon, requesting a second scoop. They

seemed to mention love less often. It was more peaceful, they had found.

As people do who are confused, Kate looked around to see how other couples managed with this question.

'Do you believe in Love?' she said to Trixie, with whom over the years and for want of deeper bonds Kate had seen an easy friendship grow.

Trixie looked vague; her defence when she was confused.

'I don't know that I do,' persisted Kate.

'You don't mean that,' said Trixie, doubtful.

'What I mean,' said Kate, 'is, What *is* love?'

'Anybody could tell you that, Kate.'

'You tell me then.'

'Why,' began Trixie. 'It's very basic, isn't it? Have you and Rex had a tiff?'

'I just want to hear what you think LOVE is.' She said it rather magnificently, thought Kate. 'All the radio stuff, the movie junk, pop songs, magazines . . . what is it?

'Love is caring for somebody . . . wanting to be with them.' Wanting to be married to them, was what Trixie meant. Kate, pressed to define, might have said exactly the same thing.[18]

It's a sensitive, intelligent and limited novel about being trapped by the culture's 'love-contract'. It's limited because the possibilities it depicts are limited, and the woman in it feels unhappy, and vaguely dissatisfied, knowing there's something beyond the contract society has offered her, but something she's never been told about, something unrealisable.

Sue McCauley's *Other Halves* begins with the middle class housewife alone (with the kid), at home, fearing a breakdown. She, like the protagonists of the stories Caffin commented on, is suffering from the extreme isolation of a woman in a relationship. The novel ends with her liberation through her movingly described love for a Maori street kid, Tug. In the final episodes she discovers the excitement of shop-lifting and offering the 'shot-up' Tug the spoils. The total (and positive) rejection of bourgeois nuclear family values comes with the affirmation of heterosexual pair bonding. As such it seems directly opposed to *the bone people*. It's a realistic novel which works within the basic fictional format of the love story – girl meets boy, they undergo misunderstandings and obstacles but work through them to a happy, if precarious, monogamous ending. Even though the protagonist rejects the values of her

Pakeha society this rejection is done through wholeheartedly accepting the romance narrative and its values. No wonder the book made a successful film. Unlike *the bone people* or *Potiki* there's no need for alternative modes of relating. *Other Halves*, with its drop-out solution, is one of the very few recent serious women's novels in New Zealand with a happy ending.

Most of the serious fiction is about the impossibility, or failure, of romance in our culture. Jean Watson's 1965 *Stand in the Rain*, a woman's 'on the road' novel, questioned the bourgeois nuclear family values. I remember it from my first reading, for its marvellously evocative open-ended last paragraphs:

> There are people who will never get used to marriage is 'why is the stew burnt and where are my clean socks and must you do that when I . . . ?'
> There are people who will always look in lighted windows and want to be there behind the safety of drawn blinds, and when they are there they'll suddenly not want it or something will bugger it for them and they will feel the road beneath their feet again, and when they're too old for that they will from time to time watch it through the window of a bus or train – someday it will get them.
> And when we sleep will the road unwind dreamlike before us?[19]

But the heroine takes off on the road because she's in love with the Barry Crump-ish Abungus. She lives his lifestyle – skinning possums, casual labour, on the move. She is not following a goal of her own, or rather, Abungus is her goal. By choosing the man she chooses her destiny.

The French feminists, Cixous particularly, argue that the new women's writing must come from the female body itself, the female libido, 'jouissance'. A woman's sexual pleasure and energy, they suggest, will be the site for the new writing. Speaking of Irigaray, Kristeva and Montrelay, the critic Silverman writes:

> They see the body as a pre-cultural given which plays a determinate role in female existence – as enjoying a privileged relation to her own being, and consequently to jouissance (a pleasure which radically exceeds cultural laws and limits).[20]

Their theories radicalise the erotic and eroticise writing:

She must write her self, because this is the invention of a *new insurgent* writing which, when the moment of her liberation has come, will allow her to carry out the indispensable ruptures and transformations in her history – . By writing her self, woman will return to the body which has been more than confiscated from her – censor the body and you censor breath and speech at the same time.

Write your self. Your body must be heard. Only then will the immense resources of the unconscious spring forth.[21]

Almost everything is yet to be written by women about feminity: about their sexuality, that is, its infinite and mobile complexity, about their eroticization. . . . A woman's body, with its thousand and one thresholds of ardor – once, by smashing yokes and censors she lets it articulate the profusion of meanings that run through it in every direction – will make the old single-grooved mother tongue reverberate with more than one language.[22]

This is exciting stuff, but from this perspective both Hulme and Frame are disconcerting. Our two most innovative female writers, who have rejected traditional gender roles, have also rejected female 'jouissance'. Hulme's marvellous autobiographical poem *He Hoha* is written from and about the female body. It begins:

Bones tuned, the body sings–

See me,
I am wide with swimmer's muscle, and a bulk and luggage I
    carry curdled on hips;
I am as fat-rich as a titi-chick, ready for the far ocean flight.

See me,
I have skilled fingers with minimal scars, broad feet that caress
    beaches,
ears that catch the music of ghosts, eyes that see the landlight, a
    pristine womb
untouched except by years of bleeding, a tame unsteady heart.

But *the bone people* is not about women's sexuality – 'its infinite and mobile complexity, about their eroticization.' And Hulme herself has adopted a lifestyle many would consider basically male – on the Abungus model. It's tempting to read Hulme's rejection of women's relational stance as the inevitable response to the entrapment of woman's sexuality into the love contract, into pair bonding. Our fictions, both popular and serious, teach us that our sexuality is good as long as it leads to coupledom. To see just how thoroughly this paradigm has us in its thrall we have only to look at lesbian fiction – novels written by women for women. The Naiad Press, the Mills and Boon of lesbian fiction, give us the happy-ever-after *Desert Hearts* version of popular romances and the more 'serious' novels give us the failure of the love contract. Kate Millett's powerful autobiographical novels *Flying* and *Sita* show us a woman, who, though as a lesbian she has broken her society's gender expectations, is still trapped by what Dowling would call her 'excessive affiliative needs'.

But is Hulme's and Frame's rejection the necessary first step to break free from the phallocentric symbolic order?

I know from discussing *the bone people* with students that many women readers find its final commensal vision unconvincing and unsatisfactory. And as a Pakeha woman I don't relate to the happy-ever-after of the whanau – the final vision of the extended family and the communal vision. So while I find *the bone people* and *Potiki* the most exciting novels yet written in New Zealand, their solutions are not mine. Brought up on love stories, being the product of a culture whose women's writing is about relationships, I'd like to believe we can reclaim the love story.

Don't many of us believe that our ability to be more loving, more empathetic, more sensitive than men, is something more than socially conditioned qualities aimed at making us good wives and mothers? Having, with Gilligan, a strong personal belief in the positive value of women's relational stance, and having, with Cixous, a belief in what she calls erotogeneity, in eroticism, in the power of jouissance, I want to believe that women can write great fiction, can create new narratives out of their sexual and relational selves. I find Cixous exciting because she is suggesting this possibility. What would women's eroticism, and women's fiction, freed of social and cultural conditioning be like? The resemblances and interrelations between our fictions and our lives – the fact that the paradigms of one reflect and influence the other suggest that perhaps in order to write differently we will have to begin to live differently.

Right: *Marie Shannon*, The Rat in the Lounge (Self Portrait), *black and white photograph in three parts, 1985. Detail shown above. National Art Gallery*

82

Chapter 5

WOMEN AND ART
Anne Kirker

Traditionally, inside represents female, outside, male. We have
broadly accepted the male concern with facade and monument,
the female concern with function and environment, the male
concern with permanence and structural imposition, the female
concern with adaptability and psychological needs; the male
concern with public image, the female resistance to
specialization; the male concern with abstract theory, the female
concern with biography and autobiography. These stereotypes
are more often proved right than wrong. (Lucy R. Lippard,
From the Center, feminist essays on women's art, New York
1976.)

With the rise of the Women's Art Movement in New Zealand
during the 1970s, which paralleled similar developments in
the United States, feminists began vigorously to redress the
neglect of their gender and make visible a qualitatively different range of experience from that encountered by men. Exhibitions have been mounted, articles written, workshops and
seminars staged as a means to recast women's presence in the
visual arts. The serious commitment by recent commentators
to research the nature of female creativity as it has been shaped
by social and political forces in the past has gone hand in hand

with the production by artists of images that are consciously evolved expressions of feminism. Today it is no longer necessary to assert that there has been a continuing tradition of accomplished women artists in this country or that fresh insights are constantly being manifested by them. It is instructive, nevertheless, to be reminded of certain facts.

From an art historical perspective, there is no doubt that under the aegis of a male-dominated society women have been either effaced from official accounts or grossly misrepresented. Art writing has usually placed women in a subsidiary role to men and although feminism has had at least a handful of male supporters over the last half-century, there are still influential voices which silence the achievement of women artists. This essay sets a phallocentric view of the work of several New Zealand-born women against the reality of their lives and aspirations. Beginning with the nineteenth century and moving through to the present, I shall attempt to clarify some of the conflicts they faced in pursuing careers as artists, trace the way in which their efforts were often belittled or misinterpreted and identify the contradictions that inevitably arose in moving from one type of life to another.

The very word 'career' belongs to the public sphere of human activity and has traditionally been linked with masculine endeavour. The word 'women' has more often been equated with the private domain and assigned a lesser order of significance. Here, then, is the most obvious dilemma that underlies the creative pursuits of women regarding themselves as professional artists. They have suffered under the rules of patriarchy, for it has been men, not women, who have written the language of art. It is no mean victory that the women I discuss continued and managed to assert themselves in a man's world with their work.

Emily Harris (1837?–1925) is one of the few early colonial women whose names have featured in New Zealand biographies. As with other female artists of last century, she was classed as a genteel amateur pursuing those accomplishments which were deemed the mark of every well-bred Victorian lady. But Emily Harris considered herself a serious painter who sold her flower studies and decorated furniture and drapes to bring money into the family. Initially her artistic interests had been fostered by her father, Edwin Harris, a civil engineer and surveyor from New Plymouth who painted for recreation.

To escape the Taranaki wars, the Harrises moved to Nelson where Emily ran an infant school with her two younger sisters. She persisted nevertheless with her preferred vocation.

By the 1880s, Emily Harris was exhibiting her interpretations of New Zealand flowers and plants, but at the same time taking on as many private drawing pupils as she could manage, to offset the expense. In the eyes of society, she was a success, participating in prestigious shows not only in her own country, but abroad. In Melbourne for example, her work was accepted at the International Exhibition of 1880, and in London she was included in the 1886 Indian and Colonial Exhibition. The artist attracted many awards, but making her way as a single woman, reliant upon her own resources, was far from easy. Her interest in flower studies, a recurring preoccupation with most pioneer women artists, probably stemmed as much from convenience as preference. Flower studies fitted the expectations of 'appropriate' female creativity in the new society.

Flowers were very accessible objects of beauty which could be plucked, kept for days and painted between bouts of domestic duty. If a woman of Emily Harris's talent did not share with the men of her era (such as John Gully, J. C. Richmond and W. M. Hodgkins), the opportunity to travel and draw and paint the landscape, then it is not surprising that a practical solution was to value what was close at hand and commonplace. Although Harris, and other women of her generation, derived tremendous aesthetic satisfaction from the study of native flowers and plants, they were undeniably prevented from taking part in the broader experiences of their male counterparts.

An entry in Emily Harris's diary of 1886 reveals a creative impulse that, given different circumstances, could well have seen her maturing as a landscape painter.

> Got up before six a.m. saw the most lovely sunrise that I ever remember to have seen. Clouds fleecy and rosy, in the midst of the clouds here and there the purest and most perfect pale blue, beautiful yellow light below the rosy clouds, the Matai hills deep purple, the trees in the foreground dark, it was well worth getting up for, although I did not get up for that but to wash my clothes, which I have not had a chance of doing for five weeks or more....[1]

Time allocated to all manner of domestic, teaching and social duties cut severely into the time available for art-making.

Emily Harris, Aristotelia racemosa: Makomako, *watercolour. Alexander Turnbull Library*

Although Harris and her sisters were unmarried, their father was widowed and it was left to his daughters to run the household and keep up appearances – 'Strive with all my might I cannot get on with my own paintings', she laments in her diary. When Emily Harris did manage to produce enough items for an exhibition, she faced difficulties in ensuring both their safe transport and a sympathetic presentation. She may have attracted prizes but she suffered from reviewers who praised her work as 'pretty', a term that would hardly have been accorded to a landscape painting by a male artist.

In 1890, when Emily Harris was in her early fifties, she published in Nelson three illustrated books on New Zealand flowers, ferns and berries which featured hand-coloured lithographs. These book illustrations underline the fact that she developed as a practitioner of the decorative arts, a field in which women have traditionally excelled. But the so-called 'minor arts', which include not only book illustration but also textile design and the ornamentation of functional objects, have generally been less conducive to lasting public acclaim and fortune than painting and sculpture. These areas have been viewed as 'high art' endeavours and more particularly the domain of men. Emily Harris was hampered by the nineteenth-century conventions which did not condone women's involvement in creative pursuits outside the useful. She was a victim of circumscribed expectations of women in a patriarchal society.

Wider opportunities emerged for aspiring artists in the wake of industrialisation and urban expansion in New Zealand. From 1880 to the mid 1920s, art schools, public galleries and also energetic art societies were established in the main centres. Women from well-to-do middle class backgrounds could take advantage of these facilities and travel to Europe for study. These apparent openings could be misleading, as many talented artists had to curtail their training (abroad especially), to return home and play the part that custom required. Even though these women were usually single, they were called upon to nurse elderly relatives, mind nieces and nephews, and generally assist in running the household. Dorothy Richmond (1861–1935) for instance, went to and from London and Cornwall to Nelson over twenty years. She juggled family obligations with the stimulus of working in the company of highly experienced painters. It was only after the death of her father in 1898 that she was able to enjoy an extended period in England.

Flora Scales (1887–1985) decided at the age of forty to test herself as a painter outside New Zealand. Looking back, we can now see that she was part of the 1920s exodus of artists who made a conscious effort to escape from the insularity and ignorance of their native country, where even the products of the Impressionists were treated with suspicion. In 1928, Scales attended André Lhôte's studio in Paris and was introduced to Cubism, starting to experiment with a geometric formula for her compositions. During the following few years she sketched and painted in and around Paris and on the south coast of France.

Born within a year of Flora Scales, John Weeks springs more readily to mind as the archetypal New Zealander who sought training abroad and brought back an advanced method of painting. Weeks also attended the Académie Montparnasse where Lhôte presided. He returned to Auckland in 1929, and became a dominant figure in its artistic life. Scales, however, continued with her investigations abroad, travelling to Munich at the beginning of the 1930s to study at the Hans Hofmann School which enjoyed an international reputation for its advanced theories on art. When the artist came back to New Zealand briefly in 1934, she gave a number of informal lessons to the young Toss Woollaston which certainly encouraged him (and his close colleague Colin McCahon) to become innovative artists. But whereas Weeks was seen as an influential force in New Zealand painting during the 1930s and 1940s, it has only been since the 1970s that Flora Scales has gained a measure of recognition here.

There are a number of reasons for this. Unlike John Weeks, she did not remain in this country to pursue her vocation. Instead she returned to Europe while still in her forties and only succumbed to New Zealand in old age. She saw little point in sending work back for exhibition; even in the northern hemisphere the artist regarded the process of offering her oils for public view as 'irrelevant' and an interruption to her personal artistic development. Scales's highly disciplined approach to painting gave little heed to seeking outside acclaim; instead, she put all her energy into exploring, with quiet intensity, a range of formal solutions to pictorial problems.

In 1934, Woollaston wrote to a friend: 'Her attitude seems to be that to draw and paint is better than to discuss drawing and painting.'[2] This indication of the privacy of Flora Scales's creativity is matched by the deliberately understated nature of her imagery. Small, shimmering landscapes, such as *Bay Landscape, St. Ives, Cornwall* (c.1968–70), as well as flower studies and portraits, make up the bulk of this artist's oeuvre. She was like one of the French 'Nabis' who had absorbed the structural lessons of Cubism. Unpretentious, her small oils quietly reveal their subjects, devoid of virtuosity or facile effects.

In the 1930s, Rita Angus (1908–70) emerged as a painter who, like Flora Scales, saw little merit in compromising her talent in order to extract acceptance from society at large. Her formative years coincided with the Depression, and economic restrictions curbed any thoughts of training abroad. Instead, New Zealand witnessed a desire among artists for self-identification within their own country. A regionalist viewpoint asserted itself early on through the meticulous Canterbury landscapes in oils and watercolours that Angus produced in her late twenties and early thirties. She began to paint portraits of close friends and members of her family which were deeply personal and often included symbols which had particular meaning for the subject. These reached a high point with *Portrait of Betty Curnow* (1942) where the sitter is shown in the context of her living room, surrounded by objects which we readily identify with that generation.[3]

Rita Angus carved out a career for herself at a time when, socially and politically, it could not have been harder. The 1930s saw not only a decline in the pattern of steady social and economic growth but also an accompanying erosion of women's rights. These rights had included opportunities for women to participate in a sphere of activity beyond the home. The Second World War served as the hiatus between the earlier situation and the increasing expectation that a woman's role was to focus on childrearing and domesticity. Women artists became more and more marginalised and belittled until the 1970s, when a concerted feminist awareness asserted itself.

While still a student, Angus married Alfred Cook, but the relationship was shortlived and the couple separated in 1934. It was a classic example of two artists living together in a conventional marriage and one of them, invariably the woman, feeling obliged to relinquish a career in order to conform to the role of nurturer and homemaker. Rita Angus, recognising the creative woman's dilemma, decided not to stifle her talent but to disengage herself from emotional ties and pursue painting above all else. It is small wonder that she was regarded as an 'outsider' and became virtually a recluse.

Angus nevertheless kept working and she regularly exhibited with the Canterbury Society of Arts and The Group in Christchurch. Her direct luminous style was not generally singled out for comment by the local press; instead, it was admired and collected by a small group of discriminating and devoted friends. The paintings on canvas, and meticulous watercolours (her particular forte) did not command wide public attention until the 1960s – a few years before the artist's death.

Fog, Hawke's Bay (1966–68) was acquired by the Auckland City Art Gallery soon after it was painted and is typical of the oils Rita Angus evolved from a specific locality which was very familiar to her. Rather than being a blasé summary of appearances, however, her composition maintains the integrity of the subject, at the same time imbuing it with a tight formal structure. Individual shapes (such as the farmyard sheds) are distorted to give a sense of their totality and each brilliant tone is intentionally balanced against another. In acknowledging that the places and people she knew well were the very crux of her art, Rita Angus turned away from complete abstraction, a trend that had been gaining momentum in New Zealand art since the 1950s. It was as if she needed to retain the appearance of things to express her deep concern for humanity.

It is an interesting fact that women painters in this country have tended to work outside strictly abstract modes. Their male counterparts have revelled in the geometry and sharp edges of shapes that seem hermetic and answerable only to masculine perceptions. Even when the artist Gretchen Albrecht (b. 1943) began producing her 'hemispheres' in the early 1980s, these canvases came 'from a "well" of feelings, thoughts, responses to experiences'.[4] In their pared-down state, the twin quadrants of separate colours bolted together were not divorced from fundamental human attributes and steered clear of formalist doctrines. For her project *Seasonal* (1985–86), Albrecht's four canvases bore titles rich in connotations to Nature – 'Blossom', 'Arbour', 'Orchard (for Keats)', and 'Exile'. They were anything but 'a proclamation of painting's autonomy from the world, such as we have seen, say, in the paintings of Mrkusich or Peebles'.[5]

Up to this point, Gretchen Albrecht had singlemindedly pursued her career, in spite of suffering a measure of humiliation along the way. While a student at Elam at the beginning of the 1960s, she became pregnant and married. Male examiners at the art school apparently did not 'trust' pictures by pregnant women and she failed her paper in painting the head and figure from life. Fortunately, the artist had one ally among the staff – Kurt von Meier, who lectured in art history. He encouraged her to study other women artists such as the expatriate New Zealander Frances Hodgkins, and Paula Modersohn-Becker and Sonia Delaunay. In 1964 Albrecht held her first exhibition (at the Ikon Gallery, Auckland) and started to register with the art establishment as a painter of promise. Behind the scenes, her personal life was fraught as she coped with an unhappy marriage, then divorce, followed by the trials of bringing up a small child.

Between 1965 and 1967, she started making fabric collages from odds and ends of materials left over from dressmaking, then turned to felt to make bold simplified forms in bright contrasting colours. These pictures introduced the 'single shape, single colour' idea which led to the artist's subsequent imagery. The 1970s witnessed her 'table cloth' and 'garden' series which, although essentially abstract, were still linked to the visible world. Employing a stain painting technique, Gretchen Albrecht created expressive and very beautiful canvases in which vibrant colours overlapped or bled into one another. They evinced a theme based on the artist's immediate environment which transformed the commonplace into something lyrical and intense.

A trip to the United States and Europe in 1978–79 prompted the artist to re-evaluate her work and she began to experiment with a more ordered formula for carrying the potent hues. Instead of using a conventional brush to indicate gesture, she scraped pigment on the canvas in wide arcs with a squeegee, thus creating 'hemispheres' which consciously related in scale to her own body and that of her viewers. She wanted to engage in a direct rapport with others.

Right up to the present, female experience has tended to promote artistic imagery which reflects the private domain, that very domain which is belittled or discounted under the rule of patriarchal expectations. Since Emily Harris's day, women have generally painted from inside their lives, responding to the people, places and things which belong to their personal circumstances. By contrast, male painters have earned recognition for public subjects and masculine themes.

There is another effect of the privatisation of women's lives as artists. Not only is their art taken less seriously but they have less opportunity to pursue it in depth. The roles of dutiful daughter and wife in the confined world of the home have until recently prevented talented women from having continuous access to the sources of good training and an invigorating dialogue with other artists.

One of the first painters in this country to publicise the oppression of domesticity was Jacqueline Fahey (b.1929). Newly married and expecting her first child, she produced a number of works in 1958 and 1959 which met a hostile reception when exhibited with The Group in Christchurch soon afterwards. It was left to a sympathetic sculptor (Anthony Stones), to redress the bigotry and incomprehension:

> Could the male painter have noticed this enormous world of frustration boxed in the sprawl of suburbia? Whereas the male 'social realists' see heroics at the kitchen sink these paintings view the same world candidly, bare of idealization. The simple symbols – tea-cup, light bulb, window, bird and bulky bare forearmed figures – are set in compositions which cram these components to make the suggestion of claustrophobia complete, and the unease of women eloquent.[6]

Fahey has continued to challenge the myth of the domestic idyll with imagery that in technique might appear gauche and unsophisticated but which is deliberate. Her work is about social realism, not about genteel accomplishment. *Mother and Daughter Quarrelling* (1977), *My Skirts in Your Room* (1980), *I Dreamt About The Day My Father, the Old Soldier, Died* (1981–2) are typical of the titles given to paintings which focus on events that are autobiographical and personal, yet relevant on a broader front, particularly to women.

The same can be said of themes addressed by Robin White (b.1946) which revolve around people who feature prominently in her life. *Florence at Home, Te Puke* (1976) is one of several portraits of her mother couched in a highly detailed regionalist style. It goes much further than rendering a likeness, clearly evoking the tragic dilemma of many women of an older generation who are trapped by domesticity. Here an elderly woman, wearing her uniform (a spotless apron), stares vacantly through the window of her suburban home. The building is by far the most prominent feature of this picture and it seems

Jacqueline Fahey, The Ruined Dinner Party, *oil painting, 1986. Private Collection*

to imprison the figure. Every aspect of the composition has a regimented precision about it and a sense of confinement.

In the 1970s White consistently exhibited her paintings and screenprints in this country and built up a steady reputation. Her visually straightforward interpretations of New Zealanders in relation to their environment were acquired by private and public collections alike but one suspects that the subtler points of her social commentaries were often overlooked. The fact that the artist has been actively involved with the Baha'i faith since 1971 is not widely known and she has only alluded to it explicitly in her work at the beginning of the 1980s with a series of prints called *The Black Standard over Victory Beach*. White's and her husband's commitment to their religion has been such that, since 1982, they have lived on Tarawa in Kiribati, assisting the Baha'i community.

Removed from a western lifestyle, Robin White has adapted to an environment with few of the comforts she previously enjoyed as of right in New Zealand. Rather than trying to continue her former method of painting on large canvases, or producing immaculate screenprints, she has turned to woodblock prints as an appropriate means of reflecting her life at Kiribati. 'I feel I am still, essentially, working for a New Zealand audience. I am a New Zealander who left New Zealand and went to work on a small coral atoll. This is what my work is about and seems to me to be the only honest approach I can take, at the moment'.[7]

The woodblocks for the series of images titled *Beginners Guide to Gilbertese* (1984) were prepared in Kiribati and later editioned at Carole Shepheard's studio in Auckland. Small and intimate, the prints depict the day-to-day routine – sleeping on a mat, washing clothes in a bucket – interwoven with symbols that evoke a specifically Polynesian culture. The contrast between them and the declamatory figurative work, fashionable among many painters today, prompted the director of the sixth Biennale of Sydney (1986) to include White among the New Zealand contingent. This could be seen as a pat on the back from the patriarchy, with her icon-like images perceived rather as a 'sorbet' in the exhibition, a refreshing insert between the main courses of an elaborate meal. From a different perspective, Robin White's recent imagery can be equated with the feminist search for public meaning in private life. Not grandiose, it represents alternative values to those espoused by

a capitalist society, concentrating on the richness of close personal ties between woman and man and between two peoples
united in their celebration of an economical, spiritual lifestyle.

The ranking of artists' reputations in New Zealand has been
largely man-made. Until the rise of the Women's Art Movement, the ubiquitous male critic acted as the intermediary
between creator and consumer and, depending on his point of
view, he could endorse or dismiss their efforts. In Emily Harris's day, the term 'pretty' was commonplace in describing
work by women. So too were the notions of limitedness,
decorativeness, industriousness and prettiness. As pointed out
by Rozsika Parker and Griselda Pollock, 'The phrase "woman
artist" does not describe an artist of the female sex, but a kind
of artist that is distinct and clearly different from the great
artist.'[8] Often the only way critics could praise a woman was
to say that 'she paints like a man'.
    Maud Sherwood (1880–1956), who made a name for herself
in Australia during the 1930s, was seen as 'an exponent of
virile but reverent draughtsmanship and a master of watercolour technique'.[9] The insistent maleness of critical metaphor
testifies to the overt masculine presence in antipodean culture
from the 1930s to well past the Second World War. A. R. D.
Fairburn, whose misogyny was never revealed more clearly
than in 'The Woman Problem' his essay of 1967, often conde-
scended to the 'feminine' in his art reviews. He wrote in 1944:
'I admire the way Miss Brown [Helen Brown (b.1917)] des-
pises pretty colour, and uses a combination of dull shades to
produce a genuine richness. She is very free with her brush and
broad in her style – an excellent thing in a woman.'[10] Ten years
later, a reporter for the *Dominion* in Wellington attempted to
assess an exhibition of one of the few women evolving a
geometric, abstract style. 'It has been said there are tender-
minded and tough-minded cubists. The paintings by Louise
Henderson, now on view to the public in the Architectural
Centre Gallery, Lambton Quay, are undoubtedly of the
tender-minded kind. The abstraction in these paintings is carried to a simple decorative end, having a "still life" effect.'[11]
No doubt the Mondrian-like imagery that Milan Mrkusich
was producing at the time would have been perceived by such
a commentator as 'tough-minded'!
    In the late 1960s, a summary was published in a fashionable

95

journal of the New Zealand 'art scene' by Hamish Keith, then keeper at the Auckland City Art Gallery. It featured photographs of the 'leading personalities' from three of the country's metropolitan centres. From Auckland only one woman (Pauline Thompson) was represented out of a group of fifteen; from Wellington no woman featured; and in Christchurch Vivian Bishop was the sole female.[12]

It is not surprising, then, to find that, in order to be recognised by the art establishment, women had to be seen to be cultivating styles which emulated those of their male colleagues. Pauline Thompson (b.1942) used flat areas of colour, undulating lines and patterned areas of polka dots, characteristic of Pop Art, for several years after leaving art school. Almost certainly this use of 'international' imagery added credence to her ability in the eyes of those wielding power in the visual arts. It was a different matter when she changed from large formats, using watercolour for images that responded to her involvement with the Sufi religion and her interest in biology. Sexual organic forms and a regenerative interest in cyclic symbolism were the hallmarks of these paintings and the numerous drawings that accompanied them. Thompson faded from public view – '1972–79, is the period in which I am popularly supposed to have confined my activities to childrearing. The plain fact is that these cyclic symbols and cellular forms were not greeted with any delight by dealers who saw them.'[13]

Art critics and administrators still fail to appreciate the unusual, the personal and autobiographical. In particular there is a resistance among male viewers to overt sexual and political statements in feminist art. To declare oneself a feminist artist remains a courageous act as it invites estrangement and often antagonism from the public arena. The term 'Feminist artist' gained currency among a number of New Zealand women in the mid 1970s who began researching their female identity and establishing alternative subjects in art. The key factor became content not style, and in a wave of feminist exhibitions (beginning in Christchurch) the Women's Art Movement gained momentum. Juliet Batten pointed out 'This was not the sort of art New Zealand was used to receiving from its women artists. . . . Women artists who were well established before the new movement began to have an impact have often been the most vocal in their denial, although there are others whose work has been transformed by the new challenge.'[14] Two examples immediately spring to mind of women who embraced the new implications for their work – Marté Szirmay and Claudia Pond Eyley.

Shortly after graduating from the Elam School in Auckland, Marté Szirmay (b.1946) won the prestigious Smirnoff Sculpture Award (1969) for a monumental outdoor piece in Newmarket. Two curved interlocking forms made from polished aluminium successfully fulfilled expectations for an abstract statement that was publicly accessible. This ambitious project was followed over the next ten years by smaller sheetmetal works which reiterated the semi-circular and curved elements of the earlier piece. By 1978 the sculptor had also begun to experiment with the medium of ground marble cast with resin. Her sheetmetal images could more easily be equated with an impersonal cosmopolitan style; the newer technique was much more private and alluded to the natural world (especially to marine life and the sea). Szirmay became preoccupied with shells as the basis of her imagery. She sees them as embodying mathematical precision as well as the 'growth spiral'. Although there is no such thing as a predetermined and absolute female imagery, there are forms that can be more readily identified with a feminine than a masculine sensibility. Circles, domes, eggs, biomorphic shapes – forms that open out – tend to belong to women's art-making rather than to men's. The shell, and the spiral concept generally, epitomises female consciousness.

In the period 1983–84 Marté Szirmay's sculpture reacted even more obviously against male ideological notions of solidity, permanence and monolithic scale when she created cast paper pieces with molten fibreglass. Using the shell concept, she evolved fragile curved shapes which appeared to be washed with sea water or suggested receptacles for liquid. Only recently, with two works she constructed for the project Sculpture I (1986) at the Auckland City Art Gallery, did Szirmay return to something approaching the monumentality of her Smirnoff sculpture. Titled *Splitting/Egg* and *The Meandering Spiral*, the works merge very feminine qualities with a commanding public presence.

Claudia Pond Eyley (b.1946) has similarly changed course in her career. 'During 1979 I began to research my New Zealand family history. . . . I read about the Women's Art Movement in America and learned about the Dinner Party Project. . . . It

Claire Johnstone performing Five Times Seven *at Outreach, 3 October 1984. Photographed by Gil Hanly.*

became clear to me that as an artist I should be relating the point of view that I experienced as a woman, and as a mother.'[15] The paintings she produced took domesticity as their subject matter and related to her home environment. More recently, Pond Eyley has developed compositions using collage elements on a shield shape which juxtapose stencilled words with pictures of special relevance to women. (See Preface.) An instance is the artist's *Shield for Mary Cassatt* (1983) which features vignettes of the American painter's work. (Cassatt is admired by feminist artists for her devotion to the theme of mother and child without falling into the trap of sentimentality.)

That women tend to be more autobiographical in their imagery than men is borne out in performance art. More particularly, the collaborative projects and the visual art diaries that have emerged in the 1980s are significant demonstrations of feminism. Many women artists wish to destroy the boundaries between 'low', 'hobby' and 'high art', motherhood and career. A public reputation within established art circles is less impor-

Marté Szirmay, Splitting/Egg, *cast alabaster/resin, stainless steel, 1986.*
Auckland City Art Gallery

tant to them than the exchange of ideas and empathy with
other women. To this end, the Women's Gallery opened in
Wellington at the beginning of 1980 and became the focus for
female creativity. During the four years it was in operation,
the gallery mounted many group exhibitions, including the
Mothers show which toured New Zealand and afterwards went
to Sydney for the Women and Arts Festival (October 1982). It
also staged performances and held collaborative workshops.

In Auckland, the Association of Women Artists has maintained a similar programme at the Outreach community arts
centre. It was here that Claire Johnstone performed a piece
called *Five Times Seven* (thirty-five years alive and looking

back) on the evening of 3 October 1984. Johnstone does not have a high profile as an artist – she has not, for instance, featured in the journal *Art New Zealand* which serves as the mouthpiece for the art establishment – yet the professionalism she brought to this project was undisputed. As basic ingredients for *Five Times Seven*, she took portions of silk, satin and similar cloth which were assembled and then reassembled to reflect patterns of personal growth. In other respects, the performance was reminiscent of patchwork quilts and the making of intricate garments, reminding one of the long involvement women have had with needlework and with the decorative arts.

Inevitably a contradiction arises through women deliberately choosing to explore their identity through art forms such as needlework, for in the process they are condemned as practitioners of a 'lesser' art. In spite of this the reclamation of devalued arts has featured as the mainspring of the work of a number of feminist artists in New Zealand. In the early 1980s, for instance, Juliet Batten created a number of small two-dimensional images under the title *Mending,* which used fabric as the chief medium. Her particular forte, however, has been as a teacher and facilitator. Batten's championship of collaborative art, as the ideal way to explore female creativity, has encouraged many women to realise their potential outside male hierarchies and power structures. She is among those artists who see the mainstream as irrelevant and seek to establish alternative models. This invariably implies a private and low-profile presence.

In her recent survey of work from 1980–85, Carole Shepheard (b.1945) published a statement which explained her attempts to 'sift out the clichéd, the foreign, the observer aspects' and replace them with 'work that clearly explores my love of the "craft" aspects of collage and assemblage'.[16] After her marriage broke up in 1979, Shepheard explored the trauma through mixed media assemblages. She sifted and selected bits and pieces of fabric and objects, uniting them with passages of paint to record states of mind and memories. This 'fragment' technique was often incorporated in a grid format and sometimes concentrated on photographs, such as in the case of *Jeanette* (1981). Soft, dark images were related to the thought patterns of a close friend, in the course of one month. A written diary served as the basis of this visual record which, although highly personal, communicated effectively when exhibited, especially to an audience of women.

The modular and serial formats of much of this artist's work fall naturally into feminist art philosophy. In that highly consequential text *From the Center* (1976) one of the essays is simply termed 'Fragments' and in it Lucy Lippard points out that 'perhaps by coincidence, perhaps not, many of the artists who have drawn a particularly unique interpretation from the grid's precise strains are women'. Carole Shepheard's assemblage work of the 1980s, like Claire Johnstone's work, has direct links with the patchwork quilt aesthetic. Patchwork by its very nature is organised as a grid with regular lines of stitching uniting each portion of fabric into a functional whole. Once considered the particular province of women, quilts speak of time, of order and care and practicality, of frugality, of making do by making.

If one were to single out a woman artist in New Zealand today whose work belongs in this world, it might well be Joanna Paul (b.1945). Her images are about confinement to the privacy of the home and 'the great meaning in ordinary things'.[17] Early on she adopted a multi-disciplined approach, resisting specialisation. She not only painted but drew, wrote poetry, took photographs and made films all of which centred on the day-to-day realities of her life. Married until recently to the painter Jeffrey Harris, she adapted her working pattern to cope with domestic demands, seizing on those short spaces left spare between the responsibilities of childrearing. In comparison to the critical attention Harris was commanding, Joanna Paul's own development tended to be overlooked in the 1970s. Her activities were much more discreet.

On a number of occasions this artist used Super 8 film to document her experiences as a mother (*Napkins* 1974), and of living at Barry's Bay on Banks Peninsula. One film, ten minutes long, recorded the change of seasons in the area and took her home and its immediate environs as the motif. A series of domesticity-inspired paintings accompanied these projects, often depicting an interior rich in the textures and varied shapes of family belongings. In 1977 Joanna Paul was responsible for initiating a number of exhibitions using the diary as a visual art form. This was the event known as *A Season's Diaries* (Victoria University Library, 1977–78) which made it possible for women to share threads of common experience. Earlier that year the artist gave her interpretation of grief in losing a child through an installation at the Canterbury Society of Arts Gallery, called *Unwrapping the Body*.

Until the Women's Art Movement gained momentum in this country Joanna Paul had suffered criticism for the varied nature of her work. To be considered a serious artist implied concentration on a single medium, such as painting. But she sees her inspiration as interwoven intimately with the ebb and flow of her own existence and that of others, responding to changes as a matter of course and referring to them in her creativity. It was not surprising to witness in April 1986 (at the Wellington City Gallery) a sequence of collage drawings termed *Fragile Communities: Intimate Maps*, which traced the history of Roseneath, a neighbourhood the artist had lived in for several months.

Tony Bellette drew a parallel between her paintings and the poetry she has written and stated that her 'art might be said to have a kind of distinct propriety about it: a sense not of what might be done on the white paper of the watercolour or the book page, but of what should not be done. It is these proprieties that permit the expression of the small, sudden joys and the immense deprivations which echo through her work.'[18]

Women artists in New Zealand today are developing talents that embrace any number of art media and subject matter. Although the efforts of some are still viewed with scepticism, others enjoy a measure of public acclaim and patronage. Their forebears, who include Emily Harris, Flora Scales and Rita Angus, to various degrees revealed themselves as women in the work they produced. What we have come to know of their lives and their creative expressions influenced New Zealand women artists later this century. For the future, we can look forward to an increasing number of women artists who are committed to their vocation and have the courage to discover new avenues in art.

Chapter 6

MILLWORKERS' WIVES*

Bev James

Feminism seeks to challenge and change the separation of public and private spheres in an effort to overcome sex inequalities. To do so it must investigate how women experience and perceive such divisions in their daily lives. In this chapter I shall focus on the family and, in particular, women's experience as wives.

The great majority of women in New Zealand spend some period of their adult life married and rearing children. Marriage is a critical event for a woman, because it places her firmly within the private sphere and defines her economic position. As Janet Finch observes, when a woman marries:

> . . . she marries not only a man but also she marries his job, and from that point onward will live out her life in the context of the job she has married.[1]

This chapter, then, examines wives' experiences of their husbands' jobs. It draws on the experiences of women living in Kawerau, a town dominated by the pulp and paper industry. From those experiences a general analysis of the relationship between public and private spheres is developed. The analysis considers not only the domination of private life by public imperatives, but also the ways in which individuals attempt to get around constraints and make the best of them.

The women range in age from young mothers to grandmothers, differ widely in their experience of paid work, and

* The material for this chapter is taken from Bev James, 1985, *Mill Wives: A study of gender relations, family and work in a single-industry town*, DPhil. thesis, Department of Sociology, Waikato University, Hamilton. I would like to express my thanks and appreciation to the women who participated in the research. Their hospitality, interest and generosity made it possible.

Kawerau, with the mill in the background. National Publicity Studios

include Maori, Pakeha and Pacific Island Polynesian women. One major experience they have in common is that they are wives of mill workers. Their husbands are directly involved in production in one of New Zealand's largest companies, a large-scale, capital-intensive industry. The men are members of the working class,[2] and this class position is a crucial, though not the sole determining factor of the women's material circumstances and social status.[3]

As the wife of a mill worker, a woman is continually aware of how the public world of industrial production influences the life of her family and household. The industry permeates the household in many ways: the family's standard of living is largely determined by the husband's wage packet, the family home is likely to be rented from or financed through the company, and the industry's occupational hierarchy furnishes the basis of a status system that pervades the community and affects social relations beyond the mill gates.

This chapter singles out two aspects of mill work for examination. One is shiftwork, an ever-present example of the way the industry determines the rhythm of both working life and domestic life. Shiftwork reaches into the household, determining the organisation of housework and meals. It structures even the most intimate aspects of domestic life. Of necessity, shiftwork is accommodated by household members and its routine becomes accepted, if not altogether enjoyed.

In contrast to the routine of shiftwork, there is the sudden, crisis event of an industrial dispute in which the mill is closed for a period of time. Its consequences spill in a dramatic and disruptive manner from the public world of the workplace into domestic life. Such a dispute upsets the accommodations wives make to maintain a divided world, throwing into doubt accepted understandings of separate spheres and complementary responsibilities for husbands and wives.

Women relate to their husbands' jobs in two distinct ways. On the one hand a man's occupation imposes many constraints on domestic life which must be managed by his wife. On the other, women's domestic work provides for the physical and other needs of the male worker so that he is able to perform his job.

Wives of men in all social classes and occupations support their husbands in their work, though the nature of that support differs, depending on the type of work the husband does and the social expectations associated with the position of wife. For example, wives of farmers and shopkeepers contribute directly to their husbands' work by producing goods and services in the family enterprise, many of which are eventually sold on the market.[4]

The wives of men in middle class and professional occupations often provide services the husband could obtain in the workplace, such as secretarial assistance. There has grown up alongside the occupations of doctor and lawyer, for example, a parallel status of the 'proper wife'.[5] Such a wife has a public part to play in representing and supporting her husband's job. His work imposes certain requirements on her, as a wife. She must carry out specific tasks demanded by his job and act in a manner befitting her husband's social status. The advantages for the wife in making his career hers are the vicarious status and benefits she enjoys from his success.

The contributions wives of working class men make to their husbands' jobs contrast with that of wives in other classes. For the wife of a working man, there is no obvious gain in status in developing a vicarious career as 'wife of ...'; she is not crucially involved in the maintenance of her husband's social status and power. Instead, her major contribution is her provision of a comfortable home life. She furnishes domestic services and emotional support, enabling her husband to return to work each day, physically and mentally refreshed.

The woman's support of her husband in his job is not just a matter of circumstance, growing out of the external constraints of his job on the organisation of the household and her dependent economic position. The wife's commitment to supporting the husband in his job also has a strong moral component. It is generally understood, by both women and men, that it is a natural and inevitable part of 'being a wife' to put the husband's occupation first. One woman in the study, a full-time housewife, emphasised why:

His job's important because that's our living.

Another woman, employed in a part-time job, made it clear that her domestic responsibilities were important. Being able to look after husband and children, in addition to holding down a job was a source of pride:

I have always made sure, and have been lucky to have had part-time jobs. I was there to cook his meals. He didn't have to stay home and prepare meals and iron because I was at work, no way. I still do all the jobs that a housewife would do. In fact, I spoil my [husband and boys].... I say, if I can't do for my three, then I must stop work, you know. So I can cope with work and still do all the things in the house as well.

Domestic work has a special moral character, derived from the fact that it is done for those with whom a woman has an emotional and intimate association. There is no law that decrees a wife is obliged to do housework, or any other unpaid work in the home. But certain standards are publicly acknowledged, and negative sanctions applied when a wife is considered to be shirking her proper domestic duties. Consider the public censure of a wife who cannot manage the household budget, whose children are not suitably attired, or whose husband has to iron his own shirts. It is not only a matter of public expectation; standards are not simply imposed from the outside. The wife is also the judge of her own performance of domestic work. She sets her own domestic standards in reference to wider public notions of propriety.

One woman, a part-time clerical worker, emphasised the importance of keeping up standards, especially if one goes out to work. Public censure of the 'working mum' can be especially harsh.

I am a little bit proud. I wouldn't like someone to come into the house and find it in a terrible mess.

Husbands are also influential in defining domestic standards. One young mother who was busy at home with her preschool children commented:

My husband doesn't like a messy house ... and if I don't do it all the time, well I suppose he would be in a bad mood.

This comment suggests how vitally the role of wife supports the man's occupation. By providing clean, tidy and comfortable surroundings a wife helps her husband to relax and regenerate himself after a stint on the factory floor. Women's domestic work is not only necessary and useful in the way it provides the backstage support for public life; it is also personally beneficial for a man to have a wife.

107

Wives are not only constrained by their husbands' jobs and expected to provide indirect support for the public industrial process. They also respond to and attempt to exert some influence on the public sphere. During an industrial dispute at the mill some wives came to question divisions between the public world of production and the domestic sphere. Some sought to use what little power they had, derived from their domestic position, to intervene in events of the workplace. In the process they asserted their right to be involved in matters beyond the private sphere.

It is important to acknowledge that, even though women act to influence public matters, they may not seek to break down divisions between public and private life. Nor do they wish to relinquish their special domestic position and concerns. They may not be convinced that public and private divisions are oppressive to women. Rather, attempts to influence public life may be a means of preserving some private autonomy, and of maintaining the great investment most women make in family life. The private sphere has been traditionally the only place in which women have been able to wield some power and obtain some security.

Millworkers' wives in Kawerau deal with shiftwork and industrial disputes in the context of a world divided between work and home life. The mill at Kawerau, epitome of the public sphere, is a strongly masculine environment. By custom and practice its labour force is predominantly male. There are few women in production jobs, in trades, in technical or administrative occupations. On the mill site women are most visible in clerical and cleaning jobs, and in the cafeteria.[6]

Women's absence from the industrial labour force is typical of single-industry towns based on the extraction or use of primary resources. This type of work requires a skilled, adult, male labour force. Consequently, employment opportunities for the unskilled, youth and women are restricted. Opportunities are particularly limited for young women leaving school, and for women of all ages seeking part-time work.

The development of secondary industry in the town has been piecemeal and slow. The dominance of the pulp and paper industry has constituted a drain on available land and housing, and exerted a pull on labour in the area. Other enterprises have been reluctant to set up business, and the conse-

quent narrow range of retail, commercial, business and public
sector employment has resulted in limited job opportunities for
women. They are mainly restricted to sales and clerical
occupations, although women with teaching and nursing
qualifications can usually find employment locally.

The mill is a powerful symbol of masculinity. One wife
expressed the feeling of many: 'it's a man's working town'.
To the wives, the men's jobs are imbued with masculinity.
The wives see the husbands' work as tough, demanding and
dangerous. One woman, whose husband works on the paper
machine indicated how she was distanced from his job by its
masculinity:

> Exactly what he does, I don't know. He works with a lot of
> fast, hard machinery. . . . I've never gone in there to see what he
> does. What I don't know won't hurt me.

Associated with a male labour force and with male attributes,
the mill is perceived by the women as quite alien to their
experience. They gain only a scanty knowledge of the workplace from their spouses. The man might bring home gossip
from work, or comment that he has had a 'bad run', but often
the occupation itself is considered 'too technical' to discuss
with a wife. Furthermore, few husbands are forthcoming
about union matters. One woman, whose husband is a trades-
man's mate, commented:

> He doesn't really say much to me because I don't really
> understand what he's talking about, machine-wise, and he
> doesn't want to worry me with things that are happening at
> work.

One husband made a special point of keeping the home as a
haven separate from his work. His wife commented:

> Quite often he wants to switch off from all work when he
> comes home . . . he tends very much to like to keep his work
> and his private life apart. He's that sort of person. I don't think
> he would like me being closely involved in any way with his
> work . . . he likes to keep home sort of his . . . he just likes to
> think 'I can go home and I can be me'. . . .

Associated with the mill and with men's work as both 'public'
and 'masculine' is the husband's wage. This 'is won in a
masculine mode in confrontation with the "real" world which

is too tough for the woman'[7] The wage is a significant part of the masculine identity shaped through work. It denotes the man as domestic provider. He has to bring the money home.

When the wage packet comes into the household decisions must be made about its management. Then differences in the husband's and the wife's relationship to money, including their access to it and their control over spending, become apparent. Typically, the money the man earns is handed over to his wife for her to manage for the benefit of the family as a whole. However, the wife's authority over money is circumscribed. She is responsible for financial decisions entailed in the daily running of the household, and must operate within the bounds of what she is given. One wife observed:

> It's all very well for a man just to say 'Well here's a $100, that'll feed that lot.' Because it just doesn't when you've got children.

In some cases the wife's access to money is restricted for both household and personal spending. Those women who did not have any income of their own were particularly reliant on the goodwill of their spouse. One woman discussed her situation:

> He'll go through and look at the bank book and wonder where the hang all the money's gone . . . he forgets about the telephone bill and the power and things. Um, he sort of thinks I'm just wasting it . . . just as well I wrote it down, so I can show him. Otherwise, he would think I was spending it all on myself.

In contrast, one woman who had worked for several years emphasised how the job gave her financial autonomy:

> Right from the time we got married I always wanted my own account. I felt independent . . . he's never queried my spending, and usually, if it's any big spending, we always talk about it.

Spouses' different access to money and the wife's lack of financial control is especially apparent when it comes to personal spending. Personal spending gives rise to a tension between self-interest on the one hand, and commitment to the collective requirements of the household on the other. Both wives with no income of their own and those earning a wage often felt that personal spending conflicted with wise management of the household budget. They felt a pressure to spend money on their children or save towards household purchases, rather than spending on themselves. One part-time worker summed up the feelings of many of the women, that their families came first:

> Whereas before [marriage] perhaps everything revolved around myself, you know, and the money that I worked for, went on myself. Whereas now I get more pleasure in giving to the kids. I'd rather work to get them more, and miss out.

Excessive personal expenditure was condemned for both spouses. But several husbands had pocket money allocated to them from the household budget. None of the wives were in this position. A wife's personal expenditure is not legitimated in the same way as her husband's; in some cases it is not a right, but a privilege bestowed by the husband. A young mother at home with pre-school children explained:

> If I have any personal expenses I just ask him and he'll give me that little bit extra just for me.

The amount a man is able to earn at the mill (more than most wives can earn anywhere), coupled with his access to housing benefits provided by the company, put him in a superior financial position to his wife. This assures him a dominant role in the control of domestic finances. A man's earnings are expressive of both his public and domestic identities. But a woman's involvement in paid work is often conceptualised in ways that affirm her primary responsibilities as domestic ones and point to conflict for wives between employment and domesticity. The women in this study saw their financial contributions to the household as secondary to their husbands', and thus as not essential to the family livelihood.

Almost all of the women had taken on a paid job, or were thinking of doing so when their children started school. But decisions about working outside the home were not influenced solely by their responsibility for childcare. Many of the women had found it difficult to combine employment and coping with the demands of their husbands' work.

It was not simply that some men saw a wife's employment as conflicting with her domestic obligations; her employment also represented an intrusion into the male domain. If a wife earns money, a man's status as breadwinner and head of the household is threatened. One husband expressed concern that the balance of power between husband and wife would be undermined. His wife, who had a part-time job, observed:

I don't think he'll ever really be too happy about me working, but he accepts it ... he still thinks the housework is my responsibility. Doesn't mean just because I've got a job I can shirk all what's at home ... his idea is that Mum should be at home. Mum should be in charge of all what's at home, and he goes out and makes the money and takes care of us all in that way ... he wants to know that he's providing for us.

The influence of a husband's job on a woman's employment decisions often starts before their marriage, during courtship and engagement. Some of the women who had grown up in and around Kawerau recalled the restricted choices of their youth. Early marriage was a sensible option, considering the nature of the town's job market which was much more favourable to male school leavers than to female. Now in her thirties, one woman talked of her own experience:

It's not so bad for the guys 'cos they've got the mill, but there's very few jobs for the girls that leave school. You've either got to hang around, or you have to leave, and go to Auckland or somewhere like that. So, the ones that do stay, the easiest way to sort of get around the whole business is to get married.

Once a couple is married, the husband's occupation becomes the principal one, always needing to be accommodated. Some of the women discussed their ambitions to re-enter the labour force, or to get on in their jobs, but they encountered difficulties in obtaining training and qualifications locally. A move away to further their ambitions was impossible for most. One woman whose part-time job provided her with little challenge commented on how a man's job could limit his wife's horizons:

I know there's a lot of women who would like to leave Kawerau ... but prising your husband out of the mill is the main obstruction ... unless he could get a job somewhere as good as the one here, he's not going to leave. There's a lot of men like that, and there's a lot of women who are having to make the most of staying put.

In addition to their loyalty to their husbands' jobs, the women were always aware of their family ties, and cited these as reasons for curtailed career ambitions. A young Maori mother expressed her aspirations:

112

I would have to go away from here to do further study ...
which I can't do ... if I had no children I might consider it.

So far, in discussing women's experiences as mill workers'
wives in Kawerau, it has become apparent that the demands of
husbands' work and raising a family combine to produce the
conditions in which the women conduct their lives. Now these
demands are further examined specifically in relation to shiftwork.

The mill operates several shiftwork systems, but my discussion is primarily concerned with the women's experiences of
the rotating three-shift system, which affects about 41 per cent
of the labour force. The three-shift system operates con-
tinuously, twenty-four hours, seven days a week. The individual worker works a shift for six days, followed by two days
off. The three shifts are: a day shift (8 a.m.–4 p.m.), an
evening shift (4 p.m.–midnight) and a night shift (midnight–
8 a.m.).

As an unchangeable part of the husband's job, shiftwork
imposes a structure around which the wife must fit her own
and her family's life. The women say 'the wife does that
shiftwork as well'. Wives deal with shiftwork's rigid schedule
by subordinating activities to it. This is the experience of one
young housewife:

> If he's on a '12 to 8' sometimes he'll sleep in the morning and
> the baby and I will go out somewhere so the house is quiet, or
> if he's awake, well he stays home and we stay home and he
> works around the house so we do things around the house. If
> he's on a '4 to 12', sometimes he sleeps in, so my housework
> gets done later.... It just depends which shift he's on.

A wife often accommodates her housework to the shiftwork
schedule, doing it early in the morning or late at night when
her husband is at work. This is done to avoid disturbing the
worker when he is asleep in the daytime. The wife may also
wish to do her housework when her husband is at work so as
to keep her time free when he is off work during the day. One
of the few advantages of shiftwork for wives is that it allows
spouses to share activities during the daytime, such as shop-
ping, childcare and leisure.

The wife's accommodation to the shiftwork schedule is most

clearly seen in the provision of meals, particularly the main meal of the day. This is usually a substantial cooked meal, distinguished from cold food or hot snacks.[8] What is eaten, when it is eaten, and who partakes of the food – all the rituals involved in the meal – tell us about divisions and connections between the public and the private domains.

Food preparation and meals are areas where women have control; they are illustrative of the woman's domestic realm of expertise, and an opportunity for a wife and mother to demonstrate her love for her family. The meal is a significant symbol of family unity. It shows the success of the family in getting together, of the father being with his family, despite the demands of the shiftwork schedule.

But paradoxically, while meals are ostensibly under women's control, they are also prepared and served in deference to the man's timetable, shaped by external forces. The organisation of the meal indicates how a wife's domestic work is structured by her husband's occupation. For example, on the evening shift, the main meal is often served at lunchtime, or in the afternoon when the children have returned from school, and before the husband leaves for work. One woman explained:

> I would run around getting everything ready for him and we'd have tea at 3. As soon as the kids come home from school we'd sit down and we'd all have dinner together. It's the only time we manage to get him, we'd have our roast dinner together at 3 o'clock.

Another woman expressed how she felt obliged to fit in with her husband's work schedule:

> I feel I have to, because they're coming home and they might be tired ... you put yourself out, don't you? ... if he's on 4 to midnight I cook him a hot meal before he goes.

The obligatory nature of the wife's work reveals not only the way it benefits industrial production in sustaining the male worker but also the way in which it is a service to the husband, done as part of the woman's duties as wife. Although some husbands cooked their own meals, most expected their wives to have food ready 'on call'. In this context the main meal can be seen as a symbol of hierarchical gender divisions of power and status. The wife's deferential status is revealed in her role;

she cooks as a service for her husband. Meals are organised around his comings and goings, and made to his taste. Women and children can make do with snacks, but a man needs a filling cooked meal to prepare him for work or to replenish him afterwards.

Cooking for the husband is a marital expectation that is seldom questioned, and the actions of two wives who refused to be at the beck and call of the industrial timetable are unusual. One husband ate many meals at the work canteen. The other woman insisted that everyone in her household prepare their own meals. The behaviour of these women challenges deep-seated ideas about the association of women with nurture and service (the canteen meal can be seen as the antithesis of the nourishing home-cooked meal). But these two were very much in the minority. Most wives did not question that they would cook for their husbands in compliance with their timetables. This not only required the provision of a proper cooked meal, but also snacks and cut lunches when required.

Wives ensure their husbands' material wellbeing by providing meals. Wives' efforts to ensure the health and emotional wellbeing of their spouses are equally important. Research indicates that nightwork and the regular change of shifts can result in physical problems and mental stress for the shiftworker.[9] Wives cope with these problems in their attempts to make a soothing and comfortable home life, so that their husbands can relax after work.

The wife is often required to minimise conflict arising from the male worker's routines and requirements, and those of other family members. This is especially acute when the children are young. Children have their own 'shifts' and routines which can be only partially accommodated to the shiftworker's timetable. One woman recalled her experience when the children were young:

> I had him doing shifts . . . plus my [pre-school] daughter had her shift as well, and then I had baby who had hers. Up at nights, and all different hours . . . where's the time for me?

Accommodating the needs of children with the demands of shiftwork was not the only problem the women identified, though it was certainly a major one. There were others, well summed up by this woman whose husband had been on shiftwork for over twenty years:

When there's children in the family, especially when there's younger children, there could be conflict, you know, when he's trying to get sleep and perhaps, the children are being unruly. There could be conflict in routines, well, mealtimes. And of course there's the social aspect too, where wives may want to go out, particularly on night shifts.

The constraints and demands of shiftwork rest heavily on the wife, and she must deal with these in her role as custodian of the family's welfare. Less obvious are any advantages the wife derives from shiftwork, or any ways in which its pressures are eased for her. However, some wives discover a certain freedom within its confines. For women with older children the evening shift offers time relatively free from domestic duties, and from their spouse's expectations of companionship. Many of the women implied that when the husband was at home, he determined how the couple would spend their time. One wife compared the relative freedom of the evening shift with the freedom of 'pleasing herself' she had experienced as a young woman before marriage. Another woman described how she used the evening shift for both individual and social activities:

> Oh, bed, book and apple, lovely! Even in the first couple of years of marriage I didn't mind shiftwork. Working women like to get together to have a natter, so at night you wouldn't like to go if your husband's there staring at the box, so, OK, shiftwork gives you the chance to do all your socialising.

Although shiftwork takes precedence in so many ways, some wives have made their own personal spaces within its demands.

Some women found other advantages in shiftwork. For them it opened up possibilities in reorganising childcare and housework. Several mentioned that their husbands did household chores and cooked meals when they were off work in the daytime. Most women also mentioned how shiftwork gave fathers the opportunity of spending more time with their children. One young mother considered that in this way shiftwork had considerably benefited her family:

> Oh they see him a lot more. I think it's brought him and the kids closer together.

Another woman reported how her return to work when the children were small had been facilitated by her husband's shiftwork:

> ... he pulled his weight at home ... on 4 to 12 and 12 to 8
> he'd do the housework in the mornings and he'd have the tea
> ready at night ... he was able to look after the children too
> prior to their going to school ... the hours worked in well ...
> there's only one week in three where I had to get a babysitter.

Yet the husband's opportunities to be with the children are curtailed when the children start school, and shiftwork encroaches on family time at the weekend. Most wives found that they still took on the major responsibility of childrearing, and some insisted that shiftwork made it easier for fathers to opt out of some duties, such as disciplining the children. Nor does shiftwork necessarily promote a greater sharing of housework between spouses. The two women who commented that they were only able to remain in paid work throughout most of their married lives because of shiftwork were unusual. For other men, the shiftwork routine justified a lack of domestic involvement, and reinforced a traditional sexual division of labour. Even those husbands who did domestic work and childcare helped rather than took full responsibility. The fact that domestic responsibilities are still largely women's, although the actual tasks may be divided more evenly in some families, indicates that the traditional sexual division of labour remains predominant.

A wife may change the impact of shiftwork on her in a personal way by persuading her husband to go on to day work. But this does not affect the structure of shiftwork in the workplace. Shiftwork is a feature of the organisation of the public world beyond wives' control. As such, it illustrates the dominance of industrial production over domestic activities.

Shiftwork is an everyday feature of the workplace that is routinely dealt with in the home. In contrast, an industrial dispute is a sudden event, intensely disruptive to both public and private life. Industrial disputes are salient, though infrequent features, of this town that make everyone acutely aware of the mill's effect on their lives. Most of the women in this study have experienced their husbands being off work because of an industrial dispute. The loss of a job for a male worker and loss of family income led the women to question their accepted understandings of marital roles and the power of public events to prescribe private lives. The domestic sphere is not an autonomous world in which individuals remain uninfluenced by outside events.

The women described the effects of a six-week dispute in the autumn of 1978.[10] They detested industrial disputes because of their immediate and personal effects on the family. One of the most shattering consequences is economic hardship. The women viewed the dispute as directly threatening their ability to be competent housekeepers. As the managers of the household budget, they were confronted with the problem of how to provide for their family's daily needs, and how to honour long-term financial commitments, without regular funds. One woman expressed it like this:

> ... it was pretty hard, you know ... trying to manage the money so it lasted ... not really knowing where the next lot of food was going to come from.

The wives who received union welfare felt the public stigma attached to their position. While priding themselves on their abilities as domestic managers, they became acutely aware of their vulnerable position. Public events were exerting a forceful influence on their domestic realm.

Lack of money was not the only problem faced by wives. The dispute also disrupted the household routine. At first the women enjoyed not having to accommodate shiftwork. But having a husband at home all day, and perhaps a bad tempered one at that, meant further unwelcome unpredictability for the women. It is difficult to get away from a dispute, in the town where the mill's employees make up over 60 per cent of the local workforce. Spouse, neighbours, friends, relatives – all are directly or indirectly involved. In such a situation a wife becomes especially sensitive to her husband's emotional state.

One woman, whose husband belonged to the union at the centre of the dispute, commented that she felt bitter about him being off work, but acknowledged the pressures he must have felt from workmates, the family and other quarters:

> It wasn't too hot on him either ... he felt sort of helpless. He was assailed from both sides.

This woman wanted information about the dispute from her husband, but in seeking it she was aware that she risked upsetting the already precarious atmosphere of the household. She observed that talk about the dispute 'just caused arguments, it was pretty counterproductive'. Another women had a similar experience:

Every husband seemed to come home with a different point of view . . . so it was very hard, you just didn't know where you were, who was telling the truth.

Although some women could talk about the dispute with their husbands, the experiences of wives quoted above were more typical. Being physically and symbolically distanced from their husbands' workplace, most wives did not have access to reliable and accurate information. Their view of events was particularly influenced by the news media, which tended to provide only superficial coverage. One wife summed up the frustrations of many:

. . . we only learn . . . what is passed around from one person to the next, and sometimes it's not accurate anyway . . . in a lot of ways we are not really enlightened.

A few wives accepted the imposition of the dispute; it was something they had no power or business to challenge. But others vehemently resented its disruption, and wanted to express their dissatisfaction publicly.

. . . us wives should speak up and say we're sick of strikes and things like this because it's really the wives and children that suffer.

The women aimed their frustruations at the unions. Blaming the union upset personal relations less than blaming a husband, and it was more accessible than the company. On the whole, the women did not support unions. There were several reasons for this. They had little direct experience of union activities, owing to their own fragmented labour force participation, and their involvement in jobs which had typically weak unions. In addition, they regarded their husbands' unions as part of the work site and thus part of the masculine sphere beyond their usual concerns.

The women believed the unions to have excessive power. Several expressed bitter resentment at what they saw as union control over their lives. One wife commented:

Living with the thought that at any one time, because of one union, that mill could shut, that't the only thing that I don't like living here, that threat of a strike always holding over your head, and it's *not* an easy thing to have to live with.

Newspaper reports of the dispute encouraged such a view by

casting the unions as the powerful party, poised to do irreparable damage to the industry and, inevitably, to the community which relied on the mill for its existence.

There were real fears for the women. They questioned the actions of the unions, but were far less critical of the company. Yet the company had suspended a large number of the mill workforce and, furthermore, there was government interference in negotiations. Both company and government had influenced the course of the dispute, and were in a more powerful economic and political position than the unions.[11]

Some wives who wanted to contribute to public debate about the dispute sought inclusion in union stopwork meetings. As justification for their involvement, they referred to the separate family responsibilities of husbands and wives. In normal circumstances these separate responsibilities would reinforce a distinction between the women's world of domesticity and the men's world of work and politics. But in this crisis, they argued that wives' domestic responsibilities provided a good reason for inclusion in public debate:

> Women put a different angle on things, 'cos they've got to put up with the hardship. I mean the kids have still got to go to school, the kids still wear out clothes, the power bill's got to be paid.

Suggestions concerning the involvement of wives in union meetings were not welcomed by union officials.[12] One to whom I spoke was scathing of wives' criticisms of unions. He did not acknowledge that the women lacked reliable information about the dispute. Nor did he accept their view of events, derived from their domestic experiences of the strike. The union official held strongly the ideal of the male breadwinner as head of the household, and opposed what he saw as wives' intrusion into the male domain of work.

Keen though many of the wives were to express their grievances publicly, they were hesitant about any collective protests. Some had discussed such action, but nothing came of it.[13] This woman's comment reflects resignation in the face of powerful forces:

> Got plenty ideas! [laughs] we could run the world quite successfully, us women. But, whether anybody'd have the guts to put it into action, I doubt it very much . . . we just console each other. Make up all the things we're gonna do. Gives us something to do [laughs].

In Kawerau public and private are starkly divided along gender
lines. The private world of the home and the family is seen as
female, and the world of the mill as male. These are physical
distinctions, observed in the spatial separation of community
from industry, in the organisation of daily activities, and in the
allocation of finances and resources that concern individuals,
families, the company and local government. Public and private divisions also embody ideas and values, which are clearly
expressed in expectations about masculine and feminine
behaviour.

The separate worlds of public and private are, however,
linked through women. As managers of the home, they must
deal with the domestic consequences of their husbands' employment in the public sphere. The household is largely organised around the man's job and there is an expectation that the
wife will contribute to his wellbeing as a worker. The wife's
servicing role becomes even more important in a time of
stress, in an industrial dispute.

As organising principles, the concepts of public and private
are helpful in making sense of life, but in some circumstances
they are inadequate. Boundaries between the two spheres often
reassure, and spell security; but they may also be restrictive. A
crisis such as an industrial dispute brings into question custom-
ary ways of organising day-to-day life and accepted beliefs.
In this chapter I have shown how the 1978 industrial dispute
exposed widely held assumptions about women's association
with the private sphere and solely domestic matters. Its effects
on families prompted some women to question their exclusion
from public decision-making and debate.

The women's response to the dispute was, on the whole,
conservative. They were critical of unions and sceptical of the
benefits of industrial action. From their personal and domestic
viewpoints, they regarded the unions' actions as opposed to
family life. Such responses are understandable. Although
money stops coming into the household when the husband is
off work, the wife still has to make ends meet. The women
regarded the dispute as directly threatening their family's economic livelihood and emotional wellbeing. The women had
much invested in domestic life. Over the years they had worked hard to establish a satisfying and secure home life for all,
and they feared their hopes and dreams were under attack.

The women's domestic responsibilities prompted some of
them to seek public expression of their grievances. They did

not want to be constrained and defined by a narrow definition of women's activities and interests that excluded them from influencing the world outside the home. During the dispute some of the women began to regard their domestic activities in a new light. They recognised the devaluation of domestic work, compared with paid work, and started to question the assumption. They were more concerned that their views should be given public validity than that their domestic contributions should be given a monetary value. These women considered that their domestic experiences gave them a fresh, and wider perspective on issues where usually only matters deemed relevant to public life are examined.

Paradoxically, the women's domestic responsibilities not only provided justification for their public involvement in the dispute, but also inhibited public expression of their views. The women were caught between action and inaction; both seemed to threaten the order and security of their home life. They felt compelled to act, perceiving that their efforts to maintain a home were being eroded by the dispute. But they were also wary of involvement in public protest. This seemed to overstep inflexible boundaries defining male and female areas of responsibility and expertise. Public action seemed to be necessary, but it also seemed to threaten the unity of the family at the very time the women were struggling to preserve their home life.

The experiences of these women highlight the contributions women make to social life through reproduction and nurturing. It has been shown that they work hard at making a satisfying home life for themselves and others. The structures and beliefs which divide our society along gender lines associate women with the private, domestic life and, in doing so, offer women security and identity. However, the divided world can also restrict women's lives. Public and private divisions tend to define women only in terms of reproduction and nurturing, despite women's actual experiences which straddle both worlds. While such divisions continue, women have to contend with more than the 'double burden' of housework and paid employment; as wives, women also contribute in various essential ways to their husband's occupations. Despite all these important contributions, there is currently no public commitment to and very little financial support for women's domestic work and childrearing. The connections between reproduction and production go unacknowledged in all areas of public life and women are largely excluded from power in the public sphere. Furthermore, many women do not see the public sphere as offering them opportunities for personal and social fulfilment. These appear to be gained only from the private sphere, yet primary association with domesticity can be limiting.

In this chapter, I have looked at the relationship between public and private spheres by starting from the 'inside', the daily lives of women as wives and mothers running a household. I have shown that ordinary domestic activities concerned with the care of individuals and the maintenance of households are public issues. We must fight against these activities being defined as solely the duties of 'private woman', if divisions between the public and private spheres are to be overcome.

Hikurangi, 1982. Photograph by Ans Westra

Chapter 7

THE INVISIBLE
WOMEN
Marilyn Waring

The majority of women live in the rural areas of developing countries, hundreds of millions of them in conditions of absolute poverty. Eighty per cent of the female populations of Afghanistan, Bangladesh, Bhutan, India, Nepal, Pakistan and Sri Lanka are found in the countryside. In China the proportion is 77 per cent, in the Koreas, Hong Kong and Mongolia 56 per cent, in South West Asia, in the region of the Persian Gulf and Peninsula 50 per cent. In Africa, eight to nine out of ten women live in the country. It is estimated that they perform 60–70 per cent of the agricultural activity of the African continent.

While the specific tasks vary, the work of rural women internationally includes childbearing and rearing, household provisioning and management (cooking, cleaning, washing clothes, household repair and manufacture, fuel gathering, provision of water) and aspects of agricultural production (much of the production processing, storage and preparation of food), livestock raising, artisan production, trade and income generation. These varied tasks are not perceived by women as falling into separate categories of familial and non-familial, domestic and economic, non-productive and productive, public or private, but as intrinsically related.

Consider the case of Tendai, a young girl in the Lowveld, in Zimbabwe. Her day starts at 4 a.m. when, barefoot, she carries a 30-litre tin to a borehole about 11 kilometres away from her home to fetch water. She will be home by 9 a.m. She will eat a little, and proceed to fetch firewood until midday. She will clean the utensils from the family's morning meal and sit preparing a lunch of sadza (ground meal) for the family. After lunch and the clearing of the dishes she will wander in the hot sun until the early evening, fetching wild vegetables for supper

125

before making the evening trip for water. Her day ends at 9 p.m. after she has prepared supper and put her young brothers and sisters to sleep.

Tendai is considered unproductive and 'unoccupied'. According to international institutions, and to patriarchal theorists, Tendai does not work, and her labour has no value.

The labour of the vast majority of women like Tendai is invisible, but this fate is not confined to the developing world. A North American or New Zealand housewife, who spends her days cleaning the bathroom, kitchen, sink and oven, clearing food and dishes from the table, cooking, cutting grass, changing infants' soiled or wet nappies, disciplining children, disposing of rubbish, dressing children, dusting, gathering clothes for washing, filling the car with fuel, going to the supermarket, repairing household items, ironing, keeping an eye on or playing with children, making beds, paying bills, caring for pets and plants, putting away toys, books, clothes etc., putting children to bed, putting in and taking out clothes from the washer or dryer, and putting clothes away, setting the table, serving a meal, sewing or mending or knitting, sweeping floors, taking the children to daycare or to school, talking with door-to-door salesmen, answering the telephone, vacuuming, washing the dishes, washing floors, weeding, shovelling snow, and wiping down the kitchen, just has to face the fact that she fills her time in a *totally* unproductive manner. She, too, is classified as 'unoccupied'.

A Survey of Rural Women in New Zealand[1] showed that, in 1981, 81 per cent of respondents did manual work on farms and that 49 per cent received no payment for this work. The numbers of those who received payment tended (a) to increase as the size of farms increased, (b) to have half or less responsibility for major policy decisions, and (c) to undertake farm tasks less regularly than those who were unpaid. (It is unlikely that these women received cash. The tax regime will see less tax levied on larger farms with larger incomes if a 'book-entry' payment is made to the wife. This operates essentially as a form of tax avoidance.)

In addition to household and farm labour tasks, 56.3 per cent of the respondents always, and 65.3 per cent sometimes, did two or more of the following tasks: answering the telephone, seeing callers, keeping farm accounts, paying bills, deciding who does what each day, listening to workers' grievances, deciding cropping or stocking policy for the coming year, policy planning and keeping stock records. Sixty-four per cent of them were not paid for this work. In the commercial world, these tasks, when paid, are called decision-making, labour relations or data collection, and carry with them status and an above-average income.

Eighty per cent of the respondents grew fruit or vegetables, 89 per cent preserved farm or garden produce, 27 per cent made bread, 73 per cent provided meals for workers, 63 per cent entertained business visitors, 53 per cent kept poultry for farmhouse needs, 24 per cent were involved in another form of 'farmhouse activity'. Seven per cent were involved in craft-work *for sale*; we can only guess at the knitting, sewing, needlework, spinning and a multitude of other crafts being undertaken for 'household consumption' in the countryside.

Sometimes, the New Zealand farm woman would be said to be 'occupied'.

The International Labour Organisation (ILO) sees occasion for those engaged in non-market subsistence production and for subsistence and unpaid workers to be regarded as 'active labour'. Housework done by members of a family in their own homes is not active labour, but 'work done by members of a family in helping the head of a family in his [sic] occupation is, even though only indirectly renumerated'. That this is 'active labour' is subject to the proviso that, in order to be defined as such, the unpaid family worker must work in non-domestic activities for at least one-third of the normal hours.

This definition excludes the great bulk of women's work – reproduction (in all its forms), raising children, domestic work and subsistence production. The activity of cooking is active labour when the cooked food is marketed, and economically inactive labour when it is not. Housework is productive when performed by a paid domestic servant, and non-productive when it is not.

In assessing who 'works' the ILO has stated that 'the activity rates for females are frequently not comparable internationally, since in many countries large numbers of women assist on farms or in family enterprises without pay, and there are differences from one country to another in the criteria adopted for determining the extent to which such workers are to be counted among the economically active.'[2]

The data are collected by way of census or survey. But data accuracy problems also surround the choice of respondent, and the concept of 'the head of the household'.

The United Nations (UN) suggests that one issue in the choice of survey respondent is 'whether to interview one person to obtain the information for an entire household or to interview each member, or at least each adult, *for himself* [italics mine]. Interview time and costs are usually much smaller if a single household respondent is used.... For selecting the household respondent, *the head or wife* is usually the preferable choice.'[3]

The presumption of a male head of household continues in all literature despite statistics released by United Nations Development Programme (UNDP) that one-third of all households on earth are headed by women. Female-headed families as a percentage of all families in OECD countries include 24.4 per cent in Sweden, 17.5 per cent in the USA, 13 per cent in France, 10.8 per cent in Australia, 10.6 per cent in Canada and 10.4 per cent in Great Britain.

Barbara Rogers reports that a check on the reliability of Indian census data revealed that, among other biases, the census, based on information given by the 'men of the household', tended to understate the participation of women in agricultural work. The Gokhale Institute, also in India, found that attempts to train men farmers and their literate sons to keep accounts were unsuccessful. The errors and omissions were greatest with regard to the use of so-called 'family labour' – namely women's and children's work.[4]

But little changes. Dennis Casley (a prominent Food and Agricultural Organisation (FAO) statistician) and Dennis Lury describe the international practice.

We prefer to call a household survey one in which the household is the final sample unit and also provides the unit of reference for the major focus of the survey. Questions may be asked of individual members of the household, but these are aimed at itemising individual components of the household activities in order to obtain the household data by aggregation. Surveys of subjects such as *fertility, child nutrition, food intake* and *energy expenditure* are surveys of *individuals* although the individuals are also household members, and membership of the household will determine, to some extent, the individual's fertility, health, and consumption habits.[5] [Italics mine.]

Since Casley and Lury also define a 'household' as 'comprising a person or group of persons, generally bound by ties of kinship, who live together under a single roof or *within a single compound,* and who share a community of life *in that they are answerable to the same head,* and share a common source of food', it should also be obvious that the perceived 'head of the household' wouldn't know the answers to these 'individual questions'!

It is difficult to escape the conclusion that the male world is concerned with the wellbeing of the community, i.e. the community of men, and that the female world is concerned with 'individuals'.

Individuals would thus be conceived of as the concern of the 'private' sphere. Women do not see a distinction in the question material between household or individual surveys; they are all intrinsically related.

But the (manifestly strained) demarcation established by Casley and Lury causes the majority of the human species to become statistically invisible. The family of man avoids confronting the absence of wellbeing in the family of women. In 1982 800 million people in the Third World were living in absolute poverty. Most of those affected are migrant workers and their families, youth, the disabled and the aged – and the majority of all those categories are women. Approximately 500 million people suffer from malnutrition; the most seriously affected are children under five and women. Twenty million people die annually of hunger-related causes and one billion endure chronic undernourishment and other poverty deprivations; the majority are women and children.

In microcosm, it is easy to find examples of this process, and reports on aid and development projects are full of them. Ruth Dixon describes a number in her paper 'Assessing the Impact of Development Projects on Women'.[6]

Following the Sahelian drought in North Africa, the lack of understanding among programme administrators of the sexual division of control over resources seriously damaged the nomadic women's economic and social positions. Dixon reports that among both Fulani and Tuareg herders, one of the major concerns expressed was that the government's programme to reconstitute herds lost in the drought was replacing cattle only for the men. Women's stock was not being replaced. This was crippling their social system, animals were unavailable for dowry and bridewealth payments, women had lost their independent property. This was apparently the unintentional result of the government programme that issued a card to the 'head of each family', and replaced animals only to the 'family head'.

Full-time wage employment for women, while offering badly needed cash incomes, can result, among other consequences, in the elimination of home garden production, with severe nutritional disadvantages for the entire family, the early cessation of infant breast feeding, and a critical shortage of agricultural labour during periods of peak demand.

A project designed to increase food production that does not take into account the sexual division of labour in agriculture, for example, can have the unintended consequences of *reducing* household food consumption. In a Kenyan land settlement scheme, women who worked long hours with their husbands (or in their husbands' extended absence) in the new irrigated rice fields had less time than before to grow traditional foods on their own garden plots, which were too small in any case to provide for the family's subsistence. While rice production increased and total incomes among participating households rose, nutritional levels fell. If the importance of women's food production had been recognised, provision could have been made for agricultural inputs such as credit, fertilisers and seeds for the garden plots as well as the rice plots, perhaps with some experiments in labour-saving collective production and marketing of traditional foodstuffs.

A Guatemalan radio campaign was aimed at two populations: illiterate highland Indians in subsistence agriculture and Spanish-speaking Latinos in the south east. Symbolised by the radio messages called 'Let's Talk, Mr Farmer', the complex experimental scheme to change agricultural knowledge, attitudes, and practices did not once identify, in a major summary document, whether women participated as farmers, radio listeners, forum discussants, community change agents, or questionnaire respondents. Women's role as agricultural producers appeared to be completely ignored.

When there is a shift in the balance of productive roles favouring male employment there is often a corresponding shift in consumption preferences. Radios, watches, beer and bicycles may have higher priority than nutritional needs of children and social welfare. The introduction of wage labour to

Kiribati, and the consequent loss of protein through the male population's failure to fish any more, have meant a massive decline in nutrition standards, and outbreaks of rickets, along with an increase in alcoholism and the consumption of imported processed foods.

But the community and country are told that a 'growth in productivity' was recorded in the economy, through the Kiribati version of the United Nations System of National Accounts (UNSNA).

The New Zealand System of National Accounts gives numerical expression to the main features of economic activity, covering production, expenditure and income distribution. The national accounts allow the aggregation of information about the transactions of the 200 000 or so 'establishments' which produce goods and services and of the 900 000 households who consume the bulk of this output.

There are two major types of transactors. The most important transactor is called the 'production unit' or 'establishment'. It may be a farm, a factory, a shop, a government department or an old people's home. It may not even have a location because it is strictly an accounting unit which brings together factors of production (land and/or labour and/or capital) and produces a good or service. It may sell its product, it may produce it for free distribution, or, as is the case with many government services, it may produce only for the common good.

These production units are grouped into twenty-five production groups. The classification distinguishes between producers that are market oriented (and divides them according to industry) and those that produce goods and services that are not normally marketed.

The non-market producers are divided into those owned by central government, those owned by local government, and those owned by private non-profit organisations who provide services for individuals and households. Also included among the non-market production groups is a class which aggregates the transactions carried out by those householders who employ labour directly for domestic purposes.

In any annual reports of the World Bank, the International Monetary Fund (IMF) or United Nations agencies and governments, there are columns of indices based on national accounts

statistics. The UN uses national accounts to assess annual contributions, and to appraise the success of regional development
programmes and aid donors use them to identify deserving
cases, 'need' being determined by 'per capita gross domestic
product' (GDP). The World Bank uses this figure to identify
nations that most urgently need economic assistance; multina-
tional corporations use the same figures to locate new areas for
overseas investment.

For individual countries the uses of national accounts and the
supporting statistics can be summarised as being in the following areas:

a) serving as a framework for the integration of economic
   statistics generally,
b) analyses of current and past developments in the national
   economy,
c) quantification of the national economy in order to determine policies related to resource allocation,
d) short- and medium-term forecasting of future trends,
e) the building of models of the economy in order to analyse
   and project the possible effects of policy and other changes
   of economic significance,
f) international comparisons of a nation's economic performance.

The National Accounts by themselves do not indicate
what economic policies a government should implement. The
appropriate size of the budget deficit or correct amount of any
taxation cuts, for example, cannot be inferred directly from the
national accounts. Policy measures are based on an understanding of how the economic system functions, and how components respond to changes in economic stimulus. The national
accounts record this pattern of economic activity. They sum-
marise past economic trends and are used as data in models of
the overall economy or production sectors for forecasting purposes. These forecasts are used by a government in considering
economic strategies and changes in government policy.

The GDP is used to monitor rates and patterns of growth, to
set priorities in policy-making, to measure the success of policies and to measure economic welfare. Activities that lie outside the production boundary, that is the vast bulk of labour in
every nation performed by unpaid women, are left out of the
GDP. It is not a large step from that point to leaving them out
of policy consideration altogether.

132

In *A System of National Accounts and Supporting Tables* published by the Statistical Office by the UN the following
appears.[7] It is the key, and only, paragraph which relates to the
universal exclusion of rural women's unpaid work from the
national accounts.

After explaining that farm households usually produce agricultural products for their own consumption as well as for the
market, and the desirability of imputing a sale by their production account to their consumption account in respect of the
value of the product which they consume, 'clearly-defined
rules' for the production boundary in 'under-developed' countries are described.

> *It is convenient* in stating these rules to draw a distinction
> between primary and other producers. In the case of primary
> producers, that is those engaged in agriculture, forestry,
> hunting, fishing, mining and quarrying, all primary production
> whether exchanged or not and all goods and services produced
> and exchanged are included in the total of production. In the
> case of other producers, that is, those engaged in all other
> industries listed in the International Standard Industrial
> Classification, the total of the primary production is included as
> for primary producers. As a result of these rules there is omitted
> from production the net amount of all non-primary production
> performed by producers outside their own trades and consumed
> by themselves. Non-primary production may be broadly
> defined as the transportation and distribution of tangible
> commodities as well as the rendering of services. . . .

The rules are in close agreement with farming imputations
made for industrialised economies. No other imputations are
made '*since primary production and the consumption of their own
produce by non-primary producers is of little or no importance*'.
[Italics mine.]

Here it is important to remember that rural women are
'housewives', not 'primary producers'.

Among the nomad people of Iran's Zagros Mountains, the
men look after the animals; it is the women who do almost
everything. They do the near-universal 'women's work' of
preparing meals and looking after the children. They haul
water into the camp on their backs. They milk and shear the
animals, mostly sheep and goats. They collect such edible
plants, berries, roots and fungi as the surroundings afford.

133

They churn butter, make cheese and yoghurt, and refine the leftover whey into the daily beverage. They spin the wool and goat hair into threads and press it into felt and make clothes, tent cloths and carpets for their families' use. From each tent household of an extended family a woman goes daily to collect firewood from the bush: on average, she spends half a day at the task, plus another hour at the camp breaking the torn-off branches of thorn bush into pieces small enough for the cooking fire.[8]

In the national economic accounts of Iran – the summary of goods and services produced in the country – the only portion of the nomad woman's work that will show up even as subsistence production is her output of woollen textiles and dairy products. If she lived in the Congo Republic instead of Iran, the accountants would also include her food-processing activities in calculating the gross domestic product, but they would omit her production of hand-crafted articles. Taiwan's bookkeepers, too, would leave out handicrafts; they would, however, assign economic value to the woman's water carrying and wood gathering. But in Nigeria, it would be argued that, in rural areas, wood and water are free goods, like air, and so are the human efforts that make them useful.

In a 1975 discussion of the non-monetary activities covered by the national accounts of seventy developing countries the activities covered least in the accounts are handicrafts, water collection, crop storage and housewives' services. Of fifteen developing countries in the Caribbean and South America, only Jamaica covered food processing in their national accounts; only four (Argentina, Haiti, Jamaica and Mexico) included handicrafts.[9]

In Africa women and men share labour in planning and caring for domestic animals. Women do 60 per cent of the marketing of excess crops and harvesting, 70 per cent of the hoeing and weeding, 80 per cent of transporting crops from farm to home, 80 per cent of crops storage, 90 per cent of carrying water and fuel and processing food crops, and 95 per cent of feeding and caring for children, men and the aged.

In accordance with the practices of defining an 'agricultural holding', the 'head of the household', a 'primary producer', and 'economic activity', only the petty marketing labour of these women is likely to be visible for development planning, socio-economic policy formulation and the establishment of national priorities.

Such invisibility is also the destiny of Pakistan women in small peasant households who work fifteen hours a day even in non-peak periods. It is a fate shared by the wife of a small farmer or farm labourer in Central America who has to start her day at 3 or 4 a.m., and for 49 per cent of all women on farms in New Zealand. It is unquestionably the case in Brazil, where interviewers were instructed that any activity declared by a housewife that was not housework should not be taken into account as this did not count as work.

Invisibility is not simply the fate of rural women.

In the international guidelines for censuses of business organisations in the mining, industrial and service sectors, all but the 'very small units' should be included. The small units are very numerous but, according to the ILO they usually account for 'only a relatively small proportion of total production. It is recommended that such small units be excluded from the population to be studied'.

In the 1971 Census of the West Godavari District in India, when the registration of lace-making as a household industry was allowed and lacemakers were classed as workers, only 6449 male and female workers in the whole Narsapur district were recorded as engaged in manufacturing.

Yet in 1977–78 8 million rupees worth of lace goods were exported from Narsapur to Australia, the Federal Republic of Germany, Italy, Denmark, Sweden, the United Kingdom, the USA, Ireland and the Netherlands. Lace worth US$1–2 million was sold in major Indian cities, mainly to tourists. According to an official statement, 95 per cent of the foreign exchange earnings from the export of handicrafts from the state of Andhra Pradish came from the lace industry of Narsapur.[10]

The more than 200 000 women who work in what is called a household industry are nowhere to be found in census statistics.

It is not as if this state of affairs is unacknowledged, or only written of by scholars such as Ester Boserup,[11] Kathleen Newland or Barbara Rogers. Economist John Kenneth Galbraith estimated the domestic services of homemakers in the United States at roughly one-quarter of the GNP in the late 1970s.[12] He also observed that the concealment or disguise of women's work serves two important functions: it makes available a permanent slaveforce to work for men, and, since what is not

135

counted is usually not noticed, economic planners are able to assume that, in the liberal sense, such women 'do not work'.

Documents that emanate from international political institutions do acknowledge a need for change, but the status of these documents is always peripheral to the central political stage.

In 1979 a UN Preparatory Committee Meeting of a non-governmental organisation (NGO) task force recommended that: 'A revised data base for national planning be established to measure the needs and activities of women. The proportion of households headed by women, the availability of water and food, and the division of labour among family members should be investigated. Women should be involved in this data collection process.'[13]

The much vaunted Report of the Independent Commission on International Development Issues under the Chairmanship of Willy Brandt acknowledged that:

> Statistical methods still largely ignore the contribution of women when it takes place within the household rather than in the labour market, and they also tend to ignore the economic contributions of women because their employment is often concentrated in the so-called 'informal sector' or is seasonal and thus difficult to measure. UN statistics also underestimate the number of households in which the woman is the de facto economic head because they use biased definitions of head of household instead of criteria reflecting actual economic contributions. Thus women remain statistically invisible. Yet their contributions are indispensable and basic.[14]

The Report of the World Conference to Review and Appraise the Achievements of the UN Decade for Women, presented at the Nairobi Conference in 1985, noted:

> The remunerated and in particular the unremunerated contributions of women to all aspects and sectors of development should be recognised, and appropriate methods should be made to measure and reflect these contributions in national accounts and economic statistics and in the gross national product. Concrete steps should be taken to quantify the unremunerated contribution of women to agriculture, food production, reproduction and household activities.[15]

There has been some acknowledgement of unpaid productivity in carefully selected areas of law in a few countries, e.g. in the principles of division of matrimonial property (but not in custody), in accident compensation régimes, in universal superannuation schemes administered by governments.

The exclusion of women's unpaid productive and reproductive work from a country's national accounts is not the only characteristic of a different form of 'value' system. The linkages are well expressed by 'Greens' parliamentarian Petra Kelly when she says: 'There is no essential difference between the rape of a woman, the conquest of a country, and the destruction of the earth. The his/story of the world records the gender of the rapists, conquerors and destroyers.'

Why is fresh air and clean water of no value, and expenditure on pollution control part of 'growth'?

Why is the production of alcohol and tobacco 'productive', and subsistence gardening for life-sustaining nutrition unproductive?

Why is women's reproduction 'uneconomic' and 'war and militarism' economic production? If reproduction is excluded as 'natural' for women, shouldn't militarism be excluded as 'natural' for men?

The tools of analysis, the basic definitions and concepts in the history of analyses of production and reproduction, have been conditioned by an unquestioned acceptance of biological determinism. While the liberal-conservative school speak of reproduction (in some of its forms) as privatised and domestic (and thus only of its micro-economic significance), the left speaks of it (in some of its forms) as having only 'use value' – as opposed to 'exchange value'. Reproduction in all its forms is not addressed within any discipline in a 'macro' sense, since it is perceived as part of 'nature' and thus not within the scope of analysis or of change.

Women's household and childcare work is seen as an extension of their physiology: they give birth because 'nature' provided them with a uterus. All the labour that goes into the production of life, including that of giving birth to a child, is not seen as the conscious interaction of a human being *with* nature, but rather as an activity *of* nature, which produces plants and animals unconsciously, and which has no control over this process.

What use is a unit of production which cannot guarantee its own continuous and regular reproduction? As a means of reproduction woman is irreplaceable wealth; reproducing the system depends on her. Gold, cloth, ivory and cattle may be desirable, but they are only able to produce and reproduce wealth in the hands of progeny. Power derives ultimately not from the possession of wealth, but from the control of reproduction.

The question of what should be included in the national accounts turns on the question of value. It is said that obvious exclusions are goods and services on which no one could put a market price because their values are spiritual, psychological, social or political. It would then be argued that women's role as socialisers, as articulators of mass and gender ideology, and as (too often the easy) collaborators in reproducing the conditions of their own subordination, has no value. Yet non–profit organisations such as churches and clubs are included as productive services in the national accounts; so are therapists and voluntary agencies where the cost of production is met by members and benefactors without being sold as a commodity commanding a price to lower the cost. Agents of social reproduction in education, law enforcement and policing are included, as are political campaigns, and administrative services of government, on the grounds that the services have an economic price in terms of the cost of labour, capital and materials to produce them.

When women are involved in the sustenance, maintenance and replacement of the labour force, and devote a fairly large part of their time, to the production of a variety of goods for household use, such as containers for food, cooking utensils, mats, carpets and clothing for the family, who dares to draw a line of demarcation between which activity is productive and which is reproductive (or non-productive?) Which activity has no value? Which has no market equivalent? Which is familial, or non-familial? Which is domestic? Which is economic? Which is public? Which is private? Which existing theory of labour or capital conceives of the linkages between the productive and reproductive sectors of women's work, let alone links them to production systems in world economies.[7]

'None' is the answer, and perpetuating the imposition of patriarchal demarcations on the female world is a grotesque and unimaginative approach to twentieth–century feminism.

Compare the dominance in political and social concerns of the process of reproduction (and particularly its control) and its inspiration of core ideological and juridical concepts (marriage, rape, suffrage, fertility, reproductive freedom, domicile, custody, inheritance), with the economic subordination of reproduction to production.

The system manages the physical reproduction of human beings, the reproduction of the producers, and social reproduction at large, through a comprehensive set of institutions, and by the ordered manipulation of the living means of reproduction, that is, women. From one theory to another, one discipline to another, one institution to another, one system to another, one country to another, 'reproduction' and 'production' and their facets are manipulated, one dominating, then the other, without consistency, except in their use to sustain the universal oppression of species female by species male.

The SNA (System of National Accounts) is, by its nature, adaptive and capable of incorporating additional data which may be required for future economic analysis. The scope of production is in fact an elastic boundary which can be expanded or contracted depending on the 'values' of the national accountants concerned, and on the purposes for which the national accounts are used.

Relations of production and reproduction are immaterial to the conceptual framework. They are relevant only to the practical problems they present for the collection of data. Since the role of an unpaid woman in production and reproduction is greater than the sum of its market-defined parts, there may be some difficulty encompassing everything she does.

This is certainly the problem that the New Zealand Department of Statistics has. The last New Zealand Census of Populations and Dwellings took place on 4 March 1986.

In 1983 when the Department of Statistics invited submissions on how the census might be altered, 257 replies were received. Forty-four submissions requested the inclusion of a question on voluntary work; twenty-eight advocated a question on unpaid household work.

All labour force questions in the 1981 Census related to those in paid work, but included unpaid relatives assisting in business and those unemployed and seeking work.

Those not in these categories were required to tick nil for hours worked, write nil for occupation, and tick Not Applicable for the name of the employing organisation, address of workplace, industry and main means of travel to work. In the question on employment status, they had to choose between retired, full-time student, housewife, or other.

The reasons advanced for the inclusion of a question on voluntary work were substantial. Voluntary work needed to be considered 'real work' and to be recognised. With pressure for shorter working weeks, job sharing, increasing numbers of unemployed, there will be major societal changes that will affect voluntary organisations in a variety of ways. A question on voluntary work in the census might assist organisations in their requests to government for assistance. Statistics could ensure effective planning for the services and number of volunteers needed. Voluntary work needed to be recognised as valid work experience, as important as paid work in reaching a realistic measure of economic and social activity in society. And such information was needed for future planning; whether for roading or childcare, full details of the population and workforce would be needed, not just details on those in 'paid work'.

It was finally decided that 'voluntary work' would be a new and separate question and would not be included with any of the existing labour force questions. This, it was argued, was primarily so that respondents were not confused by an unfamiliar question. It is also because the United Nations Statistical Commission recommends that only the 'economically active population' should be included in the labour force questions. (It is, therefore, important to remember that next time you are delivering meals on wheels or doing your Red Cross duty or helping at a nursery or serving at a fund-raising cake stall you are neither economic nor active.)

Then, the Department of Statistics reported: 'asking respondents to write down the number of hours they spend on voluntary work does rely on memory recall. Some voluntary work is affected by seasonal variation' – just like paid work, or is the insinuation that only volunteers have poor memories? Then the department claimed that 'no overseas countries are known to have included the unpaid sector of the labour force in their national accounts'. OECD studies by Derek Blades and others refute this, but it is hardly the point: no other country had the suffrage, no other country had national superannuation, no other country had a nuclear weapons-free policy.

But, on balance, the question was in and asked, 'How many hours of voluntary work do you do on a regular weekly basis?'

Submissions on the inclusion of household work (unpaid) were not too successful. The arguments used to justify inclusion had many parallels with voluntary work: to gain recognition and improve the status of those involved in unpaid household work, and to provide base data for further research in the area. It was suggested that such work should be quantified so that it can be included in the GNP, and so that account can be taken of such work when planning policies and services.

But when the question was included in pre-testing, the department said respondents had difficulty with it. For instance, they said, there was difficulty differentiating between hobbies and household work, for example, gardening and sewing. It seems to me that where there is a market equivalent and where obvious skills are involved, and where there is obvious production and even where there is (heaven forbid) pleasure in the task, it is still work.

Then, of course, there was the problem of those respondents who thought that caring for children was a twenty-four-hour job! And for many, activities overlapped or were carried out simultaneously, making their allocation difficult or inaccurate.

So a question on (unpaid) household work was not included in the 1986 Census, but there was a separate question on 'main activity'. The exact wording was:

What is your main work or activity?
1. Home duties – looking after children.
2. Home duties – not looking after children.
3. Full-time student.
4. Retired.
5. Unemployed.
6. Paid job, business, farming or profession.
7. Unpaid work in a family business.
8. Other (such as hospital patient) please state.

Well, answer that. Many women I know should tick No. 8, and write 1, 2, 5, 6, and 7 of the above 110 hours a week – which is, I suggest, the best approach.

This is the grass-roots response available, in kind, to all women. And while it may be seen as a reformist policy, it is an action of cultural creativity, and ultimately a vision of a new concept of value, and therefore revolutionary. This concept might be realised in the assessment of production and reproduction as creative or destructive. Then the national accounts might portray whose labour truly contributes to the wellbeing

141

of the community. Only a lack of will or imagination inhibits us from portraying a nation's (or the world's) accounts in this way.

The treatment of New Zealand women in the economic system is typical of their treatment internationally. Whatever the culture, level of wellbeing, ruling patriarchal ideology, race or language, the bulk of women's productive and reproductive labour is invisible. And wherever they are, when women are invisible as producers, they will be invisible as needy beneficiaries in the policies of governments that redistribute the wealth produced.

If women counted, the world's economic decisions would be made with the contributions of everyone clearly visible. The consequences of those decisions could then begin to approach a comparable lucidity; humane policies based on the needs, worth, and contributions of all humanity, as well as the needs, worth and contributions of the natural elements themselves – upon which all life on this endangered planet is dependent.

Chapter 8

LESBIAN WORLDS
Alison J. Laurie

Lesbianism has been suppressed and made invisible throughout male-dominated cultures. It has been forced into the private sphere through controlling mechanisms ranging from the regulating institutions of society which overtly exclude and oppress it to liberal tolerances which call it 'a private matter' and help to keep it hidden.

Lesbianism has been explained variously as sin, some form of mental or physical disease, or as simply a series of superficial sexual practices occurring between women in the absence of men.[1] 'How do you do it?' prurience has alternated with the question of 'Why must you do it?'. Before the second wave of feminism in the late 1960s, lesbianism had primarily been written about and described in western societies by male writers, either from a medical-psychiatric position, or as pornography for male readers.[2] In the twentieth century, lesbianism has hardly ever been criminalised, for suppressive rather than benign reasons.[3] For example, when an attempt was made to criminalise it in Britain in 1921, the House of Lords rejected the proposed legislation on the grounds that legal recognition of the possibility of sex between women would 'bring it to the notice of women who have never heard of it, never thought of it, never dreamed of it'.[4]

Because lesbianism has been denied, trivialised or made invisible, it is difficult for us to construct a herstory for ourselves, or to document the ways in which some women in every society and in every time have managed to become lesbians. We have to rely on the little evidence we have. There are indications of cross-dressing women from a number of societies. In Europe these women were sometimes caught and punished; Jeanne d' Arc is one of the women who was burnt as a witch. Others seem to have avoided discovery and lived as men in male occupations – as soldiers, sailors, tradesmen.[5]

The 'romantic friendships' of middle and upper class Amer-

Jools and Lynda Topp at the Christchurch Arts Festival, 1984. Photograph by Jan Robinson

ican and British women are recorded in their diaries, letters, novels, poems and short stories. Lillian Faderman has researched some of the writings from women of the sixteenth to the nineteenth centuries, and is prepared to call these women lesbian, though she does not believe that they were having genital sex.[6] Carroll Smith-Rosenberg, however, believes that these intense female friendships should be understood as part of a continuum of women's experience, but that they cannot be called lesbian, as the term is inappropriate within the homosocial societies of earlier times.[7]

Adrienne Rich has proposed a lesbian continuum within which she sees a variety of women's experience taking place, including activities as diverse as a baby suckling her mother's breast, to a woman dying at ninety, comforted by the hands of women.[8] The idea of this continuum is attractive, until we realise that its inclusiveness and diffuseness can be a hindrance to recognising and acknowledging lesbianism.[9] It is, however, a useful premise from which to begin. Lesbianism has always existed; every act of resistance to patriarchy embodies an aspect of lesbianism; many women's experiences include a component of unacknowledged lesbianism; and lesbians exist in both private and public worlds. From this view, the radical lesbian activist who publicly acknowledges her lesbianism links into all of the private and hidden worlds of lesbianism, both in the present and in a lesbian past which we may begin to claim and to make visible.

Further, the distinction between the public and the private world may be an artificially contrived division so far as lesbian existence is concerned. If we regard the only public world as patriarchal and heterosexual reality, we risk defining ourselves in relation to it as deviants to a norm. There are other public worlds, alternatives which we may construct for ourselves, as new perspectives which develop because of the private and personal worlds which individual lesbians and lesbian communities have experienced.

Private and public lesbian worlds exist in diverse ways. Differences of race, class and degrees of ablebodiedness mean that there is no central 'lesbian reality'. A term such as 'the public world' in itself denies the existence of, for example, Maori, Pacific Island and working class public worlds, which are invisible to the dominant culture but are accessible and public to the individuals within them.

In this chapter, therefore, I have pluralised the term 'world' in order to reflect the diversity among lesbians in Aotearoa/ New Zealand. My analysis is based on my own perspective as a Pakeha lesbian from a working class background (becoming middle class) and is a personal view.[10]

Making lesbianism visible is a difficult and dangerous activity under patriarchy. This is because patriarchy is based upon sexism, which in turn is based upon heterosexism. Heterosexism is defined by Susan Cavin as

> an ideology of patriarchy which economically sanctifies heterosexuality, especially procreative intercourse, as sacred and ordained by imaginary patriarchal gods, as the *only* normal purpose of sex; while at the same time criminalising homosexuality as a perversion, a sickness, an abnormality, or as a crime.[11]

Patriarchy requires compulsory heterosexuality, not just as occasional intercourse, but through an institutionalised system of what Janice Raymond has called 'heterorelations', such as 'traditional family roles, sexual division of labour, and gender defined child-rearing and education'. Raymond points out that 'reproduction can occur through "normal" male-female intercourse in a variety of contexts that do not presume continued heterosexuality or heterorelations outside the reproductive function.'[12]

Compulsory heterosexuality is a system which does not merely recommend heterosexuality as a preferred 'life style' or 'choice'; it is a system which propagandises and trains children into strict gender activities, away from alternative sexualities. Further, the system has the power to punish and to threaten with punishment any non-conformity to the prescribed rules and norms. The church and the state and their agents have used a variety of mechanisms to coerce and force women into continuous and institutionalised heterosexuality. Lesbians are marginal outcasts, who can be excluded from families, employment and access to housing, goods and services.

Sexism, heterosexism, racism, classism and other forms of institutionalised oppression depend upon power-over relations between an oppressor and an oppressed. The oppressor has in each instance the power to construct and define the social reality within which the oppressed will live, through the economic control of resources, institutions such as the media, the schools, or the police, and through the control of language itself. Dale Spender has discussed how 'man-made language' forces all women to communicate from within a framework which has difficulty expressing non-patriarchal concepts.[13] Taking this further, for the lesbian, the heterosexualisation of language has meant that lesbianism has been consistently hidden. The word 'woman', for example, suggests 'heterosexual woman'; the adjective 'lesbian' must always be added if the component of lesbianism is to be understood. The noun 'lesbian' has become the marked term, against the unmarked term 'woman'.

There is a clear parallel here to the way in which 'man' functions as the unmarked term for the term 'woman'. Such marked terms are often used as the repository for all the negative qualities which the oppressor wishes to disclaim. Katz suggests that the 'invention of the heterosexual' required the construction of the 'homosexual' as a sexual identity, so that this homo/hetero polarity could establish a clear boundary between 'sex evil' and 'sex good'.[14] The homosexual could then be seen as the 'bad twin' who was the 'absolute antithesis' of the heterosexual. Such controls of language are not the accidental product of social control – they are essential mechanisms which marginalise all undesirable rebels.

Patriarchy and its institutionalised heterosexism sees lesbianism as more threatening than male homosexuality.[15] The expression of male sexuality is not antithetical to sexist controls because, under patriarchy, men are required to exercise an autonomous sexuality. Some societies, such as early Greek and Arab, have been able to incorporate male homosexuality as a sexual practice which did not threaten the institutions of heterosexuality and male dominance. In Greek culture, the ideals of male love helped to reinforce male superiority and power.

Lesbians, however, are independent women, 'loose women' as Janice Raymond says.[16] Because we are not owned by a man, we are women who are seen as being outside male controls. Such women are greatly feared by the patriarchy: uncontrolled female sexuality may lead to uncontrolled motherhood, to the refusal of marriage and motherhood, to demands for economic and social autonomy and to an undermining and a destruction of male supremacist society.

Heterosexism, like sexism, racism and classism, is built upon power and dominance, oppression and subjection, benefit for some at the expense of others.[17] Such systems and their institutions cannot merely be reformed; they must be transformed. Lesbianism is the place from which all women may question and challenge the patriarchy. As Adrienne Rich has pointed out:

> Any theory or cultural/political creation that treats lesbian existence as a marginal or less 'natural' phenomenon, as mere 'sexual preference', or as the mirror image of either heterosexual or male homosexual relations, is profoundly weakened thereby, whatever its other contributions. Feminist theory can no longer afford merely to voice a toleration of 'lesbianism' as an 'alternative lifestyle' or make token allusions to lesbians. A feminist critique of compulsory heterosexual orientation for women is long overdue.[18]

I consider that feminisms which do not address heterosexism as a primary and basic objective remain reformist and have failed to achieve change to the degree that they have allowed heterosexism to remain unchallenged. Reformist feminisms treat the symptoms of the disease rather than the cause which remains hidden, unacknowledged and dangerous. Challenging heterosexism is as necessary as challenging sexism. The early slogan 'no woman is free until all women are free to choose to be lesbian' expressed this clearly.

One of the ways in which lesbianism is made invisible, is through heterosexualisation. As we read *history*, it would seem that there were hardly any lesbians at all. This effect is achieved by suppressing information about women's lives, so that even those women who are visible to us from the past seem to be entirely heterosexual. For example, Doris Faber wrote a book about Lorena Hickok, Eleanor Roosevelt's lover. To begin with, she tried to persuade the National Archives to suppress Eleanor Roosevelt's letters to Hickok. She considered that Eleanor Roosevelt's lesbianism should not become publicly known because she was 'a great woman'. Faber claims that Eleanor Roosevelt must not 'be placed in the contemporary gay category' in spite of her longstanding relationship with Hickok. Faber decided to write the book after the National Archives refused to suppress the letters, and she realised that 'it's going to come out'. In her book she disparages Hickok and tries to depict Eleanor Roosevelt as 'really' heterosexual.[19]

Margery Dobkin, the biographer of M. Carey Thomas, the first dean of Bryn Mawr College in the USA, and Anna Wells, biographer of the president of Mount Holyoake College, Mary Woolley, and her lover Jeanette Marks, attempt to explain why none of these women should be called 'lesbian'. They use an historical relativist argument to claim that women of the past must be seen only within the context of their own times, and that they would not have seen themselves as 'lesbian'.[20] Whether we postulate lesbian sub-cultures, communities and networks as existing through history, or whether we believe that there were only individuals and couples who existed in isolation, we must still consider how these women understood themselves. The fact that they may not have used the actual term 'lesbian', or any other word with which we are familiar, does not prove that they were unaware of a different and subversive sexual identity. Historical relativism, arguing that it is inaccurate to refer to pre-twentieth-century women as lesbian, defines lesbianism as a modern social construct which can be isolated in the present, and denied a past.

The seventeenth-century nuns Benedetta and Bartolomea are an example of this type of argument. They were tried by church authorities for lesbian sexual activities which Benedetta claimed had occurred only when she was controlled and possessed by a male angel called Splenditello. It may therefore be argued that she did not see herself as 'lesbian' in twentieth-century terms. Apart from the possibility that Benedetta lied to her inquisitors, this argument fails to consider that although lesbian identity is socially constructed in diverse ways through different cultures, it may still remain recognisably lesbian and can be claimed as such. Setting up a rigid definition of lesbian identity as a modern invention in order to disallow the lesbianism of women like Benedetta and Bartolomea is highly suspect.[21]

This kind of academic ahistoricising may seem harmless, until we realise that it serves a definite political purpose. If lesbianism is seen as a recent identity which is socially constructed, it can be denied for any and every woman of the past. This argument does not deny that some women may have had lesbian experiences. However, it places these experiences in a private world, by labelling them as sexual practice only, as

distinct from sexual identity, which would have political significance in a public world. Calling women of the past 'lesbian'
connects their lives together, and connects them to lesbians of
the present as part of a continuous and subversive process of
rebellion. This kind of visibilty represents a threat to a patriarchal view of history, intent upon depicting heterosexuality as
part of a constant and unchangeable natural order.

Whether women of the past are heterosexualised by suppressing the facts of their lesbianism, or by denying that their
sexual relationships can be defined as lesbian according to a
new and strict definition, the result is the same. Lesbianism
remains invisible, hidden within a private world, shut away
from public worlds in which all women are presumed heterosexual.

In Aotearoa/New Zealand, lesbianism has been especially
invisible. Until the late 1970s newspapers would not take
advertising in personal columns which contained the word
'lesbian' ('homosexual woman' was acceptable). In 1980 the
Wellington City Council refused to allow the Lesbian Centre
to advertise support services on its buses. During the
Homosexual Law Reform campaign in 1985–86, lesbian
groups battled with the media for visibility. On one occasion
the editor of the Television New Zealand *Sunday* programme
refused to call me a 'lesbian-feminist', arbitrarily deleting the
'lesbian' part.

New Zealand women of the past are all seen as heterosexual.
Katherine Mansfield, our best-known writer, has now been
called 'bisexual',[22] but few researchers have been prepared to
discuss her lesbianism openly, or to depict her twenty-year
relationship with Ida Baker in any but the most disparaging
terms. Yet Manfield herself was well aware of her homosexuality, and the argument that she would not have defined
herself in this way is inappropriate. Antony Alpers reproduces the letter that Mansfield wrote in 1909, where she ago-
nises over 'my secret from the world' which she shares with
'Wilde' and which is 'a degradation so unspeakable that – one
perceives the dignity in pistols'. Alpers further suggests that
Mrs Beauchamp cut Katherine out of her will when she realised that Ida Baker and her daughter were 'lesbian friends'.
This implies that Mansfield's lesbianism was by no means a
secret, that her difficult relations with her family can, in part,
be attributed to it, and that any biographer or critic should see
her lesbianism as integral to an understanding of her life.[23]

It is not only the lives of famous women which have been heterosexualised. Heterosexuality is always presumed for every woman, even in the face of evidence to the contrary. It is important that specific questions are asked about women's experiences with other women;[24] writers and researchers who omit these questions are actively contributing to the suppression of lesbianism. Most books about women in Aotearoa/New Zealand do not include any reference to lesbian experience. Although research has yet to be carried out here, overseas work indicates many areas in which to search for earlier lesbian lives.[25] There are the professions such as nursing and teaching, for example, and the unknown number of nineteenth-century women who cross-dressed and led lesbian lives of adventure on goldfields, in sailing ships, on farms and in forests.[26]

It is important that we insist upon lesbian visibility for both past and present women. This visibility requires not only that we use the word lesbian but also that we refuse to allow women's lives to be heterosexualised or heterosexual assumptions to be made about women. Where lesbianism is relegated to a private world of secret pleasures, it is seen as nonthreatening and can be trivialised.

The patriarchy has a number of mechanisms to ensure that women who make their lesbianism public will be punished. Acknowledged lesbians risk loss of employment, credibility and status, rejection by family and friends, problems with housing, loss of children (custody has been denied to lesbian mothers), loss of ordinary access to public places which can and do bar obvious lesbians from their premises, loss of access to the media, to certain kinds of training (teaching, for example) and to promotion. All these punishments have been applied.

These mechanisms are also used against groups oppressed for reasons of class and race. Class and race are difficult to hide so the mechanisms operate more consistently against these groups than they do against lesbians, some of whom may be able to pretend that they are heterosexual in order to avoid punishment. Lesbians who exercise such an option pay the consequences of living a double life and of fearing discovery. Blatant lesbians experience the immediate consequences of stepping out of line.

In effect, all women are kept in line and controlled by the

threat of being called lesbian and being treated as such. This ensures that women are prevented from realising the connections which are possible between them, outside the hetero-relations which have been forced on women. Any woman who values other women above men defies these prescriptions. Patriarchal myth insists that female-bonding is rare, at the same time as patriarchal controls vilify or trivialise all female-to-female relations. Mothers, for example become mothers-in-law and lose their daughters to the hetero-connections of husbands and sons. Patriarchy has always feared strong female-to-female connections. Janice Raymond, for instance, describes how nunneries and other communities of women have frequently been dismantled.[27]

Within the feminist movement itself attitudes to lesbianism are ambivalent. Many of the central issues of feminism are concerned with heterosexual reform. They are issues which are intended to improve heterosexuality and to make it less oppressive without addressing the structures and institutions of heterosexism. For example, contraception, safe legal abortion, childcare, custody, part-time work and so on are often presented entirely from within a heterosexual framework. All of these issues affect lesbians, either directly or indirectly, from a different position. The question of self-determination is involved, and a resistance to heterosexism – but this perspective is seldom discussed publicly by the movement. Feminist organisations have often feared lesbian visibility, explaining this fear by insisting that the particular issue is the most important matter, and that an inclusion of lesbianism would destroy chances of success.[28]

Punishment and the threat of punishment are highly successful techniques. They ensure that lesbianism remains invisible, and that few women will be prepared to risk the consequences of visibility. There are also rewards and privileges available for women who publicly conform to the demands of heterosexist society. Heterosexual privilege includes an absence of punishment, possible access to male resources and power through the man or men to whom a woman is attached, some protection from sexual harassment by other men, and a recognised if inferior place within the patriarchal system. It also depends upon the race and class privilege she and the man to whom she is attached may have. Heterosexual privilege in itself cuts across other forms of institutionalised oppression to ensure that in all societies heterosexual women as a group will be more highly valued by patriarchy than are lesbians.

What are the benefits of being a lesbian?

Becoming a lesbian is a discovery of a self which is not defined in opposition to another in a binary and confrontational division of the world.[29] Lesbian relationships do not in themselves involve institutionalised power differences or sets of expectations as do relationships between men and women (though differences of race, class, age, or ablebodiedness can create other institutionalised imbalances). This is not to say that lesbian relationships are perfect and blissful, or to create unrealistic myths about relations between women. If, however, a lesbian role-plays or dominates, she does so as an individual, not because of a fixed structure which reinforces and supports her behaviour.

While stepping out of line involves punishment and a loss of heterosexual privilege, it also enables a woman to create a woman-centred and identified world for herself, from within which she may value other women freely and establish important connections with them.[30] The limitations which have been placed upon all women are constricting and damaging and the loss of heterosexual privilege may be experienced as liberating where new values have replaced patriarchal dependencies. Further, alternative lesbian worlds are being developed which allow women new and different possibilities.

Some lesbians are building alternatives to patriarchy and its institutions through the development of separate lesbian domains. These alternatives include the creation of music, poetry, writing, art, design, crafts, spirituality, food, environments and forms of language and thought which challenge male ideologies. These cultural developments are based on the view that because patriarchy has colonised every aspect of our lives, liberation can be achieved only through a deliberate process of decolonisation. Opportunities to examine and question actions, ideas and assumptions to determine what and who may benefit from them are an essential part of this process.

As lesbianism is not a monolithic culture, the contradictions and complexities of diverse lesbian identities and worlds may be explored within this process. Decolonisation helps to establish space, either as actual living environments, or as areas of the mind from which new and different perspectives may develop.

Actual living situations vary considerably. Some lesbians, in Aotearoa/New Zealand and elsewhere, have established communities on lesbian land, though this requires sufficient race and class privilege to have access to finance. Numbers of other lesbians live in women-only households in cities and towns, and have reduced their close contacts with men to a practical minimum. The question of how or whether to bring up children within these households is the subject of on-going debate.

Regardless of living situations, for most lesbians the importance of lesbian culture-making is the challenge which it presents to the assumptions of heterosexism. The decolonisation of mental space allows new questions to be asked, and new solutions to be proposed. Lesbian culture-making bridges the division between private and public worlds by creating alternative communication structures for lesbians. These have involved establishing lesbian printing and publishing, lesbian record companies, and the production of lesbian books, magazines, records, video and audio tapes. The development of communication channels has been essential as access to patriarchal systems has been limited and unreliable. Most of these developments have taken place in the USA and in Europe. However, in Aotearoa/New Zealand, lesbian magazines such as *Circle* (since 1973) and *Lesbians In Print* are produced, a weekly lesbian radio programme is broadcast on Access Radio in Wellington, local lesbian music is available and video collectives are producing video tapes. Further, the establishment of women's bookshops has meant that lesbians have access to overseas lesbian material.

These alternative communication channels mainly reach those lesbians who are aware of their lesbianism. Lesbian culture-making has also provided an operational base from which to construct avenues of connection and influence into the institutions of the patriarchy, in order to reach women who have been isolated and cut off from other lesbians. Using the media, holding public demonstrations, putting out information about lesbianism through educational institutions and programmes are some of the things which have been done, in spite of opposition and difficulty. Such activities can become collaborative and reformist, providing a platform for tokenism. For example, getting individual lesbians into positions of influence within the power structures of society does not guarantee a benefit to other lesbians. However, individual lesbians in such positions can provide increased visibility for lesbianism, and can also help effect some change within the institutions of patriarchy if they feel responsible and accountable to other lesbians.

Lesbian political groups have, during the past fifteen years in this country, operated across the public/private distinction, basing political analysis on lesbian experience and sexual politics.[31] These groups have had a variety of different aims – fighting heterosexism, increasing visibility, improving conditions for lesbians under the present system, and making connections between different forms of oppression through anti-racism work, for example. Lesbian-controlled information and support services, like Lesbian Line in some centres, lesbian social and sports clubs, lesbian self-help groups, as well as regular lesbian events such as summer camps and developing lesbian archives all provide avenues for reaching other lesbians and learning about each others' lives.

Creating alternative worlds does not necessarily require the immediate dismantling and replacing of the structures of patriarchy. This task cannot be accomplished at present. But it does require a questioning of the division between private and public worlds, through the development of new perspectives and value systems. While we recognise the power of the public worlds of the patriarchy and continue to confront and subvert these, creating our own lesbian worlds furthers the breaking down of the public/private dichotomy.

Lesbianism challenges both private and public worlds, and in many ways breaks down the distinction between them. Private worlds may transform public worlds by eventually establishing alternatives – not to a public norm of patriarchy, to co-exist as an appendage to the real, but as a new and transformed reality. The early movement emphasised the importance of the personal as political. The personal and private reality of every woman is a political process, moving either into patriarchal colonisation, or towards autonomy and independence. The existence of any lesbian, whether secretly closeted or publicly known, is in itself a political statement – and is a threat and a challenge to male supremacy and to patriarchy. Because of this, the division between the private and the public worlds of lesbianism is in some ways artificial and unreal. There are powerful links and connections between these worlds, which subvert and undermine the institutions of sexism and heterosexism. The development of independent lesbian structures and services, through open lesbian communities, has provided some of these links and connections, but every other manifestation of lesbian visibility and existence does the same, wherever and however it occurs.

The greatest threat to all women is the suppression of knowledge about lesbianism; and the greatest threat to patriarchy and to the institutions of sexism is the existence of either public or private lesbian worlds.

Chapter 9

WOMB MAKERS AND WOMB BREAKERS

Women and Religion

Catherine Benland

Big signs saying 'keep out, women' and a few saying 'keep out, men' have long been a feature of the religious landscape – just as they have in every other area of human society. Why? And is this immutable?

In this chapter, I shall begin by presenting an hypothesis which could account for the deep origin of the divisions between women and men in all human societies – an origin so ancient that myths from the dawn of history shed light on it, yet so current that it is also illuminated by modern psychological theories. I will turn to my own religious experience, that of other New Zealand women, and that of women generally. Finally I suggest that just as myths describe our plight, so they can inspire hope.

Let us start with New Zealand's two main myths of origin. The Maori myth is narrated by the Matriarch in Witi Ihimaera's novel of the same name.[1] The way she begins her telling of the ancient stories illuminates the real significance of all myths:

> Ah, mokopuna, but your life began even before you were born in Waituhi. You may have taken your first breath here but, ara, you have eternity in you also. Your life, yes, began even before the stairway to Heaven was built.

To locate one's personal beginning, identity and raison d'être in myth is to understand deeply that the truth in religious myths lies in our lifetime, not in the distant past. The Maori

Robyn Kahukiwa, Te Po and Papatuanuku, *pencil on paper, 31 × 32 cm.*
National Art Gallery

creation myth can serve a dual purpose: it not only accounts for our planet and everything on it, and for the nature of society, but also supplies symbolically our earliest foetal and infantile memories which we cannot access with language but which are within us and affect us profoundly. The same can be said of the major Pakeha (non-Maori) myth of origin, the Eden story.

Both begin with an absence of form and order: the time before one's conception and the development of physical memory cells, when nothing mattered. Both begin in darkness: that of the womb. In the Maori myth-telling, our world is born from the womb of the darkness, Te Po.

Both record wistfully a safe place, a divine forcefield of immense potency. In the Maori myth, one of the original offspring is reluctant to leave that place, so warm, moist and static, reluctant to have the mother hurt (as mothers are, in birthing). In the Pakeha myth, the place is a walled garden from which exit necessitates violent expulsion.

But the price that must be paid to have life and maturity is birth, a thrusting apart. In the Maori myth, the offspring cannot grow because they are cramped, restricted and confined within the embrace of the primeval parents, so they push them away, causing pain and grief. In the Pakeha myth, the primeval mother herself seeks life, the fruit of one tree, plus knowledge, the fruit of another – even though adult maturity means she will have to undergo the pain of birthgiving and the misogyny of men. Not only is she responsible for taking the first step towards her own maturity, she is also responsible for the primeval man's expulsion from the womb of Eden. And he can never forgive her in all the subsequent millennia.

In most creation myths, including the Maori one, the original matrix or environment is female (though this is not clear in English translations of Genesis). The growing infant is utterly dependent on woman in most societies: omnipotent all-beloved mother, source of nourishment, comfort and protection. But then comes the grief of realising that the infant self is not identical with but is a separate person from the mother self. And anger, despair and panic come when the infant experiences hunger, thirst and pain which no human mother can prevent. In both men and women, this infantile, helpless rage is the likely origin of both mythic and actual misogyny: the need to punish, reject, blame, exclude, ward off, repress and control the female. It is the likely origin for the mythical Maori term for the female reproductive organs – 'the house of misfortune and disaster' – and for the devouring destructive goddesses like the Semitic Lilith, the Indian Kali and the American Coatlicue.[2]

But in a sexist society, a remedy is at hand. The infant discovers that there is someone stronger and more powerful who can control this fickle and dangerous mother-goddess: the father. A boy's disappointment when he realises he can never produce a baby is abated by the prospect that he will inherit male status and privileges, including the ownership of a female mate – like a second mother but this time safely kept in bounds.

A girl does not experience the grief of expecting never to birth offspring but she must come to terms with the fact that she herself will come to embody all that she feared and resented in the person who gave her infant care. She may welcome external control, although she will have to expect the low status and powerlessness her own mother experienced when she, too, becomes a wife and mother.

Religions have always offered mechanisms to help people deal with these personal creation experiences and accept the social roles determined by their sex. Men can be birthgivers in religion by rituals such as baptism; they provide a clean 'born-again' start with male midwives and nourishers to erase the unclean birthing and lactating controlled by females. In some religions, boys, denied menstruation, experience genital bleeding through circumcision, and can prove physical fortitude, as a birthgiver does, through tattoo or initiation ordeals at puberty.

The debt to the mother can be paid off by ensuring that all access to all goods is through males so that females who receive anything good must give thanks to males both human and divine. In Maori myth, the divine son who initiated the hurting of the mother, Earth, comforts her with raiment of forests and jewels of lakes and seas. In Pakeha myth, the divine son gives his mother and all women, salvation.

The potency and sacredness of that original motherland can be totally transferred through religion to a Father God who can be accessed. The power of this Father God to punish or reward can be controlled by male religious experts (tohunga, priests) through ritual, liturgy and sacrament. Goodness, highness and

sacredness (tapu) are thus deemed male and all that is corrupti-
ble matter, low and profane (noa), is deemed female. So the
earth and everything in it comes under male control and can be
exploited to benefit males.

It may seem that the services that religion can provide have a
pay-off only for men. Not so – there is psychological relief for
women too. The female's infantile experience is identical to the
male's: it makes sense to her too to have the motherland
controlled by force. Even though she herself is motherland
incarnate, she fears her own potential. So she accepts a Father
God, the Church Fathers, and exclusion from the ecclesiastic
public sphere. Since she is able to experience real menstruation,
real birthing and real nurturing, there seems to be balance if
men take over spiritual bleeding (for instance, Maui's bait,
Jesus' scourging), spiritual birthing and spiritual nourishing.

Then there is the ordering of sexual relations. Both men and
women can have childish fear and guilt because sexual intercourse may be painful for the mother and seems dirty. A
prudish religion that does not celebrate sexuality but represses
and controls it, sanctioning it only within rigid limits and
within an aura of uncleanness, can feel right and proper.
Through religion, taboos can be broken vicariously. The incest
taboo between fathers and daughters can be broken: Tane
mates with Hineahuone and with Hinetitama; God the Father
impregnates his daughter, Mary. The incest taboo between
mothers and sons can similarly be broken, for example, by
contemplating the love between the Mother of God and God
the Son, which no wife ever altered. Jealousy of parental intimacy can be escaped by separating the parents (as in Maori
myth) or by not permitting God to have a spouse at all.

The pay-offs and coping strategies provided by religion can
permeate a whole culture so that they are available for all, not
just for active members of institutional religion. Whether or
not you personally were taught religious myths which account
for your mindset and mental furniture makes no difference to
the physical and social realities that underlie the myths. You
still inherit what they describe: for men, access to a place in the
public sphere and a role that is world-exploiting, society-
making, and history-producing; for women, confinement in
the private sphere and a role that is safe and nurturing.

Women attempt to create a safe womb in their homes for
their husbands, their children and themselves; they are the

womb makers. Judy Garland said of her life: 'Sometimes it seems as if I've been in bondage since I was a foetus.'[3] Men take on both the rewards and the guilt of being womb breakers and of venturing forth into the fatherland that is the public sphere.

It may be significant that in the Maori myth, the seventy offspring responsible for breaking forth to growth and the world were all male. In the Pakeha myth, it is a female who is responsible for the human acquisition of knowledge and the world, but unlike her seventy male counterparts she is not remembered by her descendants as good and divine but as bad and mortal. She, along with all her daughters ever since, is made a scapegoat because she usurped a male prerogative and became the first human rebel, the first history maker, the first womb breaker.

So we have inherited a social and religious order in which the womb makers are female and the womb breakers are male and which punishes those who cross or try to remove the barrier between. But the myths describe; they need not pre-scribe. They can be seen as warnings not as laws. Sex-deter-mined destinies are not immutable provided we can attain the wisdom and maturity to understand their deep causes. We must let go of infantile demands. We cannot return to the womb. God set an angel at the gates; when Maui tried to crawl back up through the vagina of the Goddess to gain immortal rebirth he was crushed between her thighs. Nor is it wise to waste our lives longing for an after-death return to mother-land (Hinenuitepo) or fatherland (Jehovah).

Although religion has played a major role in condoning and perpetuating what Dorothy Dinnerstein terms 'pathological sexual arrangements and human malaise', 'the heterosexual stasis needed by mother-raised people', or 'the male–female collaboration to keep history mad',[4] there is much more to religion. Because of the real power of myth, symbol, art, liturgy, ritual and communal spirituality to inspire people and affect their actions, religion could begin to offer the healing that people need for sanity, maturity, and fulfilment, and that the world needs for survival and justice. But will it? The prophets have always been available in every generation but are they being listened to? I turn now to institutional religion, as I have experienced it, here in New Zealand, and to what it is doing about its daughters who are currently prophesying and who are rejecting gender-defined roles.

But before you read the rest of this chapter, I want to state my bias. Many academics present themselves as above bias and untouched by personal experience. But to feminist theologians, such claims are always false in writing about religion.[5] Those making them are refusing to acknowledge their own experience of living and thinking within a particular physical body and within a particular family and household. Who you are affects your selection of criteria, data and values. Such claims of objectivity are an example of denying validity to the private sphere, and of valuing the cerebral more than the emotional, physical, social and domestic.

Although I've studied most of the religious groups in New Zealand academically, I haven't experienced personally what it is like to be a New Zealand woman in a Jewish, Buddhist, Hindu or Moslem community, or in such communities as Ratana, Jehovah's Witnesses, ISKON (Hare Krishna followers), the Unification Church ('Moonies'), Mormons, Rastafarians, or Baha'i. Much of what I say may well have parallels within the experience of people in such communities, but generalisations in the rest of this chapter are not intended to include them.

I am a fifth-generation New Zealander of mixed ancestry but the religious world in which I was reared and through which my schooling was filtered was Irish Catholicism. For the second half of my life to date I have been Protestant (Religious Society of Friends, or Quakers). I've had many ecumenical religious experiences, both Pakeha and Maori, and some experience of neo-pagan ritual[6] and post-Christian feminist spirituality,[7] but mainstream Christianity has been my primary source of religious experience.

However, the religion that has dominated New Zealand society since it joined the western world has been Christianity and, since the arrival of Europeans, the Judaeo-Christian heritage of their ancestors has deeply influenced all New Zealanders, both Maori and Pakeha, both Christian and non-Christian.

My earliest recognition of the division between 'public for males' and 'private for females' was when I was about seven, and the boys in my class started training to be altar boys. An

163

altar boy or acolyte helped the priest during Mass (the central liturgical event), answering the Latin responses on behalf of the silent congregation who remained on a lower level on the far side of the barrier at the boundary of the sanctuary (or holy territory).

I longed to perform this service. Much later, I dared to long, not merely to help, but to be the priest. The altar boys were so integral to the event, so visibly and tangibly participating, while I knelt unnoticed, unnecessary, inessential, and so much further away physically from the sweet presence of Jesus nestling in the little womb-like tabernacle.

It was not that women were prevented from getting too close to the tabernacle. Women did enter the sanctuary to clean the brass, replace the candles, renew the flower arrangements, vacuum, and take the linen (beautifully embroidered by anonymous women) away for washing, starching, mending and ironing. I used to go sometimes with my mother, and the little red light would be burning indicating that a consecrated host (that is, Jesus) was present while we worked. Nor were women prohibited from touching the sacred bread (baked by anonymous nuns) for in Communion it was placed on our tongues and digested in our bodies.

So in private, when no one was in the pews, no liturgy was taking place and there was menial work to be done, females could enter the sacred space. But in public, when the community was watching and important sacred events were being brought about, only males could enter the sacred space. There was only one exception to this in the life-cycle of a female – her wedding day, when ownership of her was transferred from father to husband.

The subject of altar girls came up recently in the Catholic press,[8] and although much has changed it seems that the Sacred Congregation in Rome still prohibits altar girls. In response to an article by Veritas in the *Tablet*, a correspondent (Answerman) wrote: 'What is involved here is not doctrinal Magisterial teaching, but discipline and the rights of the Church through her [sic] proper organs to regulate the liturgy. Also obviously involved is our duty to obey – even if we do not like the rule.' What I think is involved is whether a seven-year-old child has 'proper organs' below the waist to take a minor role in the public domain of institutional church life!

Since the reforms of Vatican II, women have been allowed

WOMB MAKERS AND WOMB BREAKERS

to read sections of the liturgy, preach, and even dispense the Eucharist. Yet recently when I attended the Mass to celebrate the 125th anniversary of St Mary's Convent where I had been both pupil and first full-time lay teacher, I was struck by the sight of about thirty white-gowned males at the altar, creating a religious event for a predominantly female congregation. There must have been 1000 women watching all those men on the altar. After two decades of feminism how many, I wondered, were still oblivious to the dichotomy?

Probably the most public religious event to occur in New Zealand for some years was the visit of the Pope. Again women were conspicuous by their absence from centre stage. The public mass held in Auckland was criticised by one organiser who pulled out, disillusioned at the prospect of the Pope 'surrounded by male clerics, male Maori concert party, and by local worthies – predominantly male'. Sister Judith Couper described the planned scene as having the Pope in the centre with fifty priests on one side and another fifty priests on the other side: 'For me just to be there and look at that just reeks of male-dominated church and I just can't see how it doesn't to everybody else.' Denied any public role, Wellington nuns decided not to be available as domestic servants for the Pope; the papal representative resident here imported nuns from the Phillippines to serve him.[9]

There is nothing new in the churches reserving the public domain for men and requiring women to function in the private domain. In the Catholic church, one must be male to set foot on the ladder which climbs from priest to bishop to cardinal to Pope. Though one title of the Pope is 'Servant of the Servants of God', his visit to New Zealand was as a head of state, a lord, a king. The cardinals are princes of the church – there are no princesses. In most of the Protestant churches, though the hierarchies are simplified, most elders, overseers, ministers, priests and bishops have been male.[10]

Should a good woman seek the chance to be a 'princess' of the church? A double standard operates here: a male can seek entry to an ecclesiastical hierarchy and his motives are not suspect. It is true that the desire for power and status is no proof of true vocation to leadership – whether it be parish priest, prime minister, or magistrate. A correspondent to the *New Zealand Listener* calls it a 'thoroughly disreputable motivation' and suggests that women claiming a call to ordination should simply assume that they 'hadn't heard Him correctly'![11] Yet the white Anglo-Saxon Protestant (WASP) male rulers of the western world could attribute such motivation to all outsiders: Jewish, Maori, working class, female. There remains the possibility that an outsider *can* receive a divine call to attempt entry to the public sphere of institutional religion and shoulder the responsibilities formerly or usually entrusted only to a particular caste.

What sort of responsibilities do churches prefer to entrust to males? Men decide who may belong and who is to be excluded from the religious community. Though women raise most of the money in most New Zealand parishes, men hold the purse strings. Men decide how the huge financial resources of Christendom are to be spent or invested and how to use the resources of land, property and personnel. Man devised the rituals, chose the symbols and decided the intellectual framework of doctrine and theology that underpins Christian identity. Men wrote the words of the liturgies just as men wrote the sacred Scriptures on which the liturgies depend. Formal public expressions of communal belief and worship have been controlled by men.

All this is in the public domain: what of the private domain? What has New Zealand's main religion done for the self-image of women? What has it affirmed and what has it denied or condemned? Like all the other patriarchal religions, Christianity has a long tradition of telling women they are unclean, guilty as daughters of Eve, ashamed, punished by childbirth, mentally inferior, physically weak, deformed or mutated, ineligible to be symbols of divinity or priesthood, incapable of sanctity or wisdom, emotionally unstable, in need of protection and male guidance and supervision, and fit primarily to follow or serve. If all this were true, then indeed women would not be fit to operate in the public sphere and it would be well to keep them shut up.

Virtues expected of Christian women include obedience without question, self-sacrifice, meekness, chastity and asexuality, patience, acceptance of patriarchal leadership, generosity and humility. Men who have few of these virtues can still have high standing in Christian communities. They are not virtues which fit in easily with leadership roles, breadwinning, money-making, profit-making, promotion seeking, authority wielding, politics or war-making. These virtues do, however, suit the roles of domestic servant, cleaner, nurse, teacher, dependant-minder, charity patron, nun or service worker – the traditional roles for Christian women which the Pakeha pioneers introduced to this country.

Women are affirmed by mainstream New Zealand religion as equal to men in the sight of God. But in the sight of men, they are affirmed primarily for being heterosexual, married and child-producing or for being chaste celibates (though the prestige of celibacy is waning). Nothing in the tradition affirms lay spinsters, childless wives, lesbians, or women whose raison d'être is located in the public rather than the private sphere.

> Women tend to view a woman who wishes to do non-traditional women's work as a bit forward or suspect.... With respect to lay preaching, which is traditionally a male sphere, I have found myself viewed by some members of both sexes as a bit odd for being so forward in taking this up....[12]

It is sad but true that the oppressed learn to oppress their own kind – the black overseer of slaves, the South African black policeman, the female head typist, the child abuser who was an incest victim, the Maori competing with a Pacific Islander at work. Mary Daly noted: 'Often in the late sixties I encountered hostility in women, not towards the patriarchs whose misogynism I exposed, but towards me for exposing it.'[13] Women's acceptance of limits is so hard-won that a suggestion that limits be removed is resented and resisted. The system of sexist division among church members has operated for centuries. Many would say it has stood the test of time and operated well; they forget the private, unresearched, unrecorded agony of the misfits, the frustrated, the unfulfilled and the outcasts. It has operated for so long that it feels 'natural'; many would say it is the way God wants it.

There is a sort of practical wisdom in the resistance of religious communities to change – whether the challenge be feminist, pacifist, Marxist, or any other kind of '-ist'. A church has a corporate identity which, if chipped away at too roughly or too quickly, may disintegrate altogether. One can regret that our ancestors wove certain threads in the fabric, but removing those threads just might cause the whole cloth to unravel. Social workers in foreign parts face a similar problem: introducing antibiotics or discouraging female circumcision may weaken the status of the chief or witch doctor and, before you know where you are, the elders' authority is broken, the young drift to the cities and the whole rich culture starts to disappear from the face of the earth.

Indeed, my study of feminist theology indicates that once a few pebbles are thrown it's not long before you have a whole avalanche bearing down on you. Reforms such as female lay readers, cosmetic changes to pronouns in church language, new Bible translations and the ordination of women open the door to huge challenges to basic doctrines such as the Fall, Atonement, Incarnation and Redemption.[14] One starts by saying, 'Can women please have a bigger slice of the cake?' and ends up by saying, 'Let's bake a new cake using a totally different recipe and new ingredients.'

If you have not yet ventured into the whirlpool waters of feminist theology, you should be warned that you run the risk of 'losing your faith'. The corollary is, of course, that another faith may enter the vacuum. Or, while some beliefs may be lost, a more durable base for commitment to life and trust in goodness may be found. Mary Daly writes of the terror of leaving as *error*: the belief that 'the church has something special to offer, that something irreplaceable is bestowed upon women by and through the churchly godfathers, and that leaving the church means spiritual death.' She recommends 'Leap after Leap of Living Faith' to those propelled by desperation to exorcise gynocidal patriarchal religion.[15]

The fear of venturing into such territory is that of all who break new ground in thought: 'What if, when I've destroyed my heritage, I find only an abyss – nothing to put in the place of what I've rejected?' Few thinkers have the existential courage of a Mary Daly to venture into theological outer space 'where no man has gone before', alone, all contact with ground control lost, no charts, no life-support system, nothing but personal integrity and desire for truth. Church studies of how to tackle sexism have remarked on this resistance to change:

> Fear. Fear of change. Fear of women by men, fear of women in the ordained ministry, fear that women in decision-making offices in the church will threaten women in the home. The fear, often hidden, of women's sexuality, together with the suspicion on the part of women that all men want to keep them

under. Fear. Fear. Fear. This was the word most often
mentioned as the major obstacle to creation of the new
community.[16]

Few women these days are unaware of the social changes being
demanded and brought about by the women's movement.
Whether they accept or reject feminist values and perceptions,
they will be aware that the new attitudes are relevant to their
religious commitment. This awareness is likely to be unwelcome and disturbing, and many women prefer to fence off
their religious commitment safely by rigid orthodoxy rather
than expose it to the eroding, iconoclastic challenges of new
religious ideas.
Within her church, home and marriage, however, the
woman who is publicly content with the status and roles
assigned to her by churchmen and by male-authored, male-
interpreted Scriptures may well be considerably discontented.
She may perceive this discontent as sin in herself or as disloyal-
ty, or as an unnatural personal peculiarity. Her solution may
be to escape into depression, institutional zeal or private mys-
tical fervour. Or it may be to work patiently for change in her
marriage, her parenting role, her chances to find payment for
her labour. In her religious community she may seek change
through unthreatening 'proper' channels such as churchwomen's organisations, discussion groups, committees, or that
underestimated sphere of women's influence – conversation.
I understand deeply the Christian women who subscribe to
the New Zealand Christian women's magazine, *Above Rubies*,
which affirms submissive housewives, and who travelled in
busloads to defy Ann Hercus and friends at the 1984 New
Zealand Women's Forums.[17] One's sense of identity is possibly
one's most precious possession, and if this is inextricably
bound up with one's roles as mother, wife and daughter as
ordained by God, then resisting change becomes a matter of
life and death. No one welcomes radical surgery on their sense
of identity. When the surgeon is a parvenue female politician,
she is no match for the local male pastor or priest whose
authority comes from a Heavenly Father.
In a world of fathers who denigrate women, a churchwoman can find great solace in being the child of a loving
Father who is more powerful than the human kind. In a world
where a husband may beat, exploit and desert you, it is a great

consolation to have a 'Spouse of the Soul', gentle Jesus meek and mild (and safely asexual). When your own mother lacks social status or economic power, you can turn to Mary, Queen of Heaven. When the powerful warmongers take your sons to whom you devoted decades of labour, it is a comfort to worship a Son who came alive again after being executed.

Most of all, Christian religion provides churchwomen with an equality and freedom in their private spirituality as 'honorary males' which most human institutions deny them, and which, indeed, they may fear to possess in the public sphere. A parasitic dependence and existential cowardice are justified. And the vulnerability of women while gestating and child-rearing is provided for if they agree to Christian matrimony.

The dutiful churchwoman receives much social approval from both women and men, from kin and community: there have been few, if any, alternative sources of such affirmation. And the corollary has been that the non-conforming daughter of the Church received such social disapproval that her livelihood and even her life itself was threatened. There is every incentive to find a way of adapting to patriarchal religion, and every assistance from the Church.

I learned from earliest childhood how a Christian female must adapt to a difference between theory and practice and between doctrine and personal experience. I was clearly taught, for instance, that God is not male (except as incarnated in Jesus) and indeed has no personal sexuality at all. All the millions of references to 'Him', 'He', 'His', 'King', 'Lord', 'Master' weren't a deliberate celebration of maleness and it was just a coincidence that they affirmed churchmen and excluded femaleness from the forcefield of divinity and sanctity. The tradition just happened to have opted for male symbolism and language. No offence was intended to the other half of the human race.

As for the different work roles within the Church and within Christian families, the point was not that the public sphere was for men and the private for women, but that everybody worked hard. So it was easy to accept the different roles of men and women as natural and sensible. They seemed fair, each of my parents seemed to like their roles and take a pride in them, and if one disliked a particular job, one could always spin straw into gold by 'offering it up for the holy souls in Purgatory'. Because one could never be perfect in the roles assigned to churchwomen, there wasn't much time or space to notice that it was the roles themselves rather than the people trying to fill them that left a lot to be desired.

When I look back on my Catholic childhood, I find much to be grateful for and no one to blame. You simply accept the way things are when there is so much to do and you yourself can never do enough. And the people who are handing down the tradition to you love you and are concerned for you to make good. It would be churlish and ungrateful to wish un-done their training of you in your roles as daughter, sister, mother, wife and occupier of pews. When the approved roles of 'a good Christian woman' were so necessary and so valued by all the important people in your life, why yearn for something unapproved and inaccessible like studying theology in a seminary or preaching from a pulpit or devising and conduct-ing rituals or deciding what is doctrine and what is heresy? For the yearning can only lead to lonely non-conformity.

Ann Scheibner sees non-conformist churchwomen as having three options:

> One would be to renounce the institution and all its works. This path ... seems honest enough if one is prepared to be a mystic or a prophet in the wilderness.... It provides no help for those still wrestling with their demons and their angels within the institutional framework. The second option would be to ignore the dilemma ... one does the best one can under the circumstances. The third option is to see the Church's institutional form ... as an opportunity for special witness and vocation in the closing decades of the twentieth century.[18]

The non-conformist woman who takes the first option may simply repress all that religion ever meant to her, or she may find her way to the new forms of feminist neo-paganism, or she may, like Mary Daly, become a voice screeching in the wilderness to those with the courage to hear. Inevitably, she will feel pain:

> I become an exile and a traveller who has learned to take refreshment from any puddle that looks halfway clean.... It is a matter of sorrow that I recognise the church, especially the traditional institution, is not a primary base for me. In fact, I have had to give myself temporary leave of absence because it is not a strengthening home, but a ground for struggle. I cannot afford to be battered, belittled, and undermined ... I do not

need to spend time in a place where I hear language that fails to include me, where I hear God described in the oppressive categories of patriarchy.[19]

The women who take the second option become reformist. They hope that tinkering with the language, the doctrines and the rituals will fix everything, leaving the essence of the tradition purified and valid. What is so valuable and revolutionary about these women is that they are giving weight, authority and worth to their own spiritual insights and leadings. A feminist theologian comments on Sharon Emswiler, who co-authored a guide to non-sexist hymns, prayers and liturgies: 'It is important to note that the impetus to write the book and alter the images comes from her experience in sexist church services. In actual fact, she is treating her private experience as sufficient authority to change sacred scripture and tradition. This is a truly radical move which Emswiler will not admit even to herself.'[20]

The third option is that taken by radicals – lay, nuns and ministers – who stay with the Church, much to its embarrassment, demanding entry without delay to its public sphere. It is also that taken by the feminist thinkers, philosophers, theologians and visionaries who write and speak and act from within institutional churches rather than from without. The young men are dreaming dreams and the daughters are prophesying:

> Tom Driver: We look for a Christ to emerge, and we wonder where she is. It is as if we had lost, way back in infancy, our sister Christ, or as if we are waiting for her to be born.[21]

> Rosemary Radford Ruether: With Jesus' death, God the Heavenly Ruler has left the heavens and has been poured out upon the earth with his blood. A new God is being born in our hearts to teach us to level the heavens and exalt the earth and create a new world without masters and slaves, rulers and subjects.[22]

All three options are valid. Churchwomen must affirm each other's choice and not dissipate strength by stoning each other. They also need affirmation from feminists outside the churches who have hitherto trashed them as apolitical cop-outs. Increasingly, though much tacit or vicious male opposition remains, support is coming from men:

> As a man who presently works for the church I am experiencing a growing frustration with our male silence and

inability to confront the patriarchal church . . . I am taught by
the church that repentance is the process by which we are put
right with God and involves going to the root cause of all
evil. . . . I'm aware that we are beginning to do this for our
white racism but for our sexism? Silence! The church is us,
whether we like it or not. We white men built it and actively
control it. To think we can ever leave it is largely semantic – it's
in us. This spiritual guest is going to require us men to develop
new ways of relating to women, new ways of supporting each
other, and a new theology.[23]

There is no going back to the simpler cosy time before our
twentieth-century prophets disturbed our religious complacency.
Once consciousness has been raised it cannot be lowered, though
of course the ensuing demand for change can be suppressed, as the
Ayatollah Khomeini has proved, or postponed, as the fundamental evangelical sects in New Zealand are attempting. The
mainstream churches in New Zealand are committed to eradicat-
ing sexism although it is not yet a high priority. By and large it is
being left to women to set the pace, and few women are single-
minded enough to pour their whole energy into this particular
struggle. While the churches proceed on a two-steps-forward-
one-step-back basis, many women must be content with personal
rather than communal solutions, with compromises or escapes.

Some are frankly pessimistic and blunt:

If I am honest, I, as a Pakeha woman, don't hold out much
hope for the church. Despite its own words of justice, love
hope, etc, it is unwilling and unable to face and dismantle the
unjust intrigues and intricacies of its own institutional power. I
do not believe it has the humility to allow measurement,
judgement, or assessment of its performance by criteria outside
its own patriarchal and racist smugness.[24]

Other are optimistic but resigned to slow progress:

Since its formation in 1979, M.O.W. (Movement for the
Ordination of Women) has been patient and polite, suffragist
rather than suffragette. . . . If we go on about how hurt we are
they say that is typical of women. You have to keep pressing
but not be hysterical.[25]

Others are simply charging ahead despite all opposition – like
Susan Adams, one of New Zealand's few woman priests:

As women look for new models in the church in Aotearoa, we are exploring a variety of different ways of working. These include ministries outside the traditional parish framework, in issues of health, peace, racism. They include ways of working together in teams. We are searching for forms of responsibility and accountability where there is no hierarchy of authority. As women we want to claim our freedom to choose new lifestyles, new sets of values, and to move beyond the ways of being and acting imposed by a male history. We claim the freedom to participate in God's struggle for justice.[26]

Feminists outside the churches matter too. It is important that they do not discount the deep religious reasons for the exclusion of women from so many public spheres outside institutional religion; nor put down those trying to transform the still powerful world religions; nor fail to ground the women's movement on a profound analysis of human psychology (psyche meaning spirit).

This chapter has been concerned with vested interests – located in our minds, in our own bodies, in our social and religious structures. What might be the prerequisites of a different order in which both men and women would have ease of entry to both public and private spheres?

1. Men would share infant care with women so that a major cause of misogyny could be removed. Fathers would not be seen as controllers of mothers but as equal partners in the successes of childrearing, and in the failures.

2. The role of ever-available scapegoat would be lifted from women (and not transferred to any other group). People would learn to admit to and own their negativity – fear, guilt, failure, frustration, alienation, stupidity and error – and to cope with it in honest, healthy ways.

3. People would come to terms with physical sexual processes, accept their own bodies and celebrate them as good and holy.

4. The original sin of alienation between men and women would be healed by the realisation that in the Spirit there is neither sexism, racism or classism. We could give Hinetitama her due as the woman who dared to remove herself from the primeval Husband/Father/Lord. She turned her back on him and alone prepared a spiritual haven for the human race.[27] We could give Eve her due as the womb breaker who gave

humankind not only birth, but the world beyond the womb, and moral maturity to make of that world what we willed. We could give Jesus his due as a man who failed in the public sphere himself yet who consistently treated women as capable of operating in that sphere.[28]

5. Women would share with men the enterprise, the risks, the guilt, and the labour of world-making for they could bring to it millennia of nurturing and cherishing experience.

Then, indeed, many of the old myths would be a record of our past, not a description of our present, or a prescription for our future. And the new myths that are already being written would start to come true:

> Meanwhile, back in the garden, Adam was puzzled by Eve's comings and goings, and disturbed by what he sensed to be her new attitude towards him. He talked to God about it, and God, having his own problems with Adam and a somewhat broader perspective, was able to help out a little – but he was confused too. Something had failed to go according to plan . . . 'I am who I am,' thought God, 'but I must become who I will become.' And God and Adam were expectant and afraid the day Eve and Lilith returned to the garden, bursting with possibilities, ready to rebuild it together.[29]

Reclaim the Night *poster. Women's Liberation Movement/Women's Studies Association*

Chapter 10

THE OLDEST
PROFESSION*

Jan Robinson

Prostitution is hailed by many as the world's oldest profession,
yet its practitioners are unlikely ever to be accorded the same
status as other 'professionals'. The problem of locating prostitutes in the occupational hierarchy has been a perennial one,
primarily because of the disjunction between their income and
their social standing. In addition, the social position of women
sex-workers has tended to rise and fall according to changes in
the economy or the sex ratio of the population.[1] Yet historians
often write as though prostitution has existed in the same form
throughout the centuries.[2]

In New Zealand as elsewhere the evolution of prostitution
under capitalism has highlighted the vulnerability of women to
exploitation. In this chapter I shall compare prostitution in the
Victorian era with its organisation now, in the 1980s. My aim
is to demonstrate the extent to which laws on prostitution
reflect particular sexual ideologies and conceptions of womanhood. I shall examine this legislation in the context of the
policing of prostitution, both past and present. The police, as
interpreters and enforcers of the law, can be viewed as the
public manifestation of the statute books, and it is in the
relationship between police and prostitutes that the ideologies
constraining all women become apparent.

Sexuality cannot usefully be analysed without reference to
its social and historical contexts.[3] In New Zealand today, it is
grossly misleading to view sex as something sought after and
negotiated entirely in private. The mode, style and structure of

* I would like to thank all those who have contributed to my understanding of the organisation of prostitution in New Zealand, in particular
the women workers and police vice squad members who agreed to be
interviewed and who commented so usefully on previous drafts of this
chapter.

sexual discourse derives directly from public sphere activity; the underlying ideologies may be obscured in part by the drapes over the bedroom windows, but the fact that sexual acts usually occur in private should not deceive us into thinking of them as privately determined. In considering prostitution I shall be focusing on sexual transactions primarily as they occur in the public sphere.

Under New Zealand law prostitution itself is not a criminal offence. However, a range of offences exist which may be committed in association with acts of prostitution.[4] The most common offences are soliciting, which refers to the offering of one's body for the purpose of prostitution in a public place (Summary Offences Act 1981, s.26) and brothel-keeping, which involves the managing of rooms or any kind of place for the purposes of prostitution, whether by one woman or more (Crimes Act 1961, s.147). It is also illegal for anyone to live wholly or in part on the earnings of the prostitution of another person (Crimes Act 1961 s.148(a)), or for anyone to engage for reward in the procuring of any woman or girl to have sex with a man who is not her husband (Crimes Act 1961, s.149). The offence of soliciting is subject to a maximum fine of $200 while all the rest of these offences carry with them terms of imprisonment for up to five years. Any of these charges could also be brought against the managers or workers of a massage parlour, with the Massage Parlours Act 1978 providing for the licensing and regular investigation of massage parlours in an expressed bid to eliminate prostitution from this area.[5]

Current policing practices, however, suggest that the laws are used primarily as regulatory measures, and are applied more stringently to certain groups of prostitutes than others. The total number of convictions for offences associated with prostitution is low,[6] partly because of the difficulties of detection now that so much prostitution is organised from massage parlours or private houses, but largely because it ranks very low in police priorities.[7] In Wellington, for example, where most of the contemporary research for this chapter was done, the vice squad numbers only three men, whose responsibilities include not only prostitution but also videos and bookmaking. The 'thin blue line' is very thin at this end of the spectrum. This reflects current police thinking which aims at regulation rather than repression of prostitution, and which reflects more the desire to fulfil a public expectation that vice will not be tolerated rather than any moral crusade.

The prostitution industry itself is stratified in ways which are closely associated with levels of police control.

At the bottom of the hierarchy are the 'molls' – truckie molls, bikie molls, groupie molls and, most commonly, ship molls.[8] In the 1950s widespread concern over ship girls led to their frequent arrest on vagrancy charges and their detention in girls' homes 'for their own protection'.[9] Today the police estimate that a large number of girls and women fall into this category but they are very hard to detect. Many have regular relationships with particular men on fishing boats and coastal traders,[10] they come and go from the ships in taxis, and the 'payment' they receive for services rendered may be in the form of gifts or bags of groceries rather than cash. Most captains tolerate having the women on board, even to the extent of allowing them to travel on the ship around New Zealand coastal waters, because they keep the men happy and prevent fighting. Should fights break out over the women themselves, however, then their stay on board may be abruptly terminated.

There are also reputed to be large numbers of back-street 'knocking shops' supplying a full range of sexual services for a fee. Again, these rank low in the hierarchy but are organised in such a casual and discreet manner that the police have little knowledge of them or control over their operation. Occasionally landlords have been known to enter into arrangements with such women, capitalising on their awareness of the illegality of the trade either by charging exorbitantly high rentals or trying to organise a cut for themselves with 'freebies' on the side.

Next up the hierarchy are the streetwalkers who, although relatively few in number, are more heavily policed than most other prostitutes. They attract police attention by their public visibility, which means they are just as easily 'picked up' by the police as they are by a client. The majority of streetwalkers in New Zealand today are transvestites or transsexuals. Wellington police, for example, estimate only about ten women in that city to be regularly soliciting on the streets. These women may be streetwalkers because they are unable to work in the massage parlours (either because they are under age or have convictions for drugs or prostitution), and are vulnerable to violence and harassment.

The police maintain that streetwalkers, particularly transvestites, are more heavily policed because of the public nuisance element of their street trading practices; in Auckland the vice squad will often do an early evening 'cream run' to establish who is out working and will attempt to 'tidy up the streets a little'. Justifying police action in terms of public nuisance derives from a belief in the sanctity of the private sphere[11] and a commitment to preserving a public façade of sobriety and decorum. Wanton women hustling on street corners threaten public perceptions of social order. The police, in responding to the alarm bells of moral indignation and outrage, fulfil what is essentially a street-sweeping role.

Escort agencies rank next in the hierarchy. Most are run by men and employ women who are often described as 'failed' or 'reject' parlour workers. These agencies are extremely difficult to police because the liaisons are made over the telephone and any sexual transactions are quietly negotiated on legally designated 'private' premises. Often this involves the heavy casual use of hotel or motel bedrooms – one inner-city Christchurch motelier boasted a 120 per cent occupancy rate as a result of this trade!

Even more obscured from police attention are the women who work as 'hostesses' in either clubs or hotels. Several prominent Wellington hotels tolerate women regularly frequenting the bars to pick up guests for 'dinner and afters'.[12] There is also a discreet private club catering for politicians, company executives and the like, employing women to provide company, conversation and 'whatever else the gentleman desires'.

Massage parlour workers are next in the ranking order and, as with the streetwalkers, tend to be a transient and highly mobile population. The provisions outlined in the Massage Parlours Act 1978 enable the police to regulate to some extent who works in the parlours. But while the Act appears to provide for a carefully controlled industry, there are various loopholes which mean prostitution may not be detected.[13] The police also employ wide discretion in their enforcement of the Act. For instance, while the Act stipulates that a woman cannot be employed in a parlour if she has any drug convictions obtained in the preceding ten years, the police will sometimes overlook her convictions if she is able to demonstrate that such involvement occurred during her misspent youth and that she is now 'clean'. There are also some massage parlours which provide an out-call service, but the women workers often fear rape or violence and may stipulate that any such liaison must occur in at least a semi-public setting (such as a hotel or motel) rather than involve their going to the client's home.

The women at the top of the hierarchy are the discreet, high class call-girls who operate exclusively in the private arena. They seldom advertise publicly, and usually have a small regular clientele built up through word of mouth. These women work independently 'and at a level which escapes police notice entirely.

Essentially, therefore, the policing of prostitution in contemporary New Zealand is associated largely with the context in which the profession is conducted. The women whose lives are most vulnerable to police intervention and regulation are the streetwalkers and massage parlour workers, whose relationships with their clients are negotiated in easily accessible public settings. Although streetwalkers and ship girls are both low in the prostitution hierarchy, the latter are relatively immune from police scrutiny now that they tend to arrange contacts in advance on board the vessels or form liaisons in downtown pubs rather than tout for business on the wharves. It is the open proclamation of sex as a purchasable commodity which promotes public indignation and attracts police attention, for the belief is still strong that matters of sexuality are more properly private activities.

How does the contemporary organisation and policing of prostitution compare with nineteenth-century practices?[14]

The existence of prostitution in the colony was noted with grave concern in the 1860s, when it was feared that many of the young women emigrating to New Zealand would be 'out on the streets' the day they left the ship. After a police brothel return estimated there to be forty-two prostitutes living in Christchurch in 1869, a recommendation was made to the House of Representatives that 'An Act for the Suppression of Vice and the Prevention of Contagious Diseases' be introduced immediately. That year saw the passing of the Contagious Diseases Act, which stipulated that any woman who the police had 'good reason to believe' to be a common prostitute could be ordered to report for medical examination and, if she had venereal disease, subsequently detained in a female reformatory.[15] The Act gave the police widespread discretion in determining who was a 'common prostitute', a discretion which was evident in the enforcement of the law.

Prostitutes on the streets were particularly vulnerable to the police, especially if they conducted themselves in such a way as to constitute a public nuisance. In giving evidence against Martha Jones in 1869,

> Inspector Pender said prisoner was a great nuisance – in fact, the worst of her class. Wherever she resided, she was the head of all rows and disturbances, and in the streets she was a constant source of annoyance to the police.[16]

The women were categorised on police brothel registers as behaving in one of three ways – in a 'quiet' manner, a 'rowdy' manner, or 'indifferently'. The 'rowdy' women were obviously regarded as the most troublesome, attracted the most police attention and were most likely to be dealt with punitively by the courts.[17] In contrast, quiet prostitutes could expect a measure of leniency, as in 1870 when, following a Christchurch brothel raid, the charges against one of the women were dropped when evidence was produced showing her to be of 'quiet behaviour'.[18] Then, as now, the police seemed concerned about the context in which prostitution services were offered. The existence of prostitution is more easily tolerated if the women concerned operate quietly from behind closed doors.

A major concern in the nineteenth century was the detrimental moral effect that public visibility of prostitutes would have on the community's women and children. Concerned Canterbury gentlemen wrote letters to the paper protesting over the way in which their 'respectable' wives and daughters were jostled on the streets by wanton women and drunken men,[19] and the belief was strong that the presence of immoral women would result in the contamination and corruption of the young. A similar attitude is apparent today in the response to streetwalkers, although the emphasis may have altered with changes in the moral climate. Today, in the post-Kinsey era, it is the presence of transvestites and transsexuals in particular that threatens, for while sexuality may now be acknowledged, it is acceptable only in its heterosexual form.

The fear of disease (evident in the passage of the Contagious Diseases Act) was also used as a reason to regulate prostitutes' lives in the nineteenth century. In contemporary New Zealand the medical argument is advanced for the same purpose, and this has been given greater impetus by the AIDS scare. Most prostitutes, especially those working in parlours or the escort/hostess business, are very disease conscious and insist on the wearing of condoms for all sexual acts.[20]

The link made in the nineteenth century between prostitution and 'the demon drink' has been largely replaced today by concern over drug abuse or drug trading among prostitutes. A real fear exists that drugs could be successfully distributed through the massage parlours, and police officers will sometimes use women working there as informants.

Underlying these issues has always been a commitment to the regulation of public sphere activity. Prostitutes working privately have had minimal chances of detection or intervention compared with those who operate more blatantly. The significance of social class must be acknowledged here for, as one contemporary prostitute has put it: 'high class whores just don't get busted'.[21] It is true that high class brothels, catering discreetly for a respectable clientele, are much less likely to come under police surveillance than are street whores, a pattern evident both last century and in more recent times. The 1893 Return of Brothels in Christchurch was headed by a list of six women who worked at Abbey Villa, a brothel run 'quietly' for Canterbury's male gentry and where no convictions had been recorded against any of the 'inmates'. The women from Abbey Villa appear to have been treated much as the hostesses from Wellington's private club are today, being relatively immune from prosecution. The only recent police action taken against this club resulted from complaints by neighbours over traffic disturbance and impaired parking access in the street outside – the owner now requests patrons to operate a car-pool system up the hill to his house![22]

The relevance of social class, however, resides more in the way it governs a prostitute's choice or ability to operate in or out of the public arena rather than in providing any direct link between class and prosecution. Class position mediates the way in which women experience public and private divisions in their lives;[23] the working class prostitute with relative lack of access to private space may negotiate publicly what her middle class sister is able to arrange with more discretion elsewhere.

Essentially, it is not prostitution itself which provokes antagonism and intervention but prostitution conducted blatantly and in public. Prostitution behind closed doors is typically not seen as a problem, but the case of massage parlours raises some interesting contradictions. The growth of massage parlours in the 1970s effectively removed much of the prostitution trade from the streets. Although this meant in practice that the industry became somewhat more privatised, it did not mean that the women involved were beyond the long arm of the law. Concerns about such parlours being associated with crime, drugs, disease and general moral decay led to their being redefined in law as *public* places in order to facilitate their regulation under such legal provisions as those contained in the Massage Parlours Act 1978.

The owner of Wellington's élite private club is determined to resist all efforts to have his establishment redefined as a massage parlour, since such a move would give the police greater control over his staff and premises as well as opening the door to any member of the public who requested entry, thereby curtailing his efforts to provide a discreet service for those whose status cannot allow them 'indiscretions'.

The issue of prostitution highlights some of the anomalies that lie behind the separation of life into public and private spheres. In the nineteenth-century moral order, the prostitute challenged the sexual division of labour and the ideologies derived from it. Effectively, she shifted what was a private activity into the public sphere, and, moreover, removed herself from the domestic to the commercial arena at the same time. In so doing the prostitute tore apart the fundamental linkages seen as existing between the concepts of 'woman', 'wife', 'family', 'home' and 'private'. The challenge she thereby presented to the gender order resulted in the prostitute being socially ostracised and labelled as deviant.

Not only did she reject the privatised domestic role set down for her but, in taking sex out of the private domain and into the public, she exposed the power and exchange dimensions which were usually obscured within the domestic setting. In other words, she highlighted the reality of sex as a commodity when other long-accepted practices of exchanging sex for goods and services such as food, shelter, housekeeping and so forth had been much less obvious.[24] The new ideology of romantic love which arose during the nineteenth century effectively disguised the more blatant exchange and property functions of marriage and legitimated the power dimension of the relationship under a guise of paternalistic protection for the 'weaker sex'. The sexual value system which evolved identified 'good normal natural sex' as that which was heterosexual, marital, monogamous, reproductive, non-commercial, and private.[25] So prostitution was condemned.

This condemnation was not sustained purely on moral or religious grounds. The nineteeth century had witnessed growing secularisation as society's foundations were shaken by evolutionary theory, and medicine and psychiatry were now accorded greater status and assumed extensive control over sexuality.[26] Unacceptable behaviour could now be condemned not only as 'sinful' but as 'sick', as symptomatic of mental disease or defectiveness. Belief in the ideology of natural female passivity was so strong that the prostitute must be defined as 'sick'. Thus the argument was advanced that she suffered from the over-production of male hormones.[27]

Such an argument was consistent also with the view that 'normal' men were sex-driven in ways which none but deviant, lascivious women could ever be. The double standard of morality which evolved condemned sexual expression by women, yet actively encouraged it by men. For women to be overtly sexual was seen as evidence of pathology or deviance. Later this argument was inverted so that deviant or criminal women were seen to be sexually motivated. One of the most recent manifestations of this line of reasoning surfaced with the debate on female involvement in terrorism. While strong political convictions are generally accepted as underlying men's involvement in such activities, women are not recognised as having political motivation. Instead, they are described as suffering from 'erotomania', an overpowering lust for sex which drives them to hijack planes and blow up buildings for the sake of being able to bed down with male terrorists at the end of it all![28]

Terrorist activity is, in a sense, a particularly extreme form of public sphere involvement. The reaction to women's participation in it has been correspondingly extreme. Ideologies of womanhood do not allow for rational motivation in such a case, and encourage the perception of this behaviour as evil and diabolical and hence linked, for women, with their sexuality.

If female delinquency is equated with sexual promiscuity, situations which are defined as likely to turn men to crime can be defined as turning women to prostitution instead. In 1968 the New Zealand Justice Department noted: 'The traits and environment that may lead a boy into crime may lead his sister into promiscuity, fecklessness or prostitution.' Thus 'the law which is invoked against females, and particularly adolescent girls, is in many cases an attempt to regulate sexual behaviour by legal sanctions.'[29] Intervention in the lives of wayward young women was justified as being 'for their own protection'. In the 1950s and 1960s hundreds of ship girls were rounded up for this reason and detained in penal institutions.

While the strength of the reaction against prostitutes may not be as great now as it was, nevertheless certain groups of prostitutes are still subject to extensive state intervention. For massage parlour workers, as we have seen, intervention is achieved through the regulatory devices contained within the Massage Parlours Act. Streetwalkers are vulnerable to the police because they operate in a public, and therefore legally controllable, setting. At present, prostitution is low in police priorities, and relatively under-enforced. However, legislation exists that would allow for a system of extensive interference and repression in the event of another moral panic, such as fundamentalist Christian media manipulation of the AIDS scare.

At the heart of a prostitute's fear is the threat her existence poses as a woman unrestrained by male control. Few prostitutes today work in conjunction with pimps, preferring to be independent physically, emotionally and economically. As an ex-prostitute said regarding the way landlords might try to benefit from her trade: 'If I'm going to sell my body I'm damned if some bloody *man* is going to get any money out of it – let him go and sell *his* bum if he's hard up!'[30] The economic independence of such women is shared by other women in our society, such as lesbians and single women, who also share a similar stigma of deviance and unacceptability.

The social cost attached to living independently is implicit in this comment from an American lesbian prostitute: 'one

186

woman alone is a whore; two women together are lesbians.'[31] Prostitutes and lesbians share a similar history of medical, religious and state intrusion into their lives. Any public declaration of their deviance has often invited state intervention and attempts at repression, with the women concerned being primarily censured not for what they have done criminally but for who they are sexually. '"Whore" and "queer" are the two accusations that symbolise lost womanhood and a lost woman is open to direct control by the state.'[32] In the American bar raids of the 1950s and early 1960s the vice squad treated both lesbians and prostitutes alike, and both groups of women typically shared common territory and common police experiences.[33]

It is not uncommon for prostitutes today to be lesbians also, some before they enter the trade but most as a result of working in it. One New Zealand massage parlour worker, for example, maintains many of the parlour women have had lesbian experiences, even those who still live with boyfriends, because 'they've got to get satisfaction somewhere'.[34] For some women the divide between their public and private sexual worlds may be very great, with their only sexual contact with men being 'on the job'.

This highlights the fact that prostitution is not primarily a sexual activity for the women involved. Earlier criminological accounts attributed strong sexual motivations to women entering prostitution,[35] and the myth still prevails in many quarters that all prostitutes must be nymphomaniacs. The motivation, however, appears to be economic rather than sexual. In the nineteenth century the options for women seeking paid employment were likely to be sweated labour in the factory or sweated labour in the home.[36] The third option of prostitution might then seem quite attractive despite the risk of disease, violence and legal vulnerability.[37] Life as a prostitute also gave the women a measure of independence compared with their servant or seamstress sisters, whose every waking hour was spent toiling for the pittance handed down from their masters or mistresses. Financially at least, then, prostitution appeared to be the least exploitative of the limited options available for such women.

Although women's opportunities in paid employment have expanded over the last century, they still have fewer chances than men of earning high wages and salaries.[38] One massage

parlour worker related how she and her friend had first tried
working as secretaries but 'got fed up at being told what to do
by men', so left and obtained jobs at a chain restaurant but that
was 'horrible' too. The next step seemed inevitable. This
woman has been employed in parlours now for four years,
typically working three days a week and expecting to earn
$350 to $400 each day. Her job satisfaction is obviously economic rather than sexual:

> This job's about as erotic as someone sticking their finger in
> your ear – all you can do is lie back and wait for them to get it
> over with. Meanwhile you think about anything – what you're
> going to have for tea, when you'll go shopping. . . .

For the women involved, therefore, prostitution is a public
sphere activity. They have their own personal relationships and
sex lives outside the job, just like any other worker. For their
male clients, however, visits to a prostitute are part of their
private existence. Discretion, if not subterfuge, usually sur-
rounds such visits. The majority of massage parlour clients
come to the parlour alone, and 60 to 70 per cent are regulars at
the same parlour, often with the same masseuse. The rest are
casuals who come for a variety of reasons: young males looking for their first sexual encounter, sailors whose boat is in
port, or the provincial rugby team out for a night on the town.

The fact that they pay means that the men often expect they
can command whatever sexual service they desire. But most
prostitutes in fact resist any suggestion that they are simply
'there to do what men tell them', and reserve for themselves a
clear boundary beyond which they refuse to go. Some, for
example refuse ever to do bondage, and some will do only
light bondage, while others will be prepared to do heavy
discipline, for a price. Most refuse to kiss their clients on the
mouth – as one expressed it, 'kissing is for pleasure'. The
women, therefore, are by no means simply there for the asking
but operate within a set of rules and expectations designed for
their own protection.[39] Difficult clients, such as those who
want to touch the women in taboo areas, are given 'punishments' which incorporate the tools of the trade – for example,
the digging in of sharp fingernails, or the 'accidental' putting
of cream or massage oil in the man's eyes.[40]

The women involved in prostitution, therefore, generally
have a very pragmatic approach to their work and most prosti-

tutes take precautions to maintain a careful distance between themselves and their clients. The use of condoms contributes towards this distance, as does the prohibition of kissing. This attitude is reinforced by the practice of adopting a professional name while retaining the use of their real names for their private lives. Distance is achieved mainly, however, through a process of emotional detachment not unlike that used by workers in other occupations to neutralise those parts of their jobs which carry a high emotional loading.[41] Just as police officers attending a sudden death can 'switch off' or handle a maggot-infested corpse with composure and even joke about it afterwards, so prostitutes handle their clients' bodies with the same lack of involvement. An Australian prostitute complained that at times this mechanism worked almost too well:

> I have been attracted to some men who come down here and I wish I could get a buzz out of them, but I don't because I'm so psyched up and switched off it just doesn't happen.[42]

Unfortunately, one of the reasons why many prostitutes are able to detach so readily is probably their experience of sexual abuse in childhood. A study of teenage prostitutes in Minneapolis found 75 per cent to be victims of incest,[43] a finding consistent with other research in this area.[44] Sexual abuse by a family member is a very direct and powerful way of teaching a young girl that her only value resides in her body. Incest survivors who become prostitutes are translating into public testimony the lessons learned in their early private lives about the value patriarchy attaches to their sexuality. Those women unable to distance themselves from their clients usually cannot afford to stay in the trade very long, and the tales are numerous of women who have been unable to 'cope' with the job's demands.

Some of the main difficulties faced by prostitutes relate not to any features of the work itself but to the social and legal status of the occupation. However degrading the work itself may be, the prostitute suffers a double degradation in that she is also legally and morally condemned for the way she earns her money. Some prostitutes, like some lesbians, are still 'in the closet' and even members of their families may not know the nature of their work. Many landlords refuse a prostitute as a tenant; others are only too willing to have her – if the money (and the sex) is right. She lacks credibility. Her testimony in court is often viewed as questionable, and her lifestyle is seen as inviting abuse and violence. Should she fall victim to the ultimate violence and be murdered, the prostitute knows her life is thought to be less valuable than her more respectable sister's.[45] She is unable to spend money as she wishes as anyone whom she visibly 'supports' risks prosecution for living off the earnings of prostitution. No union exists to campaign on her behalf for better pay, greater protection or improved working conditions. The profession shares much in common with other 'women's work'. Massage parlours, for instance, are typically located in buildings owned or leased by men but are worked almost exclusively by women; the exorbitant rents charged provide a secure, fixed income for the men while the women work long hours in a tightly controlled industry where they lack job security and risk legal censure.

The women who work as prostitutes are performing a mundane, often boring job. That their experiences are not particularly glamorous or erotic is reflected in the everyday manner with which they discuss their profession, turning the taboo world of sexuality into casual coffee-time talk – 'Are you into leather?', 'What about greek?' 'If we've got to go down on them at least let's make the condoms strawberry flavoured!'

In researching for this chapter I found that I, too, became desensitised to the language taboos and accepted the prostitutes' discussion of the trade. What was previously seldom spoken of became easily acknowledged; the private world of sex became public because for these women it is a pragmatic, down-to-earth reality, with no mystique attached. The glamour and excitement associated with romanticised views of sexuality disappeared beneath considerations of health risks, fee scales, safety measures and so on. I had entered a work environment and these were union issues.

I was confronted by the issue of exploitation. Were these women any more exploited than their sisters in other occupations? Initially it was easy to be distracted by the high wages they earned and their own assertions of being more exploiting than exploited.[46] However, my feeling now is that these women are highly exploited, for it is ultimately men who are defining women's assets as residing in their sexuality and then capitalising on and benefiting from this social construction.

In patriarchal societies the power dimension in relationships between the sexes becomes the critical one. I found issues of power and control to be ambiguous at times within the prostitutes' world. In their day-to-day relationships with clients these women have developed survival strategies which allow them to establish the rules governing the sexual transactions which occur. However, the overall context within which such exchanges take place clearly removes power and autonomy from the prostitute, placing her in a position of relative dependency and vulnerability. Her job exists because of male definitions of who women are and what they are worth, and those who ultimately are advantaged by the prostitute's existence are not the women themselves but men. It is not just the clients who benefit, or even the male parlour owners and profit-makers, but all men. Men's power depends on the continued definition of women as sexually valuable exchange commodities.

The exploitation of the prostitute is only an extreme example of the exploitation experienced by all women. Under patriarchy men have owned women's bodies, and the legacy of that relationship remains in the price-tag attached to sex as a purchasable commodity. The undervaluing of women's intelligence, creativity and other abilities is related directly to the high market value attached to female sexuality. The prostitute acknowledges that she is, as one woman expressed it, 'sitting on a goldmine' and makes herself available not for long-term purchase, as in marriage, but for short-term hire. When she parades up the street in her low-cut dress and high heels, the prostitute is displaying her wares publicly in the same manner as her more 'respectable' sister does in presenting herself for selection at the debutantes' ball or in dressing up for the office party.

The prostitute is but at one end of the continuum of commercialised sexuality, and the antagonism directed towards her derives from her open acknowledgement of the price-tag attached to women's bodies. In effect, she makes visible the bargains we prefer to keep invisible, and exposes in public the realities we would rather keep private. Her existence discomforts us all, for in her we see our own collusion with patriarchy, and are forced to acknowledge that the public world of the prostitute is part of the private reality of us all.

191

Women against nuclear war, Aotea Square, 24 May 1983. Photograph by Marti Friedlander

Chapter 11

WOMEN AND THE STATE

Katherine Saville-Smith

The only institution with the mandate to govern our society and to set its social and economic direction is the state. What the state does is therefore always important, whether or not it appears to be interventionist. The policies of the state impinge on our everyday lives and consequently we are all engaged in 'coping' with the state. To do this consciously or unconsciously we analyse the state, we try to 'make sense' of it. This chapter is part of that process. My object is twofold: first to account for the ways in which others have 'made sense' of state policies towards women, and secondly, to assess the impact of those policies on the position of women.

These everyday theories of the state are rarely explicit or systematically expounded. Rather, they become exposed in the course of struggles over issues that involve the state. Thus in the bitter public debates which accompanied the introduction of legislation concerning such issues as equal pay, access to abortion and contraception, the protection of women from male physical and sexual violence (particularly that perpetuated by husbands), the division of marital property and the freedom of sexual orientation, particular views of the state and its intentions towards women were presented by both conservative and radical groups. Because these debates were primarily concerned with the content of policy, they did not provide a context in which popular understandings of the state could be coherently expressed. The announcement by the fourth Labour government of its intention to establish a Ministry of Women's Affairs provided for the first time a suitable context in which popular ideas about the state and its relationship to women could be systematically declared. The debate centred not merely on the content of particular policies but on the very structure of the state itself and the degree to which it was committed to pursuing the interests of women.

The controversy which surrounded the establishment of the Ministry of Women's Affairs simply distilled and revealed prevailing visions of the state and the impact of its policies on women. What is intriguing are the contradictions in different groups' perceptions of the direction of the state's policies concerning women. The question is whether these merely reflect different interpretations of state policies or real contradictions in the structure and operation of the state.

My argument is that one cannot explain contradictory understandings of the state and its policies towards women as mere interpretations which reflect the vested interests of opposing groups. There are real ambiguities in the way in which the state acts towards women and real inconsistencies in the consequences for women of state policies. These, I will suggest, derive from the frequently antagonistic demands placed on the state by gender and class élites. At this stage, however, I want to consider in more detail the nature of popular descriptions of the state and its activities as they were presented during the establishment of the Ministry of Women's Affairs.

It was predictable that the proposal of a ministry to pursue the interests of women would engender a strong response from radicals and conservatives alike. For those not directly involved in the debate, however, it must have been rather bewildering to find not only the extreme right opposed to the ministry but also feminists treating the development with as much caution as enthusiasm. Both responses were grounded in particular visions of the state.

The right was uniformly negative in its appraisal of the ministry which was accused of giving women formal rights of advocacy denied to men. It was also suggested that it would become a 'front' for amorphously defined but allegedly conspiracist groups determined to undermine 'traditional' values and gender relations inside and outside the family.

Responses from Pakeha liberal and feminist groups were more favourable, but if the Labour government had expected the proposal to be welcomed unequivocally by radical groups, it was to be disappointed. Maori women were concerned that their history and their experiences were to be neglected, and warned that the ministry could become one more state department used to nullify and co-opt the initiative of Maori women.[1] Pakeha feminists similarly suspected that the ministry might be used to maintain structures of male dominance. Such fears derive directly from traditional feminist analyses of the state.

It is true that feminists have traditionally turned to the state for action in dismantling the structures of gender inequality, and the ministry was greeted as a significant advance in both the state's recognition of women and as a passage into the policy-making process. However, many feminists have been sceptical of the state's intentions, and their encounters with it have been largely by necessity. The fact that feminists have mobilised parliament to reform discriminatory laws does not indicate that feminists believe that the state acts in women's interests, or that a state ministry 'for' women will be advantageous.

In the parliamentary debate about the formation of the ministry, this scepticism focused on two main issues; the fear of women being denied real influence by being given power in specifically feminine spheres of activity, secondly, the efficacy of state bureaucratic and legislative strategies in dismantling sex inequalities.[2]

A complete exegesis of the parliamentary debate concerning the ministry is not appropriate here. The reader must decide whether the National Party opposition to the ministry constructively represented feminist concerns or simply an inspired co-optation of feminist discourse for party political ends. Likewise, only time will tell whether or not the ministry becomes a token, impotent in the struggle for gender equality. What is significant is that the parliamentary debate revealed the degree to which feminist analysis has infiltrated popular thought and, secondly, the real tension among feminists towards state intervention and legislative reform. This tension derives from a contradiction between the necessity for feminists to deal with the state in their struggle to dismantle discriminations enshrined in the law and a feminist theoretical analysis of the state which identifies it as a major bulwark of the male power.[3]

This is not simply a contradiction within feminism. It reflects actual ambiguities in state action. State social and economic policies have maintained the gender-based separation of the public and private spheres and, by extension, gender in-

195

equalities. Nevertheless, the state has, often at the instigation
and guidance of feminists, instituted a variety of legislative
reforms over the last century which have extended to women
the rights of citizenship enjoyed by men. The tensions experienced by feminists in their dealings with the state cannot therefore be ascribed simply to conflicts between theory and practice, or between idealism and pragmatism. Instead, they derive
from inconsistencies in the direction of state policy and its
outcomes for women. These also underlie the apparently irreconcilable differences between the right's and feminist understandings of the state.

Both feminists and those aligned wih the right, particularly
in that loose coalition fallaciously referred to as the 'Moral
Majority', share a significant common understanding. Both see
gender relations as primarily structured through family relations and around a gender-based separation of the public and
private spheres. Both agree that men are primarily associated
with the public sphere, the world of paid labour, and that
women are associated with the private, the world of home and
family. Men are seen as primary income earners while women
are ultimately expected to be secondary income earners. The
nuclear family in its rigid form is predicated on women as
wives and mothers being dependent on male breadwinners. Of
course, feminists and those on the right have very different
understandings of the impact of such a structure on women.
They do agree that such a structure exists and shapes gender
relations; what they do *not* agree on is the impact of the state
and state policies on that structure.

For feminists the policies of the state not only maintain
gender inequalities but do so by maintaining or reproducing
the gender-based division between the public and private
spheres. According to the right, however, the state, far from
maintaining this structure of gender relations, has eroded gender divisions and threatened the primacy of the mother-wife
role for women, women's unique status in our society and the
sanctity of the home.

For the right, the Ministry represented the creation of one
more weapon in the state's arsenal of attack against traditional
gender relations and the family. For feminists the ministry
potentially represented a means by which feminist pressures on
the state to divest men of their power over women might be
diffused. The argument I wish to pursue in the remainder of

this chapter is that both these explanations of the state are valid, but that neither grasps the essential character of the state and its operation.

The fundamental characteristic of the state is that it operates in a contradictory institutional position. These contradictions condition state policies and create both inconsistencies in the policies themselves and in the effects of those policies on gender relations. The state simultaneously reproduces and endangers the gender-based division of the public and private spheres. This will be demonstrated through an examination of some aspects of social welfare policy.

The state in New Zealand has long been involved in supplementing the disposable income of New Zealanders. It has done so indirectly through its public works, funding of education, housing and health services and the maintenance of the communications and transport infrastructure. More directly, the state has a long tradition of providing incentives to business and farming interests and cash transfers to individuals administered through the social security system. It is this system which is of most concern, first because the recipients of social welfare payments are overwhelmingly women and, secondly, because it is here that the contradictions in state operation are most pronounced.

The over-representation of women among social welfare beneficiaries bears directly on the impact the state has on the gender separation of the public and private spheres. For, as both conservatives and feminists agree, the basic element in that division is the dependency of women as mother-wives on a male breadwinner. According to the right, the significant fiscal relationship between women and the state is a threat to the sexual division of labour within the family and to men's 'natural' authority over women. Feminists argue that the state's welfare provisions reflect and ratify women's dependence on men, both symbolically and materially.

Of all welfare payments, the Domestic Purposes Benefit (DPB) epitomises for both right and feminists these seemingly mutually exclusive processes. This payment will therefore be the focus of much of my discussion. First, however, I want to make some more general observations regarding state policy as it pertains to gender relations in New Zealand.

The idea that social welfare systems significantly redistribute wealth has long been discredited.[4] Nevertheless, the continued and systematic impoverishment of women in New Zealand is a damning indictment of a state which presents itself as committed to ensuring equal opportunities and dignity for all its citizens.[5] All indicators of wealth show women to be disadvantaged relative to men. In 1981 over 60 per cent of adult women in New Zealand had incomes of less than $5000 a year. Of adult men only 24.8 per cent suffered the same fate.[6]

These figures reflect the large proportion of married women who have no independent incomes and are totally dependent on their husbands for economic support, the large proportion of women engaged in part-time paid labour, and the inequalities of earning power between men and women in full-time paid labour. In 1981 women earned a median income only 65 per cent of the male median income despite the enactment of equal pay legislation almost a decade before.[7]

The income differentials are mirrored in disparities between the accumulated wealth of women and men. The average value of estates left by women was only 79 per cent of the average value of male estates in 1982–83. Indeed, while 52 per cent of estates in that year valued less than $30 000 were female estates, the situation was reversed with estates valued over $50 000, 63 per cent of which were left by men.[8]

This impoverishment is directly connected to a sexual division of labour in which women are primarily associated with unpaid labour in the home and are expected to be dependent on a family income earned and controlled by their husbands. The state benefits from this directly. As long as women are co-habiting with men, either as legal or de facto wives, the state is safeguarded from the potential burden of supplementing the incomes of half the adult population.

The state's overt commitment to ensure through the social security system that the income of individuals is not merely the minimum to 'sustain life and health' but at a level which allows people 'to enjoy a standard of living much like that of the rest of the community' was established in 1972.[9] Benefit rates since have ostensibly been based on this principle and are indicative of the yearly income the state regards as necessary to adults.

Even using the lowest rate of benefit (the youth rate), the cost of dignity according to the state appears to be in the region of a yearly income of $4390 after-tax.[10] Almost 48 per cent of adult women in 1981 had yearly incomes of less than half this amount.[11] The state avoids dealing with this by restricting its responsibilities to maintaining the incomes of those who would be *expected* to earn an income on the labour market. Because married women are assumed to be non-earners and, even more significantly, the responsibility for their standard of living is defined as resting with their husbands, the state can and does abstain from any responsibility for them.

The Royal Commission on Social Security in 1972 may assert that ensuring that 'everyone can live with dignity' is a 'community responsibility' and that it is 'a legitimate function of the State to redistribute income',[12] but for the most impoverished group in our society, married women, no such redistribution is even attempted. The state in practice eschews any liability for the condition of women co-habiting with men and their dignity remains part of the grace and favour of men.

Not only are married women or those living in de facto relationships ineligible for income maintenance when engaged as full-time wives and mothers, but they are also denied unemployment and sickness benefits if their husbands are in paid labour. Married women's ineligibility for the sickness benefit reveals both the real fiscal interests of the state and women's vulnerability. In 1975, in recognition of the increasing proportion of married women engaged in paid labour, the sickness benefit was extended to all married persons who had lost their employment through illness, regardless of the earnings of their spouses. These payments were restricted to a period of three months and were at half the rate paid to a married person with a dependent spouse. Eight years later in 1983 the scheme was withdrawn as part of government attempts to trim its expenditure.[13]

The regulations concerning eligibility for sickness and unemployment benefits ratify the separation of the public and private spheres and the dependency of the private on the public. A similar affirmation of that structure may be found in the rules regulating the taxation system which has frequently been used, in preference to direct payments through social security, to maintain incomes.

Peggy Koopman-Boyden and Claudia Scott, in their extensive analysis of the development of family policy in New Zealand, show that the taxation system has traditionally disadvantaged married women in paid labour, particularly those with husbands earning incomes above the median wage. This is not because the tax system has specifically over-taxed married women but because it has consistently supported one-income families in preference to two-income families.[14] In other words, the taxation system is biased towards a family structure which not only encapsulates a division between the public and private but also the exchanges between those two spheres which underpin women's dependency in the family and their exploitation inside and outside it.

Those exchanges are recognised explicitly by the state in the continued availability of tax rebates for family dependants to married paid workers and to those employing paid house-keepers. These legitimate the dependency of adults working in the private sphere on those working in the public sphere. They also confirm the notion that labour carried out in the private sphere – housework and child-rearing – cannot be expected of persons employed in the public sphere. This concept, of course, informs not only the taxation system, but also the DPB, the Widow's Benefit and a variety of other state policies such as the state's consistent refusal to provide a comprehensive public childcare system.

The state's 'no-policy policy' on childcare is rationalised by sex role stereotypes[15] and has a severe impact on women's opportunities on the labour market, particularly for married women and solo mothers, especially those living in low-income households for whom paid labour is both a household and a personal necessity. The state's failure to ensure adequate and easily accessible childcare facilities forces women into piece-work, part-time and casual paid labour, forms of paid employment characterised by low wages, lack of union representation and vulnerability to the boom-recession cycles inherent in a market-driven capitalist economy.[16]

The tendency for the state to couch its welfare and taxation regulations in gender-neutral terms has been cited by the right as indicative of the state's intent to destroy the gender-based separation of the public and private spheres. In reality gender-neutral policy, such as the state policy regarding childcare, is a type of double-speak which safeguards the state from charges of sex discrimination while veiling the gender-loaded implications of its policies.

Past tax rebates for dependent spouses and children have not been contingent on the sex of the claimant. Likewise, rebates for paid housekeepers are available to wage and salary earners of either sex. Sickness and unemployment benefits are available to a spouse of either sex as long as their husband or wife is not engaged in paid labour. Even the DPB, which is popularly believed to be a 'woman's benefit', is available to any man engaged in full-time care of a child or sick relative who has no spouse or other income to support him. (There is an exception to the gender-neutrality of the DPB which I will discuss later. The Widow's Benefit is also not gender-neutral; it is restricted entirely to women.)

The state associates life in the private sphere with dependency on a breadwinner. But the state does not prescribe that the tasks which make up the mother-wife role should be undertaken by women, merely that undertaking those tasks requires full-time commitment. State income policies, then, affirm women's status as secondary income earners and dependants not because its policy is gender-specific but because state policies operate within a context that identifies the woman's role as that of mother-wife.

Consequently only a little more than 40 per cent of women under retirement age fully supported by the state received unemployment sickness or other labour force-related benefits in 1981. In that year 58.9 per cent of women supported by the state received the Widow's Benefit or DPB. The former represents not the complete exclusion of women but the marginality of women to paid labour. Similarly, the fact that in the same year less than 3 per cent of men under retirement age fully supported by the state received the DPB reflects not men's exclusion but the inconsistency of this type of dependency with male gender roles.[17]

Men may accept dependency on the state, and the state may provide men with support, but this generally occurs only if men's ability to earn an income is disrupted through illness or unemployment. Women, however, are already considered dependants, or at least potential dependants, of men. It is not the loss of, or lack of access to, paid employment which provides the context for the most significant welfare relationship between women and the state, but the loss or lack of a man! The state compensates women for the loss of a breadwinner through the Widow's Benefit or the DPB.

The state's provision of women with support through the DPB is the most important and controversial aspect of welfare both for women and for the state. More than any other policy it epitomises the contradictions inherent in the state's position. The DPB represents most graphically the acceptance, indeed encouragement, of women's dependency. It encourages women to see their security in terms of marriage and yet it also provides them with an escape from marriage while undertaking full-time childcare. For women the DPB represents both a mere transfer from one set of dependency relations to another and a release from dependency on men and a threat to patriarchal power.

This poses a real problem for the state. On the one hand, if the DPB is a more attractive alternative for women with children than co-habitation with a man, this is clearly going to confront the state with a large expenditure. On the other hand, if the state refuses to support mothers who leave their husbands, are deserted by their husbands, who are unmarried or widowed, then there will be tremendous pressure on the state to provide childcare facilities so these women can be engaged in full-time paid labour.

In terms of state expenditure, the socialisation and support of children through a family, even if subsidised through social security, is considerably cheaper than socialised childrearing. Within families it is expected that the expense of childcare for the state will be offset by parents who, because of emotional ties, will lower their own standard of living and transfer expenditure from themselves to their children. This is clearly expressed in the difference between the support the state provides to parents receiving various benefits compared with the state's support of orphan children under the care of guardians.

Parent beneficiaries receive a relatively large sum for the first child and a smaller sum for each child thereafter. In the case of the guardian caring for orphans, there is no similar decrease in support. Until October 1986, then, a solo-parent with two children would receive a total of $200.18 a week, $82.47 of which is the state's payment for child support. The guardian caring for two orphan children would, in comparison, receive $116 a week for child support. Moreover, while the former's eligibility is governed by a means test, the guardian will receive payment regardless of his or her income although the orphan's personal income will be means tested.[18]

If, as the Orphan's Benefit rate implies, it costs in real terms

$58.05 a week to raise a child,[19] then the solo parent with two children is subsidising her or his children by $33.63 a week and living on a personal income of just $4000 a year.[20] Under these circumstances it is difficult to give much credence to government claims that the two major priorities of the social security system are the fulfilling the needs of children and maintaining the dignity of adults.[21]

We know that despite the principle that beneficiaries 'should be able to enjoy a standard of living much like the rest of the community',[22] they do not. Solo-parent families in general are very badly off, whether or not the parent is a beneficiary. Only 53 per cent owned their own homes in 1981 compared with 76 per cent of two-parent families. A quarter did not own a car compared with less than 10 per cent of two-parent families without a car. Indeed, a wide range of appliances, from telephones to washing machines, are beyond the means of solo-parent families. Worst off are solo-mother households. Solo fathers are much more likely to retain their positions within paid labour, while most solo mothers are almost entirely dependent on state welfare payments. In 1981 50 per cent of families with incomes less than $8000 per annum were solo-mother households despite the fact that solo-parent households made up only 6.2 per cent of all household types in that year.[23]

If it is in the state's interest to subsidise the familial care of children rather than provide a substitute for that care, why is it that the state not only fails to provide solo parents with a more substantial income but has over the years encouraged the stigmatisation of solo mothers? It is ironic that a recent ministerial report noted piously that 'many people take it upon themselves to report relationships between single parents and others. This can cause ill-feeling in a community....'[24] Less than a decade ago the Minister of Social Welfare was exhorting the public to inform his department of solo parents who might be cohabiting.

Herein lies a fundamental contradiction for the state. While the DPB safeguards the state from having to assume the full burden of supporting children, it simultaneously provides an alternative to the traditional familial exchanges between male breadwinners and female dependants. These exchanges represent more than an economic relationship; they underlie a gender inequality which is a central component of the moral order which has dominated New Zealand society for the last hundred years. State policies, therefore, threaten the social order which legitimates the very existence of the state itself.

To understand the full extent of this contradiction it is necessary to explore in more detail this moral order, the complex interplay of interests it represents, and the contradictory imperatives that are imposed on the state in consequence.

Underpinning the public and private division is an ideology, the cult of domesticity. This identifies the private world of home as the source of stability in society, a haven from a brutal, competitive, instrumental and essentially chaotic public world. The centre of the home is the mother-wife.[25]

The state vests in women the guardianship of social morality by virtue of their mother-wife role, the ability 'to raise well-adjusted children and manage efficient households'.[26] Women's moral authority is portrayed by the cult of domesticity as founded on women's 'natural' purity and selflessness. These in turn are associated with, first, sexual continence and, secondly, with a subordination of women's individual desires to those of their husbands and children.

Those women who dare to challenge the cult of domesticity by leaving the family home or bearing and rearing children outside the nuclear family endanger a moral authority in which many women believe they have a vested interest and in which the state and dominant élites certainly have an interest.[27] The state is confronted with a dilemma in its provision of the DPB because, by definition the majority of its recipients will be women rearing children outside the nuclear family, normative gender relations and moral structures. At the same time the state cannot allow these women and children to become so impoverished that their poverty causes social concern.

The state response to this contradiction is revealed in the regulations pertaining to the DPB and its administration, the separation of the DPB from the Widow's Benefit and periodic attempts to stigmatise women receiving the DPB. All these proclaim a state attempting to give women financial support and at the same time attempting to maintain the moral authority of the mother-wife role and the control wives can exercise over men and children.

This is achieved partly by the way in which the DPB is administered. The dependency relations between men and women in the family are mirrored, and thus ratified, by the exchanges between the state and women. Just as in marriage women's economic dependency means relinquishing personal control,[28] so beneficiaries surrender their rights of privacy and independent action. The state has access to their homes, it can regularly demand information regarding their income and savings, it controls their access to paid labour and it even governs the frequency of their sexual relations. Wives exchange sexual fidelity and sexual access for financial support from their husbands. The state also demands, if not celibacy, then the lack of a regular sexual relationship with a male from the women it supports.

Ambiguities in the definition of a de facto relationship have been used by the state as justification for regular and close examination of beneficiaries' living conditions. The Domestic Purposes Review Committee in 1977 encouraged this by stating that 'There will always be those who try to beat the system ... in a clearly de facto marriage situation ... we do not advocate "snooping".... However, a social worker, in the course of regular contact with a beneficiary, will often sense the development of such a relationship.'[29]

The distress caused by the state's investigations into the sexual relations of beneficiaries has been frequently condemned. But these investigations are consistent with the notion that women trade both their domestic labour and control over their bodies for financial support. The husband's pursuit of a wife's monogamy is usually undertaken in private; the state merely pursues this exchange in a more public arena.

The second strategy is to make marriage more attractive. The Ministerial Task Force on Income Maintenance argued that 'a single parent should remain eligible for all or part of the benefit for a period while the [marriage/de facto] relationship is being established', because if a relationship does develop 'the cost of supporting the family' is transferred from the state to the new partner.[30] This appears antithetical to a belief in the sanctity of marriage. In fact all the traditional assumptions about gender relations are encapsulated within such a recommendation. While couched in gender-neutral terms, it implies that the beneficiary will be a dependant on a new marriage partner, who is assumed to be a breadwinner. Even in 1986 women with children were defined by the state as dependants either on the state itself or (preferably for the state) on men.

The third strategy is to make a clear distinction between the different 'types' of women rearing children with state support. In New Zealand this is manifest in a dual system of state support for women: the DPB on one hand and the Widow's Benefit on the other. The recipients of the former are typified and stigmatised as the 'selfish' and 'undeserving' for they have made choices to leave the structure of gender relations in the nuclear family. Recipients of the Widow's Benefit are typified as the unfortunate. Widows pose no threat to gender relations, for their position outside the nuclear family is imposed on them by accident or nature. Thus while in 1977 the Domestic Purposes Benefit Review Committee ensured that initial payments of the DPB were reduced, they made no argument to reduce the Widow's Benefit rates.

Initial rates of the DPB were reduced on the grounds that existing benefit rates were 'high enough to facilitate the break up of marriages which might otherwise be saved'[31] and diminish 'the fear of pregnancy ... [when] the amount of money that can be received from the benefit is higher than what the girl herself could earn in *normal* employment [my emphasis].'[32] DPB recipients are thus characterised as either lacking in commitment to their marriages or promiscuous and work shy.

The reduction in the initial DPB rate was presented as a strategy to limit divorce and restrain the increasing number of ex-nuptial births. Its failure to do either, however, has not stopped many people, including politicians, from arguing that limits on the DPB's availability would halt an alleged breakdown of the nuclear family. Given that such strategies are proven to be ineffective – and in any case the state could not induce penury on this scale – these pronouncements can only be understood as part of a discourse designed to mitigate the effects of the DPB on the moral authority of traditional family structures.

They can also be seen as punitive measures against women who dare to raise children outside the structure of the nuclear family. Although recent state publications have been less draconian in tone, there is little recognition that solo mothers, DPB recipients, have very low standards of living, and there is no indication of real commitment to change.[33]

These same policy papers have also questioned the validity

of 'woman alone' provisions,[34] which allow women without dependants, under retirement age but over fifty years of age (or forty years for the Widow's Benefit) who have lost the support of their husbands to claim the DPB or Widow's Benefit. As of March 1986, over 70 per cent of women on the Widow's Benefit had no dependent children, while just over 4 per cent of DPB recipients had no dependants.[35] This support is based on the idea that women, after long periods of full-time care for dependants, are virtually unemployable. What is significant is that some women receive state support without making themselves *available* for paid employment. This makes women quite unique.

Young people without employable skills must still be willing to accept employment if it is offered. Male DPB recipients cannot remain on the benefit after their caring function within the private sphere has ceased; they must make themselves available for paid employment. The Widow's Benefit and the 'woman alone' clauses in it and the DPB are consequently an extraordinarily blatant legitimation and prescription of women's dependency.

The 'woman alone' clauses represent both a reaffirmation of traditional exchanges between men and women and an opportunity to escape from those exchanges. However, for women the exchange of dependence on a male breadwinner for dependence on the state is fraught with contradiction. Despite the fundamental similarity between the concept of the woman/man and the woman/state exchange, the latter is necessarily bureaucratic and depersonalised. It is uncomplicated by ideologies of romantic love and real emotional attachments and fears. The intimate experience of everyday exploitation which characterises unequal gender relations in the family is avoided by the woman dependent on the state. Moreover, such women have direct control over their income once it enters the household budget. DPB recipients are in some respects similar to wage earners in that they have an individual right to determine the disposal of income. The full-time mother-wife does not have this right.

It is also significant that while the state may keep its dependants in poverty relative to male paid workers, its welfare provisions do distribute income from the public sphere of paid labour to those excluded from it. Consequently, women, precisely because they are disadvantaged in wage labour, gain particular benefits from the operation of the welfare state'.[36]

To this extent, the right correctly asserts that state welfare policies can undermine the sexual division of labour presently constituted through the family and the public/private division. Yet feminists correctly note the tendency for state policies to materially and symbolically sustain the notion of women's dependency and women's exchanges of sexual and domestic services for men's economic support.

For a woman, leaving a dependent relationship with a man and replacing it with dependency on the state means losing the intangible but real status rewards associated with the mother-wife role. She must be prepared to give up her status as a moral guardian of our society and accept being labelled as a danger to our moral order. The fact that so many women *do* accept that stigmatisation is a potent indictment of gender inequality in the family and in our society as a whole.

The state, then, simultaneously undermines and reproduces the structures which condition gender inequality in our society. How can we understand this apparent paradox? To do so, we must relinquish some of the assumptions implicit in established feminist critiques of the state.

Feminist critiques have typically portrayed state policies as assuming the dependence of women and children on men and, consequently, elevating the privatised nuclear family into both an ideal and a necessity for women's social and economic survival. A gender-based separation of the public and private spheres is beneficial to men (both as husbands and as paid workers) and to the capitalist pursuit of profit.[37] Consequently the state's active involvement in establishing the nuclear family as the dominant familial structure in our society has been said to demonstrate that the state is an institution through which male and capitalist élites exercise and impose their rule over women.[38]

This kind of argument is too simplistic. The state has its own imperatives. It is involved in the business of ruling and its existence ultimately depends on its ability to maintain public order. The fulfilment of this imperative does tend to lead the state into reproducing existing relations of domination and structures of inequality, because these are how the populace conceives of 'public order'. However, the exploitative activities of dominant élites (the structure of inequality itself) encourage conflict and competition which is inherently disruptive of social equilibrium. To maintain social order, then, the state mediates these conflicts and in doing so must at times ignore the immediate interests of dominant élites.

Moreover, despite feminist assumptions, the interests of class and sex élites are not inherently congruent. They actually confront the state with incompatible demands. The mechanisms which underlie class and race inequality cut across the interests which coalesce around gender inequality and may contradict them.

These conflicting demands on the state cannot alone explain the apparent incoherence of state actions and policies. They themselves derive from inherent contradictions embedded in the separation of the public and private and the cult of domesticity which underpins it.

For male élites, for instance, the cult of domesticity undoubtedly provides men with a whole variety of material and symbolic benefits. But it also challenges the formations of male bonding and mateship which are so characteristic of New Zealand Pakeha male culture. Significantly, however, the cult of domesticity does provide the state with a potent means of social control. As Jock Phillips points out, 'family responsibilities served as the greatest check on male culture, a guarantee that its disreputable excesses would be kept firmly within ritualised and defined boundaries.... No permanent male anarchs were allowed.'[39] In these circumstances it is hardly surprising that state policy welfare payments to women should have contradictory implications for men as individuals and as a sex. For while the DPB certainly relieves some men of the burden of supporting the women with whom they have had sexual relations, it also gives all women potential alternatives to being or remaining married. This must be seen as providing women with a very real basis of resistance and grounds for negotiation within the family.

For the capitalist élite the cult of domesticity is equally ambiguous. The identification of women as secondary income earners has enabled capitalist employers to exploit women as a reserve army of labour. But male workers have been able to use the dependence of women and children as justification for higher wages which are not in the immediate interests of capitalists in pursuit of profit. The state's legislation of minimum wages can be seen as antagonistic to capital, but advantaging men, as workers, for whom the control of the family wage gives dominance within marital relations.[40] The state's provision, through the Family Allowance (1926), the Family Benefit (1946) and the Family Care and Support packages, of a minimum family income is essentially the state offsetting the costs to employers of the cult of domesticity. At the same time the state's provision of the DPB and the Widow's Benefit, which provides women with an alternative source of income from not only their husbands but potentially from paid labour as well, protects solo mothers from even more exploitation than they already suffer on the paid labour market.

The contradictions embedded in the cult of domesticity have been analysed elsewhere in this volume. My point is that the state is situated between antagonistic demands from capitalist and male élites and its own imperatives. The operation of state policies and the outcome of these policies for women reflect those conflicts. Historically women have exploited these contradictions to wrest real material and symbolic gains from the state such as the franchise and equal pay.

In conclusion, then, the state reproduces the gender-based separation of the public and private spheres and the inequalities that derive from it. But the state also endangers that structure. For feminists this contradiction must not be ignored but exposed, accentuated and used to divest dominant élites of their substantial but vulnerable power.

References

CHAPTER I: THE THEORETICAL BACKGROUND

1. Margaret Stacey says that until recently 'the division of labour as between the public and domestic arenas and within the family were taken as unproblematic, as "natural". There was no recognition that this 'naturalness' was a social construction. . . .' M. Stacey, 'The Division of Labour Revisited or Over-coming the Two Adams' in Abrams, Dean, Finch and Rock (eds), *Practice and Progress: British Sociology 1950–1980* (London: Allen and Unwin, 1981), p. 173

2. Aristotle, *Politics I, II,* 9, 11–12, quoted in Marina Warner, *Alone of All Her Sex: The Myth and Cult of the Virgin Mary* (London: Weidenfeld and Nicolson, 1976), p. 178

3. 'Aristotle's women were *idiots* in the Greek sense of the word, persons who either could not or did not participate in the "good" of public life, individuals without a voice, condemned to silence as their appointed sphere and condition.' J. B. Elshtain, *Public Man, Private Woman: Women in Social and Political Thought* (Oxford: Martin Robertson), 1981, p. 47

4. Tertullian, *Apologia,* 9:8 quoted in Marina Warner, *Alone of All Her Sex: The Myth and Cult of the Virgin Mary* (London: Weidenfeld and Nicolson, 1976), p. 178

5. S. M. Okin, *Women in Western Political Thought* (Princeton, NJ: Princeton University Press, 1979), p. 233

6. Plato wrote about private wives in *The Laws.* He wrote about women guardians in the public sphere in *The Republic* (Book 5, 4516–4526.)

7. Mill writes: 'Human beings are no longer born to their place in life . . . but are free to employ their faculties and such favourable chances as offer, to achieve the lot which may seem to them most desirable.' J. S. Mill, 'The Subjection of Women' in J. S. M. and Harriet Taylor Mill (ed. Alice Rossi), *Essays on Sex Equality* (Chicago and London: University of Chicago Press, 1970), p. 143

8. Ibid., p. 132

9. Ibid., p. 223

10. As Okin goes on to say, Mill's convictions would be undermined by the inclusion in his theory of women as the complete equals of men. Okin, *Women in Western* . . ., p. 280

11. The following discussion of Engels' theory is based on F. Engels, *The Origins of the Family, Private Property and the State* (London: Lawrence and Wishart, 1972)

12. Engels' definition of production and reproduction is contained in this passage: '. . . the determining factor in history is, in the final instance,

the production and reproduction of immediate life. This, again, is of a two-fold character. On the one side, the production of the means of subsistence, of food, clothing and shelter and the tools necessary for that production; on the other side, the production of human beings themselves, the propagation of the species.' F. Engels *The Origin of the Family, Private Property and the State* (Peking: Foreign Languages Press, 1978), p. 4

13. M. Barrett, *Women's Oppression Today* (London: Verso, 1980), p. 254

14. Ibid., p. 203

15. R. Hamilton, *The Liberation of Women* (London: Allen and Unwin, 1978), p. 40

16. Ibid., p. 47

17. See extracts from F. Engels, 'Women and Children in the Mills', in *The Woman Question. Selections from the Writings of Karl Marx, Frederick Engels, V. I. Lenin, Joseph Stalin* (New York: International Publishers Co., 1951)

18. Property, in the sense used here, refers to productive property – land, capital, plant etc. – that is used in the production of commodities. The term does not refer to items of property for personal use.

19. Radical feminists argue that fundamental biological differences between women and men, and their unequal social consequences, have resulted in the oppression of women. They regard gender relations as inherently and inevitably relations of conflict. They use the word 'patriarchy' to denote a system of universal control of women by men. Radical feminist analysis has tended to concentrate on the private sphere, and this work has been important in revealing the nature of power relations between the sexes in the family. Strategies for the liberation of women are various, but focus on the actions of women redefining, revaluing and reclaiming their lives from a male-oriented world. Radical feminists are not content simply with reform within existing social structures, but argue that the abolition of patriarchy would require change of society as a whole.

20. S. Firestone, *The Dialectic of Sex* (London: Paladin, 1972), p. 193

21. Ibid., p. 11

22. R. Arditti et al. (eds), *Test Tube Women; What Future for Motherhood?* (Boston, Mass.: Pandora Press, 1984)

23. Hester Eisenstein, *Contemporary Feminist Thought* (Sydney: Allen and Unwin, 1984), p. 106

24. Hazel Carby, 'White woman listen! Black feminism and the boundaries of sisterhood', in Centre for Contemporary Cultural Studies Birmingham, *The Empire Strikes Back. Race and Racism in 70s Britain* (London: Hutchinson, 1982), pp. 212–35

25. Sheila Rowbotham says 'It is evident that human beings live contradictions. We are not neat ideological packages.' S. Rowbotham, 'What do women want? Women-centred values and the world as it is', *Feminist Review* 20, 1985, pp. 49–69

26. Carole Pateman, 'Feminist Critiques of the Public/Private Dichotomy', in S. I. Benn and G. F. Gaus (eds) *Public and Private in Social Life* (St. Martin's: Croom Helm, 1983), p. 293

27. Investigation into the extent to which domestic work benefits capitalist productive activities has resulted in a body of work called the 'domestic labour debate.' The debate examines the contribution of domestic labour to productive activities, through reproduction of the labour force. This occurs daily, through the housewife's work in caring for the male worker; and on a generational basis, with the care of children. Secondly, part of a woman's domestic work involves reproducing the values of capitalist society. This is especially apparent in her role in the socialisation of children.

For discussion and critique of the debate see: M. Barrett, *Women's Oppression Today* (London: Verso, 1980); E. Malos, *The Politics of Housework*; M. Molyneux, 'Beyond the Domestic Labour Debate', *New Left Review*, 116, 1979, pp. 3–27

28. Barrett, *Women's Oppression Today,* p. 251

29. M. Barrett and M. McIntosh, *The Anti Social Family* (London: Verso, 1982), pp. 137–159

30. Stacey, 'The Division of Labour . . .', p. 189

31. Eisenstein (*Contemporary Feminist Thought*, p. 47), defines a woman-centred perspective as one which views women's experiences as the major focus of study and the source of dominant values for society as a whole.

32. As Rowbotham observes: '. . . women-centred values might be argued for with quite differing political emphases among different classes and in diverse historical situations.' Rowbotham, 'What Do Women Want?', p. 55

CHAPTER 2: BRIDGING THE GAP

1. Erik Olssen and Andrée Lévesque, 'Towards a History of the European Family in New Zealand' in P. G. Koopman-Boyden (ed.), *Families in New Zealand Society* (Wellington: Methuen, 1978)

2. Julia Millen, *Colonial Tears and Sweat* (Wellington: Reed, 1984), p. 62

3. Ibid., p. 61

4. Olssen and Lévesque, 'Towards a History of the European Family in New Zealand', p. 8

5. Jock Phillips, 'Mummy's Boys: Pakeha Men and Male Culture in New Zealand' in P. Bunkle and B. Hughes (eds), *Women in New Zealand Society* (Auckland: Allen and Unwin, 1980), pp. 223–29

6. Margot Roth, The New Zealand Family: Cornerstone of Colonisation MA thesis, University of Auckland, 1980

7. W. B. Sutch, *Women with a Cause* (Auckland University Press, 1973), pp. 70–72

8. Olssen and Lévesque, 'Towards a History of the European Family in New Zealand', p. 4; and Erik Olssen, 'Women, Work and Family:

1880–1926' in Bunkle and Hughes (eds) *Women in New Zealand Society*, pp. 161–67

9. Shelagh Cox and Bev James, 'Public and Private Worlds; The Theoretical Background', in the present volume.

10. Millen, *Colonial Tears and Sweat*, p. 135

11. W. B. Sutch, *Poverty and Progress in New Zealand: A Re-assessment* (Auckland: A. H. and A. W. Reed, 1969), pp. 122–130

12. Millen, *Colonial Tears and Sweat*, p. 137

13. Ibid., p. 138

14. Ibid., p. 134

15. Olssen, 'Women, Work and Family', pp. 163–67

16. Veronica Beechey, 'Women and Production: A critical analysis of some sociological theories of women's work' in Annette Kuhn and Ann Marie Wolpe (eds), *Feminism and Materialism* (London, Boston, Henley: Routledge and Kegan Paul, 1978), pp. 155–97

17. Jacqui Pearson and Elizabeth Plumridge, 'Women in the Slump' in C. Newman (ed.), *Canterbury Women since 1893* (Christchurch: Pegasus, 1979)

18. Ibid., p. 133

19. Olssen and Lévesque, 'Towards a History of the European Family in New Zealand', p. 14

20. Eve Ebbett, *Victoria's Daughters: New Zealand Women of the Thirties* (Wellington: Reed, 1981), 1971, p. 5

21. Department of Statistics, *New Zealand Census of Population and Dwellings, Industries and Occupations*, p. 5

22. Eve Ebbett, *While the Boys Were Away: New Zealand Women in World War II* (Wellington: Reed, 1984); and Lauris Edmond (ed) *Women in Wartime* (Wellington: Government Printer, 1986)

23. Helen Cook, 'The Myth of Post War Reconstruction: The Aspirations and Realities of a Post-War Generation of Wives and Mothers' in C. Philipson (ed.), *Women's Studies: Conference Papers '84*, (Auckland: Women's Studies Association NZ (Inc.), 1985)

24. Helen Cook, 'Images and Illusions of Harmony: The 1950s Wife and Mother', *NZ Women's Studies Journal*, Vol. 1, No. 2, April 1985

25. Ibid., p. 89

26. Department of Statistics, *New Zealand Official Yearbook 1985* (Wellington: Government Printer, 1985), p. 70

27. Helen Cook, 'The Myth of Post War Reconstruction'. p. 72

28. Ibid., p. 69

29. David Pearson and David Thorns, *Eclipse of Equality* (Sydney: Allen and Unwin, 1983), p. 178

30. Department of Statistics, *New Zealand Official Yearbook 1985,* p. 870

31. Ibid., pp. 989–91

32. Ibid., pp. 865–68

33. Ibid., p. 866

34. Ibid., p. 989

35. Mary O'Regan, 'Apprenticeships – jobs for the boys?', *Broadsheet,* no. 83, October 1980; and Ann Else, 'Working our way up: a survey of a decade of Women's Work', *Broadsheet,* no. 131, July/Aug., 1985, pp. 25–26

36. Information on apprenticeships: personal communication, Department of Labour; information on women lawyers: Department of Statistics, *New Zealand Official Yearbook 1985,* pp. 865–66

37. Department of Statistics, *NZ Census of Population and Dwellings 1981,* Bulletin 2, pp. 33–35

38. Ibid.

39. Ibid., p. 24

40. Ibid., p. 39

41. Population Monitoring Group, *The New Zealand Population: Change, Composition and Policy Implications,* Population Monitoring Group Report No. 4, NZ Planning Council, 1986, p. 20

42. Ibid., pp. 20–21

43. Alison Clark, *Part-time Work in New Zealand,* Planning Paper No. 25, New Zealand Planning Council, 1986, p. 9

44. Ibid., pp. 25–31

45. Susan Shipley, *Women's Employment and Unemployment: a research report* (Palmerston North: Department of Sociology, Massey University and the Society for Research on Women, 1982), p. xi

46. Ibid., p. 82

47. Clark, *Part-time Work in New Zealand,* p. 21

48. Shirley Dex, *The Sexual Division of Work* (Brighton: Wheatsheaf and Harvester, 1985), p. 186

49. Society for Research on Women, Christchurch Branch, *Jobs, Children and Chores: A Study of Mothers in Paid Employment in the Christchurch Area* (Christchurch: S.R.O.W., 1984), p. 56

50. Sylvia Dixon, The Growth of Part-time Employment: Cause or Solution to Sex Inequalities, MA thesis, University of Canterbury, 1985, pp. 1–31

51. Clark, *Part-time Work in New Zealand,* pp. 11–13

52. Prue Hyman, 'Perspectives on Equal Pay for Work of Equal Value' in *Equal Pay for Work of Equal Value: A Woman's Issue,* Centre for Continuing Education, Victoria University of Wellington, 1986

53. Dixon, *The Growth of Part-time Employment,* p. 229

54. Population Monitoring Group, *The New Zealand Population: Change, Composition and Policy Implications,* pp. 19–20

55. Department of Statistics, *NZ Official Yearbook 1985*, p. 992
56. In February 1987 the average ordinary time weekly earnings for men were $439.75. Women's equivalent earnings were $336.72. *Quarterly Survey of Employment*, Department of Labour, February 1987
57. Department of Labour, *Quarterly Survey of Employment*, February 1985
58. Alison Gray, *The Jones Men: 100 New Zealand Men Talk About Their Lives* (Wellington: Reed, 1983), pp. 77–86
59. Ibid., pp. 83–84
60. Society for Research on Women, *Women and Money* (Wellington: S.R.O.W., 1982)
61. Anne Phillips and Barbara Taylor, 'Sex and Skill' in Feminist Review (ed.), *Waged Work: A Reader* (London: Virago, 1986), p. 55
62. Roberta Hill, in From Hot Metal to Cold Type: Labour Process Theory and the New Technology, PhD thesis in Sociology, University of Canterbury, 1983, pp. 270–97
63. Ibid., p. 324
64. Ibid., p. 327
65. Roberta Hill and Rosemary Novitz, 'Class, Gender and Technological Change,' paper presented to the Annual Conference of the Sociological Association, University of Waikato, Hamilton, December 1985
66. Ibid., p. 17
67. Dex, *The Sexual Division of Labour*, pp. 99–104
68. Ibid., p. 103
69. Mary Hancock, *It Doesn't Seem to Matter What Happens to Women: A Study of the Effects on Women of the Collapse and Takeover of Mosgiel Ltd* (Hamilton: Working Women's Council, 1981)
70. Shipley, *Women's Employment and Unemployment*, p. 197
71. Brendon Thompson, 'Job Stealers?', *NZ Listener*, 11 July 1981, p. 62
72. Department of Statistics, *NZ Official Yearbook 1985*, p. 993
73. Population Monitoring Group, *The New Zealand Population*, p. 21
74. Department of Statistics, *NZ Census of Population and Dwellings*, Bulletin 2, pp. 18–20
75. Department of Statistics, *NZ Official Yearbook 1985*, p. 994
76. Ibid.
77. Population Monitoring Group, *The New Zealand Population*, p. 22
78. Kathleen Gallagher and others, 'Women Outworkers', *Race Gender Class*, No. 2, Dec. 1985, p. 37
79. Karl du Fresne, 'Assembly Lines of One', *NZ Listener*, 29 August 1981; and Gallagher et al., 'Women Outworkers', pp. 39–41
80. Gallagher et al., 'Women Outworkers', pp. 37–38
81. Ibid.

82. Quoted in J. Humphries, 'Class struggle and the persistence of the working class family', in A. H. Amsden (ed.), *The Economics of Women and Work* (Harmondsworth: Penguin, 1977), p. 142

83. Ann Oakley, *The Sociology of Housework*, (London: Martin Robinson, 1974); Pauline Hunt, *Gender and Class Consciousness,* (London: Macmillan, 1980); Meg Luxton, *More Than a Labour of Love: Three Generations of Women's Work in the Home* (Toronto: The Women's Press, 1980); Ellen Malos (ed.), *The Politics of Housework* (London: Allison and Busby, 1980); Janet Finch and Dulcie Groves (eds), *A Labour of Love: Women, Work and Caring* (London: Routledge and Kegan Paul, 1983); and Ann Game and Rosemary Pringle, 'The labour process of consumption: Housework', in *Gender at Work*, pp. 119–40

84. Mary O'Brien, *The Politics of Reproduction*, (Boston: Routledge and Kegan Paul, 1981); Katherine J. Saville-Smith, Reproducers and Producers: A Model for the Analysis of Women, MA thesis, University of Canterbury, 1982; Brian Roper, Production and Reproduction: A Theoretical Investigation of the Material Basis of Women's Transhistorical Subordination, MA thesis, University of Canterbury, 1985

85. Belinda Trainor, The Politics of Reproduction, MA thesis in Political Science, University of Canterbury, 1984

86. Bettina Cass, 'Women's Place in the Class Structure' in E.L. Wheelwright and K. Buckley (eds), *Essays in the Political Economy of Australian Capitalism,* Vol. 3, (Sydney: Australian and New Zealand Book Company, 1978); and Heidi Hartmann, 'The Family as the Locus of Gender, Class, and Political Struggle: The Example of Housework', *Signs,* Vol. 6, No. 3, Spring 1981

87. Department of Statistics, *NZ Census of Population and Dwellings 1981*, Bulletin 2, Table 5, p. 18

88. Claudia Bell and Vivienne Adair, *Women and Change: A Study of New Zealand Women* (Wellington: National Council of Women, 1985), p. 49

89. Alison Gray, *The Jones Men,* p. 86

90. Anne Meade, Margaret Rosemergy and Raylee Johnston, 'How Children Affect Family Style: The Hidden Contract', *NZ Women's Studies Journal*, Vol. 1, No. 2, April 1985, p. 27

91. Rosemary Novitz, 'Marital and Familial Roles in New Zealand: The Challenge of the Women's Liberation Movement' in P. G. Koopman-Boyden (ed.), *Families in New Zealand Society*, p. 82

92. Max Abbott and Peggy Koopman-Boyden, 'Expectations and Predictors of Division of Labour within Marriage', *NZ Psychologist*, Vol. 10, No. 1, May 1981; and Peggy Koopman-Boyden and Max Abbott, 'Expectations for Household Task Allocation and Actual Task Allocation: A New Zealand Study', *Journal of Marriage and the Family*, February 1985, pp. 211–19

93. Jane Ritchie, *Child Rearing Patterns: Further Studies,* Psychology Research Series, No. 11, University of Waikato, Hamilton, 1979

217

94. Garth Fletcher, 'Division of Labour in the New Zealand Family', *NZ Psychologist*, Vol. 7, No. 2, November 1978

95. Eric Pawson and Garth Cant, 'Re-defining Work: The Role of Informal Household Activities' in R. D. Bedford and A. P. Sturman (eds), *Canterbury at the Crossroads*, New Zealand Geographical Society, Misc. Series, 1983

96. Shirley Dex, *The Sexual Division of Labour*, p. 75

97. Peggy G. Koopman-Boyden, 'The Elderly in the Family' in *Families in New Zealand Society*, p. 65; and Alan Walker, 'Care for elderly people: a conflict between women and the state' in Janet Finch and Dulcie Groves, *A Labour of Love*, pp. 106–28

98. Social Monitoring Group, *Birth to Death*, New Zealand Planning Council, Wellington, 1985, p. 66; and Ministry of Women's Affairs, 'Patterns of Change', October 1986

99. Social Monitoring Group, *Birth to Death*, pp. 66–67

100. Ann Oakley, *Taking It Like A Woman* (London: Flamingo, Fontana Paperbacks, 1984), p. 187

CHAPTER 3: TO US THE DREAMERS ARE IMPORTANT

1. A tukutuku panel is a wooden framework made up of slats through which pingao blades are threaded back and forth to make a design.

CHAPTER 4: PRIVATE LIVES AND PUBLIC FICTIONS

1. Hélène Cixous, 'Sorties' in Elaine Marks and Isabelle de Courtivon (eds), *New French Feminisms* (Amherst: University of Massachusetts, 1980), pp. 90–91

2. Keri Hulme, *the bone people* p. 2

3. Hélène Cixous, 'The Laugh of the Medusa' in Marks and de Courtivon, *New French Feminisms*, p. 249

4. Shona Smith, 'Keri Hulme: Breaking Ground', *Untold* 2, Spring 1984, pp. 44–9

5. Keri Hulme, *the bone people*, p. 7

6. Hélène Cixous, 'The Laugh of the Medusa' in Marks and de Courtivon, *New French Feminisms*, p. 264

7. Colette Dowling, *The Cinderella Complex: Women's Hidden Fear of Independence* (USA: Summit Books, 1981)

8. Carol Gilligan, *In a Different Voice* (Cambridge, Massachusetts, 1982) pp. 156, 159

9. Marilyn Duckworth, *Married Alive*, pp. 165–66

10. Lauris Edmond, *High Country Weather* pp. 159–160

11. Elizabeth Caffin, *New Zealand Listener*, 3–9 May, 1986, p. 51

12. Rachel Brownstein, *Becoming a Heroine: Reading about Women in Novels* (New York: Viking Press, 1982), p. xix

13. Janice A. Radway, *Reading the Romance: Women, Patriarchy, and Popular Literature* (Chapel Hill: University of North Carolina Press, 1984), p. 207

14. Kathleen Blake, *Love and the Woman Question in Victorian Literature: the Art of Self-Postponement* (Brighton: Sussex 1983), p. xi

15. Janice A. Radway, *Reading the Romance*, p. 138

16. Adrienne Rich, 'Anne Sexton' in *On Lies, Secrets and Silence: Selected Prose 1966–1978* (New York: Norton, 1979), pp. 122 and 123

17. Margaret Sutherland, *The Love Contract*, p. 29

18. Ibid., p. 154

19. Jean Watson, *Stand in the Rain*, p. 150

20. Kaja Silverman, 'Histoire d'O. The Construction of a Female Subject' in Carole S. Vance (ed), *Pleasure and Danger: Exploring Female Sexuality* (Boston: Routledge and Kegan Paul, 1984), p. 321

21. Hélène Cixous, 'The Laugh of the Medusa' in Marks and de Courtivon (eds) *New French Feminisms*, p. 250

22. Ibid., p. 256

CHAPTER 5: WOMEN AND ART

1. Emily Harris Diaries 1885–1890, MS Papers 1284, Alexander Turnbull Library.

2. Quoted by Barbi de Lange, 'Flora Scales: The Woman and Her Work', *Art New Zealand*, No. 37, 1985, p. 49

3. This oil is owned by the Auckland City Art Gallery.

4. Leonard Bell, 'Concentrating Colour', *New Zealand Listener*, 27 August 1983, p. 54

5. Francis Pound, 'Albrecht's Seasonal', introduction to exhibition catalogue, Auckland City Art Gallery, 1985–86

6. Anthony Stones, 'The Paintings of Jackie Fahey', *Mate,* December 1980, pp. 25–8

7. Letter from Robin White to the author, 15 October 1985

8. Rozsika Parker and Griselda Pollock, *Old Mistresses: Women, Art and Ideology* (New York: 1981), p. 114

9. Foreword to the catalogue of an exhibition of watercolours by Maud Sherwood, The Macquarie Galleries (Sydney), August 1933

10. A. R. D. Fairburn, *Art in New Zealand*, No. 64, June 1944, p. 17

11. *Dominion*, 1 June 1955

12. Hamish Keith, 'The Art Scene', *Vogue New Zealand,* Summer 1968

13. Letter from Pauline Thompson to the author, 22 March 1985

14. Juliet Batten, 'Emerging from the Underground: The Women's Art Movement in New Zealand', *Spiral* No. 5, 1982, p. 25

15. Quoted in 'New Zealand Feminist Artists', *Broadsheet*, No. 110, 1983, p. 23

16. 'Carole Shepheard/Claudia Pond Eyley: A Survey of Work 1980–85', Wellington City Gallery, January–March, 1986

17. Statement in the exhibition catalogue to 'Six Women Artists', Robert McDougall Art Gallery, Christchurch 1975

18. Tony Bellette, 'Joanna Paul: Words and Pictures', *Art New Zealand*, No. 26, 1983, p. 45

CHAPTER 6: MILLWORKERS' WIVES

1. J. Finch, *Married to the Job. Wives' Incorporation into Men's Work*, (London: Allen and Unwin, 1983), p. 1

2. The study uses the model of class outlined in R. Steven, 'Towards a class analysis of New Zealand', *Australian and New Zealand Journal of Sociology*, 14, 2, 1978. pp. 113–29

3. In this chapter I do not propose to debate the issues involved in defining women in class terms. I am, however, aware of the lack of applicability of conventional class analyses to women's experiences. These analyses assume that a woman takes her class position from her husband or father. Consequently, men and women are defined quite differently in class terms. Men's class position is directly defined by economic criteria. In contrast a woman's place in the stratification system is mediated and conditioned by personal relationships through kinship and marriage. (For elaboration of this argument, see C. Delphy, *Close to Home. A Materialist Analysis of Women's Oppression* (London: Hutchinson, 1984), pp. 28–39.) Such an approach is not entirely satisfactory. It ignores the fact that many women participate in the labour force in their own right and therefore have their own independent economic position.

A second criticism is that by assigning a class position to a non-employed woman on the basis of her husband's occupation, it is assumed that her status is equal to his. This ignores the evidence that women in general do not enjoy equality with their husbands. Social inequalities within society as a whole affect relations between the sexes, and within marriage itself there are differences in power and status between husbands and wives. This is apparent in the ways domestic finances are arranged in families. Later in the chapter it will be shown that husbands typically have greater economic power and wives are in a position of economic dependence. Bearing in mind the complex relationship of class and gender inequalities, I argue that in the context of Kawerau and its industry, the husband's economic situation is a major influence on his wife's life. For my discussion, the most important idea is that the women are wives of working class men. They are vitally affected by the circumstances of his occupation; for example, his earning power, his hours of work, the responsibilities and privileges of his job, and decisions made in the workplace by workers and management.

4. C. Delphy, *Close to Home. A Materialist Analysis of Women's Oppression*, (London: Hutchinson, 1984), pp. 94–5

5. H. Callan, 'Introduction', in H. Callan and S. Ardener (eds), *The Incorporated Wife* (London: Croom Helm, 1984), p. 3. Also see H.

Papanek, 'Men, women and work: Reflections on the two-person career', *American Journal of Sociology*, 78, 4, 1973, pp. 852-72

6. Until 1982 women were prevented from nightwork in the industry, under legislation based on ILO Convention 89. A change in the law in 1982 enabled women to do shiftwork and nightwork in factories under the same conditions as men (see Anon., 'Recent developments affecting women's employment', *Labour and Employment Gazette*, 32, 4, 1982, pp. 2-3). However, despite such changes, women have not entered production jobs in the industry.

7. P. Willis, 'Shop floor culture, masculinity and the wage form', in J. Clarke et al. (eds), *Working Class Culture* (London: Hutchinson, 1979), p. 197

8. For detailed discussion of the idea of the main meal, see A. Murcott, '"It's a pleasure to cook for him" Food, mealtimes and gender in some South Wales households', in E. Gamarnikow et al. (eds), *The Public and the Private* (London: Heinemann, 1983), pp. 78-90; and M. Douglas, Deciphering a meal', in M. Douglas, *Implicit Meanings. Essays in Anthropology* (London: Routledge and Kegan Paul, 1975) pp. 249-75

9. See studies by E. Phillip and S. Griew, *One Hundred Shiftworkers* Research paper no. 15, New Zealand Institute of Economic Research, 1970; and J. Carpentier and P. Cazamian, *Night Work* (Geneva, International Labour Office, 1977)

10. The dispute referred to in this chapter was the most recent one at the time of the study. A detailed account of the dispute is given in B. James, *A Report to the Kawerau Community*, Dept Sociology, Waikato, 1979, pp. 218-25. An eleven-week industrial dispute, in which one union was locked out and the rest of the labour force suspended from work, occurred from August to October in 1986. Women's responses to this dispute are discussed in B. James, '"Discourse in Dispute" Image of "class", "community" and "family" in the Kawerau Dispute': *Sites* No. 14, 1987.

11. James, *A Report to the Kawerau Community*, p. 219

12. Not all unions reacted to wives in this way. The Timberworkers Union invited wives to meetings. Many were involved in organising the union's welfare services for families affected by the strike.

13. There were no public wives' protests against the dispute in 1978. This was in contrast to the public gatherings and meeting with company management and union officials that women organised during the 1986 dispute. See James, *Sites* No. 14, for discussion of women's actions in the latter dispute.

CHAPTER 7: THE INVISIBLE WOMEN

1. 'Women in Agriculture: A Survey of Rural Women in New Zealand', *Straight Furrow*, September 1981

2. *ILO Year Book of Labour Statistics,* 1969, Table 1

3. *United Nations Handbook of Social Surveys*, Series F, No. 31, 1984

4. Barbara Rogers, *The Domestication of Women* (London: Tavistock Publications, 1981)

5. D. J. Casley and D. A. Lury, *Data Collection in Developing Countries* (Oxford: Clarendon Press, 1981)

6. Ruth Dixon, 'Assessing the Impact of Development Projects on Women', AID Programme Evaluation Discussion Paper No. 8. Office of Women in Development and Office of Evaluation Bureau for Programme and Policy Co-ordination, US Agency for International Development, May 1980

7. *A System of National Accounts and Supporting Tables,* UN Statistical Office, Studies in Methods, Series F, No. 2 Rev. 1, 1968

8. Kathleen Newland, *The Sisterhood of Man.* Worldwatch Institute

9. Derek Blades, *Non-Monetary (Subsistence) Activities in the National Accounts of Developing Countries,* OECD, 29 October 1975

10. Maria Mies, 'The Dynamics of the Sexual Division of Labour: Women Lace Workers of Narsapur', *Economic and Political Weekly,* vol. 16, no. 10, 1981

11. Ester Boserup, *Women's Role in Economic Development* (New York: St Martin's Press, 1970)

12. John Kenneth Galbraith, 'The Economics of the American Housewife', *Atlantic Monthly* Vol. 232, No. 2, August 1973

13. Third UNCSTD Preparatory Committee Meeting of the NGO Task Force on the Roles of Women, 1979

14. *North-South. A Programme for Survival* (London: Pan Books, 1980), p. 61

15. Equality, Peace, Development, UN A/Conference 1985, 116/28, para 120

CHAPTER 8: LESBIAN WORLDS

1. See Dolores Klaitch, *Woman + Woman,* William Morrow, 1974, and J. Weeks, *Coming Out: Homosexual Politics in Britain from the 19th Century to the Present,* Quartet Books, 1977, for more details.

2. See Jeanette Foster, *Sex Variant Women in Literature,* Diana Press, 1975, for early examples of this.

3. Among others, some U.S. states have criminalised lesbianism. See International Association of Lesbians and Gay Men, *The Pink Book,* 1984, for the current legal position world-wide.

4. See Weeks, *op. cit.,* pp. 106–7, quoting Lord Desart.

5. See Lynne Gifford. 'Butch we win, femme you lose: the myth of lesbian impunity', unpublished paper delivered at 1983 Women's Studies Conference, J. Katz, *Gay/Lesbian Almanac,* Harper and Row, 1984, Lillian Faderman, *Surpassing the Love of Men,* William Morrow, 1981, and Judy Grahn, *Another Mother Tongue: Gay Words, Gay Worlds,* Beacon Press, 1984, for descriptions of some of these women.

6. Lillian Faderman, 'Who hid lesbian history?' in *Frontiers* IV, no. 3, Fall, 1979, pp. 74–5

7. Carroll Smith-Rosenberg, *Disorderly Conduct: Visions of Gender in Victorian America,* Oxford University Press, 1985.

8. Adrienne Rich, 'Compulsory heterosexuality and lesbian existence', *Signs,* vol. 5, no. 4, 1981, pp. 631–60

9. See Jacquelyn Zita, 'Historical amnesia and the lesbian continuum', *Signs,* vol. 7, no. 1, 1981, pp. 172–86

10. This statement follows the resolution at the 1986 Women's Studies Association Conference that all feminists state clearly the position which they are writing from.

11. Susan Cavin, *Lesbian Origins,* Ism Press, 1986, p. 1

12. Janice Raymond, *A Passion for Friends,* Women's Press, 1986, p. 57

13. Dale Spender, *Women of Ideas and What Men Have Done to Them,* Ark Paperbacks, 1982.

14. J. Katz, *op. cit.,* p. 167

15. The emergence of the new political, male homosexual is also a threat to institutionalised heterosexism. However, homosexual behaviour (as distinct from identity) among males has been freely accepted in many societies. See Dennis Altman, *The Homosexualisation of America,* Beacon Press, 1982, Susan Cavin, *op. cit.,* J. Katz, *op. cit.,* and Weeks, *op. cit.* See also Marilyn Frye, 'A lesbian perspective on women's studies', in Margaret Cruikshank (ed.), *Lesbian Studies,* Feminist Press, 1982, on lesbian feminism and the gay rights movement, and John D'Emilio, 'Capitalism and gay identity', in Ann Snitow *et al.* (eds), *Powers of Desire: The Politics of Sexuality,* Monthly Review Press, 1983, for a discussion of capitalism and gay identity.

16. Janice Raymond, *op. cit.*

17. See Marilyn Frye, *The Politics of Reality: Essays in Feminist Theory,* The Crossing Press, 1983

18. Adrienne Rich, *op. cit.,* p. 632

19. Doris Faber, *The Life of Lorena Hickok: ER's Friend.* William Morrow, 1980, pp. 331, 352–4

20. Both writers cite Carroll Smith-Rosenberg, *op. cit.,* and all three seem to have been influenced by Michael Foucault, *The History of Sexuality,* Vol. 1, Allen Lane, 1978. In spite of the fact that the term 'lesbian' appears to have been in use since the sixth century BC, Foucault argues that the 'homosexual' first emerged as an identity from nineteenth-century discourses. The word 'homosexual' itself seems to have been invented in 1869, and considerable interest in homosexuality was shown by a number of nineteenth-century medical and psychiatric writers. These writers based their discussions on real case studies which they classified and theorised about. The writers did not invent the people – they found or 'discovered' them. Presumably there were many thousands of other homosexuals or lesbians around at the same time who avoided doctors

and therefore definition. See also Weeks, *op. cit.*, Katz, 1978, 1983, Vern Bullough, *Sexual Variance in Society and History,* University of California Press, 1976, and J. Lauritsen and D. Thorstad, *The Early Homosexual Rights Movement,* Times Change Press, 1974

21. Judith Brown, *Immodest Acts: The Life of a Lesbian Nun in Renaissance Italy,* Oxford University Press, 1986

22. 'Katherine Mansfield', *New Zealand Encyclopedia,* David Bateman, 1985, and C. A. Hankin, *Katherine Mansfield and Her Confessional Stories,* Macmillan, 1983

23. Ida Baker, *KM: The Memories of LM,* Michael Joseph, 1980; Antony Alpers, *The Life of Katherine Mansfield,* 2 nd ed., Viking Press, 1980, pp. 91, 95. Mansfield's negative attitude towards her lesbianism is not apparent in her 1907 journal entries, where she says 'O Oscar! am I peculiarly susceptible to sexual impulse? I must be, I suppose – but I rejoice,' in her descriptions of her passionate affair with Wellington artist Edith Kathleen Bendall. (J. M. Murry, ed., *Journal of Katherine Mansfield,* Constable, 1957, pp. 12–4.) Something must have changed for Katherine between 1907 and 1909, making her feel ashamed of her lesbianism, as happens with many young lesbians.

24. See Frances Doughty, 'Lesbian biography, biography of lesbians', in Cruikshank, *op. cit.*

25. A few examples of this ongoing research are published in M. Davis and E. L. Kennedy, 'Oral history and the study of sexuality in the lesbian community: Buffalo, N.Y. 1940–1960' in *Feminist Studies,* Spring 1986; *Common Lives, Lesbian Lives: A Lesbian Quarterly,* No. 1, 1981 (for Lesbians only); *Lesbian Herstory Archive News.*

26. For example, the Gay Australian Heritage series of articles gives information about Australasian cross-dressing women, including the lesbian pirates who stayed in the Bay of Islands for some time.

27. Raymond, *op. cit.*

28. Frye (*op. cit.,* 1982) discusses this process in relation to women's studies.

29. See Simone de Beauvoir, *The Second Sex,* Penguin, 1972.

30. See Raymond, *op.cit.,* for a discussion of female friendship.

31. The first lesbian political organisation in this country was Sisters for Homophile Equality, started in Christchurch and Wellington in 1973, which originally published *Circle* magazine, started the first lesbian club in Wellington (Club 41) in 1974, and set up the first women's refuge in Christchurch.

CHAPTER 9: WOMB MAKERS AND WOMB BREAKERS

1. Witi Ihimaera, *The Matriarch* (Auckland: Heinemann, 1986), p. 2. Note that the Maori creation myth also has a valuable genealogical function and that it proudly locates Maoriness in the dawn of the universe. The Eden myth does the same for Jews but has less genealogical value for Christians.

2. Te whare o aitua, te whare o mate. Accounts of goddesses, including these three, can be found in Merlin Stone, *Ancient Mirrors of Womanhood – Our Goddess and Heroine Heritage*. (USA: New Sybylline Books, 1979), vol. I and II.

3. *New Zealand Listener,* 28 September 1985, p. 100

4. Dorothy Dinnerstein, 'Mama and the Mad Megamachine' in *The Mermaid and the Minotaur – Sexual Arrangements and Human Malaise* (USA: Harper Colophon, 1977), chapter 9

5. On feminist methodology see Sheila Collins, *A Different Heaven and Earth – a Feminist Perspective on Religion.* (USA: Judson Press 1974) foreword, Also, Mary Daly, *Gyn/Ecology – the Metaethics of Radical Feminism* (USA: Beacon, 1978), pp. 22–7

6. The best introduction to this is Starhawk, *The Spiral Dance – A Rebirth of the Ancient Religion of the Great Goddess.* (USA: Harper and Row, 1979), especially chapter 13, 'Creating Religion'

7. The best introduction to this is Charlene Spretnak (ed.) *The Politics of Women's Spirituality. Essays on the Rise of Spiritual Power Within the Feminist Movement* (USA: Anchor, 1982)

8. *New Zealand Tablet:* Veritas in 21 May 1986: Answerman in 16 June 1986

9. Brian Rudman, 'Opposed to the Pope', *New Zealand Listener,* 12 July 1986, pp. 8–10

10. The church I belong to is an exception. Since the Religious Society of Friends began four centuries ago, Quakers have not had a hierarchy and all roles have been shared by all members, regardless of sex.

11. F. P. Rees, letter to the editor, *New Zealand Listener,* 2 August 1986, p. 9

12. Women's Committee of the National Council of Churches in New Zealand, *Enquiry into the Status of Women in the Church,* New Zealand, 1976. A valuable document, largely ignored, which is likely still to hold true.

13. Mary Daly, 'Autobiographical Preface to the 1975 Edition', *The Church and the Second Sex* (USA: Beacon, 1968, 1975), p. 14

14. It is tempting to expand on this condensed assertion of the extent and depth of feminist theology but it would require a lengthy digresssion from the subject of this chapter. The best radical Christology I have read is Mary Daly's *Beyond God the Father* (USA: Beacon, 1973) (even though in her later books she recanted it!).

15. Mary Daly, 'The Courage to Leave' in 'New Archaic Afterwords', 1985 preface to *The Church and the Second Sex,* p. xii

16. Betty Thompson, *A Chance to Change – Women and Men in the Church,* a report of the world Council of Churches Conference on the Community of Women and Men in the Church, Sheffield, England, 1981, (USA: Fortress/WCC, 1982), p. 95

17. Public forums which any woman could attend were organised and

financed by the government and held in all main centres throughout New Zealand. The government's policy, on women's affairs, its implementation and priorities, was discussed. Fundamental Christian sects sent busloads of their women to disrupt these forums and attack the policy.

18. Anne Scheibner, 'The Church as Institution and Community', unpublished paper, 1979, quoted by Sara Maitland, *A Map of the New Country – Women and Christianity* (U Routledge and Kegan Paul, 1983), p. 139

19. Mitzi Nairn, 'On leave from the Church', in *Central*, magazine published by Wellington Inner City Ministry, No. 2, June 1986, p. 5

20. Naomi Goldenberg, 'No Feminist Can Save God', *Changing of the Gods – Feminism and the End of Traditional Religions,* (USA: Beacon, 1979), pp. 18–19, referring to book by Sharon and Thomas Emswiler, *Women and worship – A Guide to Non-Sexist Hymns, Prayers and Liturgies* (USA: Harper and Row, 1974)

21. Tom Driver, *Christ in a Changing World – Towards an Ethical Christology* (UK: SCM Press Limited, 1981), p. 145

22. Rosemary Radford Ruether, 'The Kenosis of the Father – a Feminist Midrash in Three Acts', *Sexism and God-Talk – Towards a Feminist Theology* (USA: Beacon, 1983), p. 11

23. David Hanna, 'Men and the Church', *Touch,* magazine of New Zealand SCM and the Ecumenical Youth Movement, Issue 1, May 1986 pp. 9–10

24. Dawn Danby, 'Patriarchy and Institutionalised Power', *Accent,* (a New Zealand independent ecumenical monthly), Box 8545, Auckland, vol.2, July 1986, p. 16

25. Judith Judd, 'Women Priests – the Unholy Orders', *The Press,* Christchurch, 17 April 1986, p. 13

26. Susan Adams, 'Jesus Christ Sets Free To Serve', paper for the 1985 Christian Conference of Asia Assembly, *Vashti's Voice*, a New Zealand feminist spiritual periodical, Box 107, Auckland, May-July, 1986, pp. 5–6

27. Robyn Kahukiwa and Patricia Grace, *Wahine Toa – Women of Maori Myth* (Auckland: Collins, 1984), p. 34

28. Rachel Wahlberg, *Jesus and the Freed Woman* (USA: Paulist Press, 1978). See also her book, *Jesus According to a Woman* New York: Paulist Press, 1975.)

29. Judith Plaskow, 'The Coming of Lilith', in Carol Christ and Judith Plaskow (eds), *Womanspirit Rising – a Feminist Reader in Religion* (USA: Harper and Row, 1979), p. 207. In a Jewish myth, Lilith was created before Eve but refused to lie down under Adam on the grounds that they had been created equally and so should mate equally. She then by a trick got power over Jehovah and forced him to give her wings to escape from Eden. She went off and had orgies for ever after, producing scores of demon children. Eve was her replacement for Adam's benefit. In Plaskow's new myth, Eve becomes self-identified rather than being just an

adjunct for Adam, and the age-old enmity between the bad woman and the good woman is healed. Together they return to heal the other ancient split, between women and men, fortified by experience of the great wide world beyond the womb-like Eden.

CHAPTER 10: THE OLDEST PROFESSION

1. The very origin of institutionalised prostitution arose in Athens in approximately 594 BC as the result of a government initiative to finance the building of the Greek military (Jess Wells, *A Herstory of Prostitution in Western Europe* (Berkeley, California: Shameless Hussy Press, 1982) p. 3.

2. For examples of male histories of prostitution see: Lujo Basserman, *The Oldest Profession: A History of Prostitution* (London: Arthur Barker Ltd, 1969); Vern L. Bullough, *The History of Prostitution* (New York: University Books, 1964)

3. For a provocative article on this subject see Gayle Rubin, 'Thinking Sex: Notes for a Radical Theory of the Politics of Sexuality' in Carole S. Vance (ed.), *Pleasure and Danger: Exploring Female Sexuality* (Boston: Routledge and Kegan Paul 1984), pp. 267–319

4. 'An "act of prostitution" means the offering by a man or woman of his or her body for purposes amounting to common lewdness for payment', Massage Parlours Act 1978, s.2(2). Some police argue that the laws are aimed more at those who exploit women for the purposes of prostitution than at the women themselves, but in practice it is usually the women who are the most vulnerable to legal intervention and control.

5. *Criminal Investigation Manual,* New Zealand Police, 1985, s. 36(3)

6. In New Zealand in 1986 there were 144 brothel and prostitution-related offences, of which 88 per cent were for being a prostitute importuning, i.e. soliciting (New Zealand Police Department Statistics, 1986).

7. A recent activity survey showed the policing of vice to account for only 1 per cent of the total working hours of New Zealand detectives (*CIB Activity Survey,* New Zealand Police Department, 1985, p. 49).

8. 'Truckie molls' service the long-distance road transport drivers, accompanying them on their journeys up and down the country.

'Bikie molls' hang around with the gangs and engage in casual sex, in contrast to the women who have steady relationships with individual gang members. Gang members themselves make clear distinctions between 'mums' and 'sluts', the former being respected and protected while the latter often receive rough treatment to the extent of 'going on the block' (i.e. being gang-raped).

'Groupie molls' circulate on the fringes of the rock music industry, seeking to spend time either in hotels or on the road with the musicians and their entourage. 'Ship molls', referred to more commonly in New Zealand as 'ship girls', cater for the sexual needs of visiting sailors.

9. It was easier to prove vagrancy rather than soliciting charges, and the high numbers of women arrested and imprisoned in this way prompted

the Justice Department to later assert that '"vagrancy" as the term is applied in practice in New Zealand is largely a young woman's crime' (New Zealand Department of Justice, *Crime in New Zealand* (Wellington: Department of Justice 1968) p. 260).

10. For example, one Wellington woman has had a relationship with the same seaman for nearly twenty years, and he recently lived with her for nearly a year while studying in this country.

11. That the home is seen as private territory is highly apparent in the reluctance still expressed to 'interfere' in matters of domestic violence. The idea of a man's home being his castle has long been used to legitimate the perpetration of violence and abuse against the women and girls kept within his moatless fortress.

12. These women are not paid by the hotel but are there with the tacit consent of the management, who no doubt view the availability of these women as another hotel service likely to attract visiting businessmen to their establishment.

13. Every parlour is required by law to keep a register of its masseuses in order to assist the police in establishing that those employed meet the requirements of the Massage Parlours Act 1978 (specifically that they are over eighteen and have no convictions received in the preceding ten years for any prostitution or drug-related offences). However, if the women submit false details it is difficult to prove that the licensee knew the information included in the register to be inaccurate.

14. Because of space limitations this section is brief and restricted only to comparative material. For fuller accounts of the history of prostitution in New Zealand see: Robyn Anderson, The Hardened Frail Ones: Women and Crime in Auckland, 1845–1870, MA thesis, Auckland University, 1981; Stevan Eldred-Grigg, *Pleasures of the Flesh: Sex and Drugs in Colonial New Zealand 1840–1915* (Wellington: A. H. and A. W. Reed, 1984); Charlotte J Macdonald, 'The "Social Evil": Prostitution and the Passage of the Contagious Diseases Act (1869)' in Barbara Brookes, Charlotte Macdonald and Margaret Tennant (eds), *Women in History: Essays on European Women in New Zealand* (Wellington: Allen and Unwin, 1986); Jan Robinson, '"Of Diverse Persons, Men and Women and Whores": Women and Crime in Nineteenth Century Canterbury', MA thesis, University of Canterbury, 1983.

15. For an informative account on the operation of the Contagious Diseases Act in New Zealand see Brookes, Macdonald and Tennant, *Women in History*, pp. 13–33

16. *Lyttelton Times,* 22 June 1869

17. See Robinson, 'Of Diverse Persons', Chapter 5

18. *Lyttelton Times,* 5 August 1870

19. *Lyttelton Times,* 18 November 1867

20. Recent seminars organised by the AIDS Foundation in Auckland have been well attended by prostitutes, most of whom are very receptive

to advice on disease prevention. As well as being concerned for her own personal health, the prostitute cannot afford to have any STD (sexually transmitted disease) because of the negative repercussions on her business life should she gain a reputation for being unclean.

21. Personal communication, August 1986

22. Personal communication from club owner, April 1986

23. Shelagh Cox and Bev James, 'The Theoretical Background,' this volume

24. William Acton, *Prostitution* (London: Macgibbon and Kee, 1968, first published 1857), p. 119

25. See R. R. Reiter (ed.), *Toward an Anthropology of Women* (New York: Monthly Review Press, 1975); and Paula Weideger, *History's Mistress: A New Interpretation of a Nineteenth Century Ethnographic Classic* (Harmondsworth: Penguin, 1986) originally published as *Das Weib* (Woman) by Hermann Ploss and Max Bartel, 1885

26. Jill Julius Matthews, *Good and Mad Women: The Historical Construction of Femininity in Twentieth Century Australia* (Sydney: Allen and Unwin, 1984); Andrew T. Scull, *Museums of Madness: The Social Organisation of Insanity in Nineteenth Century England* (London: Allen Lane, 1979)

27. Susan S M. Edwards, *Female Sexuality and the Law* (Oxford: Martin Robertson, 1981) p. 24. This argument was also made about other female criminal offenders, who were portrayed as more masculine than feminine as a means of reconciling the reality of their offending with the preservation of the ideology of inherent female passivity.

28. The erotomania argument has been most strongly argued in Top Security Project No. 2. Part 4, 'The Female Terrorist and Her Impact on Policing', in *Top Security* November 1976, p. 245. It has been similarly proposed elsewhere that: 'The key to female terrorism undoubtedly lies hidden somewhere in woman's complex sexual nature', H. H. A. Cooper, 'Woman as Terrorist', in Freda Adler and Rita Simon (eds), *The Criminology of Deviant Women* (Boston: Houghton Mifflin, 1979), p. 154

29. New Zealand Department of Justice, *Crime in New Zealand*, p. 234

30. Personal communication, September 1986

31. Joan Nestle, 'Lesbians and Prostitutes: An Historical Sisterhood', *The West Side Spirit,* vol. 1, no. 6, 17 June 1985, p. 10. For this section of the chapter I am indebted to the insights contained within Joan Nestle's article.

32. Ibid., p. 13

33. One of the unfortunate consequences of the recent growth in feminist consciousness has been the severing of ties between prostitutes and lesbians as prostitutes have increasingly come to be identified as the enemy for the way in which they are seen to collude with the interests of patriarchy.

34. Personal communication, March 1986

35. For examples, see: Sheldon Glueck and Eleanor Glueck, *Five Hundred Delinquent Women* (New York: Knopf, 1934); C. Lombroso and W. Ferrero, *The Female Offender* (London: Fisher Unwin, 1895); and William I. Thomas, *The Unadjusted Girl* (New Jersey: Patterson Smith, 1969, originally published 1923)

36. For details of women's work experiences in nineteenth-century New Zealand see the following, Stevan Eldred-Grigg, *A New History of Canterbury* (Dunedin: John McIndoe, 1982); pp. 63–64; Erik Olssen, 'Women, Work and the Family, 1880–1926' in Phillida Bunkle and Beryl Hughes (eds) *Women in New Zealand Society* (Sydney: Allen and Unwin, 1980); and Margot Roth, 'Making Herstory', Parts 1, 2, and 3, in *Broadsheet*, Nos 45–47, December 1976–March 1977

37. The relative attractiveness of prostitution is reflected in the comment made by a French emancipationist in 1834 who wondered how many women became courtesans out of disgust at housework! (cited in Sheila Lewenhak, *Women and Work* (Glasgow: Fontana, 1980), p. 179).

38. In the public service, for example, women are employed in ten, mainly female, intensive low-paid occupations – thus at 31 March 1983 approximately twice as many female permanent staff earned under $16 000 a year as did male staff, and only 0.4 per cent of women earned $30 000 or more compared to 7 per cent of men (from *Affirmative Action*, PSA Research Discussion Paper No. 19, 1984, p. 14)

39. It has been suggested by those in the trade, however, that street-walkers are generally more prepared 'to do anything, anyhow, with any-one' than are parlour workers (personal communication, March, 1986).

40. Brenda Strathern, The Twilight Zone: The Study of a Deviant Sub-culture by Covert Participant Observation, MA thesis, Auckland University, 1982

41. Eileen McLeod, *Women Working: Prostitution Now* (London: Croom Helm, 1982), p. 38

42. Quoted in Roberta Perkins and Garry Bennett, *Being a Prostitute* (Sydney: Allen and Unwin, 1985), p. 97

43. Cited in Jillian Riddington and Barb Findlay, 'Prostitution: The Visible Bargain', *Broadsheet* no. 78 (April 1980), pp. 20–24

44. For example, see Gail Sheehy, *Hustling: Prostitution in our Wide Open Society* (New York: Delacorte Press, 1971)

45. As seen for example, in responses to the Yorkshire Ripper murders in England and to the succession of killings of prostitutes in Seattle and Los Angeles, and in Lyons, France (Perkins and Bennett, *Being a Prostitute*, p. 281).

46. Women prostitutes do not tend to identify with images of themselves as exploited or degraded. Many see themselves as manipulating men to their own advantage and view one-night-stands as more degrading than prostitution because of the pretence involved.

CHAPTER 11: WOMEN AND THE STATE

1. P. A. McDowell. 'Tokenism and the Ministry', *Broadsheet* 128, April 1985, pp. 28–30

2. In the debate on the State Services Amendment Act Ruth Richardson argued that women could not 'be adequately served by the creation of a separatist policy ghetto for women', because, as her colleagues pointed out, 'all issues, be they transport, delicensing or whatever, apply to women'. (New Zealand Parliamentary Debates, 1 March 1985, pp. 3370, 3381.) The creation of a specific department for women was characterised as unsound in principle and backward in practice, being likely to 'isolate women from the mainstream of society' (ibid., p. 3372).

3. M. McIntosh, 'The State and the Oppression of Women,' in A. Kuhn and A. Wolpe (eds) *Feminism and Materialism: Women and Modes of Production* (London: Routledge and Kegan Paul, 1978); C. V. Baldock and B. Cass (eds), *Women, Social Welfare and the State* (Sydney: Allen and Unwin, 1983); J. Lewis, 'Dealing with Dependency, State Practices and Social Realities, 1870–1945' in J. Lewis (ed.), *Women's Welfare/Women's Rights* (London: Croom Helm, 1983); C. Ungerson (ed.), *Women and Social Policy: A Reader* (London: Macmillan, 1985); Wilson *Women and the Welfare State* (London: Tavistock, 1977)

4. V. George and P. Wilding, *Ideology and Social Welfare* (London: Routledge and Kegan Paul, 1976); N. Ginsburg, *Class, Capital and Social Policy* (London: MacMillan, 1979); I. Gough, *The Political Economy of the Welfare State* (London: MacMillan, 1979)

5. Ministerial Task Force on Income Maintenance, *Benefit Reform* (Wellington: Ministerial Task Force on Income Maintenance, 1986), p. 4

6. Department of Statistics, *New Zealand Official Yearbook* 1985, p. 776

7. Ibid.

8. Ibid., p. 753

9. Ministerial Task Force on Income Maintenance, p. 16

10. Ibid., p. 17

11. Department of Statistics, *Yearbook,* p. 776

12. Ministerial Task Force on Income Maintenance, p. 4

13. Ibid. pp. 12–13

14. P. G. Koopman-Boyden and C. D. Scott, *The Family and Government Policy in New Zealand* (Sydney: Allen and Unwin, 1984), pp. 193–94, 205, 206

15. Ibid., p. 198

16. R. M. Hill, Women, Capitalist Crisis, and the Reserve Army of Labour, MA thesis in political science, University of Canterbury, 1979

17. Department of Statistics, *Yearbook*, p. 203

18. Ministerial Task Force on Income Maintenance, pp. 17, 62–63. Budget '85 Task Force, *Benefits, Taxes and the 1985 Budget* (Wellington: 1985), pp. 33–4

19. It is argued that the $72.47 that the solo parent receives for the first child is to subsidise the expenses of setting up a new household and that the drop to $10 for each child thereafter is a reflection of the reduced cost of supporting a second child. If this is true it seems peculiar that the state insists on paying out almost six times that amount to support an orphan child in an already established household. There is a notable lack of discussion of the Orphan's Benefit in government discussion papers, and no indication of how the rate is calculated. However, in the Budget '85 Task Force document it is stated that 'This benefit helps guardians to meet the cost of caring for children under 16 who have been orphaned' (p. 16). This appears to imply that the Orphan's Benefit is the *minimum* cost of childrearing.

20. Ministerial Task Force on Income Maintenance, p. 17

21. Such claims may be found ibid, p. 4; Budget '85 Task Force, pp. 47–48; Royal Commission on Social Security, Report on Social Security in New Zealand (Wellington: Government Printer, 1972)

22. Ministerial Task Force on Income Maintenance, p. 16

23. Department of Statistics, *Population Perspectives '81: New Zealand Census of Population and Dwellings 1981, Volume 12 (General Report)*, (Wellington: Department of Statistics, 1985), pp. 28–48

24. Ministerial Task Force on Income Maintenance, p. 42

25. E. Olssen and A. Lévesque, 'Towards a History of the European Family in New Zealand' in P. G. Koopman-Boyden (ed.), *Families in New Zealand Society* (Wellington: Methuen, 1978); E. Olssen, 'Women, Work and Family; 1880–1926' in P. Bunkle and B. Hughes (eds), *Women in New Zealand Society* (Auckland: Allen and Unwin, 1980); R. Novitz, 'Marital and Familial Roles in New Zealand: The Challenge of the Women's Liberation Movement' in Koopman-Boyden (ed.), *Families*.

26. Koopman-Boyden and Scott, *Family and Government Policy*, p. 111

27. For discussions of women acting as moral authoritarians on behalf of the state see J. Phillips, 'Mummy's Boys: Pakeha Men and Male Culture in New Zealand' in Bunkle and Hughes, *Women in New Zealand Society;* J. Donzelot, *The Policy of Families* (London: Hutchinson, 1980); Olssen, 'Women, Work and Family'; Wilson, *Women and the Welfare State*

28. R. O. Blood and D. M. Wolfe, *Husbands and Wives: The Dynamics Married Living* (Glencoe, Illinois: Free Press, 1960)

29. Domestic Purposes Benefit Review Committee, *Report of the Domestic Purposes Benefit Review Committee* (Wellington: Government Printer, 1977), p. 39

30. Ministerial Task Force on Income Maintenance, p. 42

31. Domestic Purposes Benefit Review Committee, p. 12

32. Ibid., p. 18

33. Ministerial Task Force on Income Maintenance, p. 43, Domestic Purposes Benefit Review Committee, pp. 28–9

34. Ministerial Task Force on Income Maintenance, p. 40

35. Ibid.
36. Baldock and Cass, *Women, Social Welfare,* pp. xi–xvii
37. Conference of Socialist Economists, 'Women's Domestic Labour', *On the Political Economy of Women,* CSE pamphlet, No. 2, 1977, J. Gardiner, 'Political Economy of Domestic Labour in Capitalist Society' in D. L. Barker and S. Allen (eds), *Dependence and Exploitation of Work and Marriage* (London: Longman Paul, 1976); M. Molyneaux, 'Beyond the Domestic Labour Debate', *New Left Review,* No. 1, 116, 1979
38. McIntosh, 'State and Oppression', Wilson, *Women and the Welfare State*
39. Phillips, 'Mummy's Boys' in Bunkle and Hughes, p. 236
40. Blood and Wolfe, *op. cit.*

Notes on Contributors

CATHERINE BENLAND is a director and co-founder of a Wellington advertising agency. Previously she has been a teacher, public servant, editor, politician, lecturer, programmer, managing secretary, and full-time parent. She has an honours degree in religious studies, and her primary theological interest is women's spirituality. Her own faith is a blend of pagan, Quaker and Catholic.

SHELAGH COX is a sociology lecturer at Massey University, whose studies have also included philosophy and English literature. During the time she was at home, bringing up children, she did freelance writing. She has been working in women's studies for several years and wants to develop her interest in women's potential to break down barriers between ways of life, ways of thought and academic disciplines.

BEV JAMES is a sociologist particularly interested in the use of feminist methodology. This has informed the research from which her chapter is drawn. The chapter reflects a long-term association with and continuing interest in Kawerau. She teaches at Massey University, mainly in courses dealing with gender, class and race inequalities.

ANNE KIRKER is a senior curator at the National Art Gallery in Wellington. British art of the early twentieth century and contemporary developments in the visual arts generally are her special fields of interest. A strong supporter of the women's movement, Anne Kirker was co-organiser of the New Zealand's Women Painters exhibition. She is the author of *New Zealand Women Artists* (Reed Methuen, 1986).

ALISON LAURIE came out as a lesbian in 1950s and has been active in lesbian, gay and feminist politics since the 1960s. She holds a BA Hons. from Victoria University and a Cand. Mag. from the University of Oslo in English literature and linguistics. She lived in Denmark and Norway for many years and has worked variously as a journalist, tour manager, an adult education teacher, and a women's studies tutor. She lives at Paekakariki with a patient lover and a large number of poodles.

AOREWA MCLEOD has been teaching in the English Department at Auckland University since 1970. It was only in 1983 that she started looking at New Zealand women's writing. In 1984 she began seriously wondering why she had ignored New Zealand women's fiction and why *the bone people* (published that year) worked so powerfully for her. She has always had an interest in popular literature and a distrust of the tendency to divide culture into high and low, good and bad. Aorewa McLeod is a lesbian, a feminist and has no children.

234

ROSEMARY NOVITZ is a senior lecturer in sociology at Canterbury University, teaches courses in the sociology of gender and is involved in the development of an interdisciplinary feminist studies programme. In her MA thesis she looked at the priority women give to their responsibility as mothers and its relation to their involvement in paid employment. She has two children, and since the late 1960s has juggled her public and private roles.

RANGIMARIE ROSE PERE has tribal links with Ngai Tuhoe, Ngati Ruapani, Ngati Kahungunu, Ngai Tahu-Matua, Ngati Porou and Ngati Rongomaiwahine. She received an excellent education from tribal elders and has also been educated in state teacher training institutions. She has taught in preschools, primary and secondary schools and was a research fellow in the Sociology Department at the University of Waikato. She worked in the Department of Education's advisory service in Hamilton before taking up her current position in Gisborne as a school inspector.

JAN ROBINSON has an MA in sociology and a diploma in criminology. She originally became interested in prostitution while working in a youth hostel situated next to a brothel in Amsterdam's red-light district. She later studied prostitution in nineteeth-century Canterbury. She is currently employed as a research fellow at the Institute of Criminology, Victoria University, evaluating the outcome of a new community policing initiative.

KATHERINE SAVILLE-SMITH is a sociologist at Massey University where she is involved in teaching a women's studies course. Her main research interests are New Zealand's class structure and gender relations. She is presently involved in research which includes analysis of the ways in which women participate in maintaining the bourgeoisie in New Zealand.

MARILYN WARING was a Member of the New Zealand Parliament from 1975 to 1984. During this period she was active in women's affairs both at home and abroad, and chaired the government caucus committees on the economy, health and welfare. Her publications include *Women, Politics and Power* (Allen & Unwin, 1985); she has also been a soprano soloist with the New Zealand Broadcasting Corporation, and written a screenscript for Jean Devanny's novel *The Butcher Shop*.